The Virtual Self
A Contemporary Soci

21st-Century Sociology

SERIES EDITOR: Steven Seidman, State University of New York at Albany

The *21st-Century Sociology* series provides instructors and students with key texts in sociology that speak with a distinct sociological voice and offer thoughtful and original perspectives. The texts reflect current discussions in and beyond sociology, avoiding standard textbook definitions to engage students in critical thinking and new ideas. Prominent scholars in various fields of social inquiry combine theoretical perspectives with scholarly research to present accessible syntheses for students as we move into a new millennium with implications for rapid social change.

Already published:

1 CULTURAL THEORY: AN INTRODUCTION, *Philip Smith*
2 CULTURAL SOCIOLOGY IN PRACTICE, *Laura Desfor Edles*
3 CLASSICAL SOCIAL THEORY: A CONTEMPORARY APPROACH, *Kenneth H. Tucker, Jr.*
4 MULTICULTURALISM IN A GLOBAL SOCIETY, *Peter Kivisto*
5 THE WORLD OF CITIES: PLACES IN COMPARATIVE AND HISTORICAL PERSPECTIVE, *Anthony M. Orum and Xiangming Chen*
6 ENCOUNTERING NATIONALISM, *Jyoti Puri*
7 THE VIRTUAL SELF: A CONTEMPORARY SOCIOLOGY, *Ben Agger*

Forthcoming books in series:

NEW TECHNOLOGIES AND SOCIETY, *Douglas Kellner*
RACE, CLASS, AND GENDER, *Lynn Chancer and Beverly Watkins*
QUEER LIFE, *Amber Ault*

The Virtual Self
A Contemporary Sociology

Ben Agger

Blackwell
Publishing

350 Main Street, Malden, MA 02148-5020, USA
108 Cowley Road, Oxford OX4 1JF, UK
550 Swanston Street, Carlton, Victoria 3053, Australia

First published 2004 by Blackwell Publishing Ltd

Library of Congress Cataloging-in-Publication Data

Agger, Ben.
  The virtual self / by Ben Agger.
    p. cm.
  Includes bibliographical references and index.
  ISBN 0-631-21648-0 (hb.) – ISBN 0-631-21649-9 (pbk.)
  1. Information society. I. Title.

HM851.A34 2003
303.48'33–dc21

                                        2003009903

A catalogue record for this title is available from the British Library.

Set in 10 on 13 pt Photina
by Kolam Information Services Pvt. Ltd, Pondicherry, India
Printed and bound in the United Kingdom
by MPG Books Ltd, Bodmin, Cornwall

For further information on
Blackwell Publishing, visit our website:
http://www.blackwellpublishing.com

Contents

Preface

Perhaps more than any other book I have written, this essay on contemporary sociology and society emerges from my teaching. I have lectured these ideas as I have tried to grapple with the impact of the Internet on society and culture. These are issues about which my students are more expert than I am! They are the first generation of virtual selves.

The Virtual Self is intended for use in sociology courses and in humanities courses that make thematic issues of self, theory, and culture. Virtuality, as I understand it, breaks down barriers between self and society and between disciplines. This has an upside and a downside: Institutional and intellectual differentiation afford identity and stability; yet one increasingly requires interdisciplinary knowledge in order to address what Hegelians used to call totality – a dirty word among postmodernists, unfortunately. In order to stay relevant, sociology needs to open its doors to intellectual influences beyond it.

Increasingly, I find myself in disagreement with my colleagues about what constitutes sociology. They view it as a research method, a body of findings, grant proposals. I view sociology as the story of people's lives, whose telling can be liberating. But it is not sheer biography or autobiography; it is the conceptual work of connecting self and social structure imaginatively, understanding one's life in terms of larger social forces that do not fall from the sky but are continually constructed by people who work, interact, and produce discourse. An important component of discourse today is Internet use.

I have Ken Provencher to thank for staying on my case. Blackwell is lucky to have him. I am indebted to Steve Seidman for inviting me to join his Blackwell series on twenty-first-century sociology. Parts of an earlier version of this manuscript were read by Norman Denzin, Charles Lemert, and Tim Luke. Anna Oxbury did a superb job of copy-editing.

My adorable children, Oliver and Sarah, are great kids. I have told them and read them parts of this book, especially the parts in which I embarrass them. Little is more fun than reading your work to your kids and hearing them groan! And Beth Anne not only plays tennis with me, but she discusses these ideas, and affords me a healthy perspective on things postmodern.

B. A.

CHAPTER ONE

Everyday Life in Our Wired World

Does the Internet require that we revise sociology's and social theory's categories? Have we entered postmodernity? The virtual self is connected to the world by information technologies that invade not only the home and office but the psyche. This can either trap or liberate people.

This short book introduces sociology and our wired society and culture. It can be read as an introduction to the discipline, without all the facts and figures of the 600-page intro books. It can also be read as an exploration of contemporary society. This society is like none before, and calls forth new sociological categories, such as the **virtual self**. By "virtual self" I am referring to the person connected to the world and to others through electronic means such as the Internet, television, and cell phones. Virtuality is the experience of being online and using computers; it is a state of being, referring to a particular way of experiencing and interacting with the world. (For a very optimistic account of the experience of virtuality see Nicholas Negroponte's (1996) *Being Digital*.) Although I contend that we are in a stage of history called "modernity," we require postmodern theoretical categories that help explain how our media culture and information technologies get inside our heads, position our bodies, and dictate our everyday lives, including working, parenting, schooling, traveling, shopping. This account will already sound like George Orwell's (1981) dystopian novel *1984* in which Big Brother controls people's thoughts and thus lives. But mine is not a totally dismal story for new information technologies and our media culture afford unprecedented opportunities, largely literary in nature, for taking control of our lives.

If you believe that sociology is, or should be, a science, you probably won't read any further. Truth in advertising: I believe that sociology must give up its pretense to be a science, confessing that it is poetry or fiction, which is not a cause of shame but of celebration. Sociology is better viewed as a writing style than a methodology or body of findings, as a way of arranging certain words and images on the page (or, for most of us, screen). It is a writing style that makes arguments; as such, it is rhetoric. Sociology grew out of the nineteenth-century attempt by certain classical theorists to conceptualize and then solve social problems of suffering, inequality, and alienation. In the meantime, sociology has lost its way and lost its public, its readership of intelligent but not necessarily academic people who care deeply about the life and times of the self, society and culture. One of the plot lines in the story I am about to tell involves how sociology became a profession, with its own discourse, credentials, status symbols, especially statistics and research methods. I want to de-professionalize sociology, enabling virtual citizens to acquire and promote sociological insight using the Internet as their data base and vehicle of publication.

These are the thoughts with which I begin almost every one of my classes. I decided to write this book because I wanted to summarize my ideas and make them available to students and their teachers. The series editor, Professor Steve Seidman, a noted sociological theorist at the State University of New York at Albany, had invited me to contribute a book to his new series on sociology in the twenty-first century. I had already begun to think, write, and teach about the Internet's impact on selves, especially as a parent of virtual children! As a person who drinks deeply of **critical theory**, French postmodern theory, and the emerging inter-disciplinary project of **cultural studies**, I situated my thinking in these prior theoretical traditions. (For brief discussions of these perspectives, please consult the glossary.) There were already a number of excellent books on these issues, including Dyer-Witheford's *Cyber-Marx* (1999), Poster's *What's the Matter with the Internet?* (2001), Luke's *Screens of Power* (1989), Kellner's *Media Culture* (1995) and *Media Spectacle* (2003), and Derrida's *Specters of Marx* (1994). None of these books is standard sociological fare. All of them influenced my thoughts, which emerge in this book, on whether postmodern social changes such as the Internet require new social-science appraisals of **capitalism**, modernity, the family, popular culture. As I see it, little is more important and exciting than for sociologists to engage these issues as they demonstrate the relevance of our discipline for the lives of students and citizens, kids and their parents.

To grapple with these issues, sociology must reach beyond its traditional disciplinary boundaries for intellectual tools with which to theorize the self, society, and culture. This challenges traditional sociologists, those who write and adopt the typical introductory texts, who defend our discipline and its scientific method against interdisciplinary interlopers and foreign influences. Although I don't believe that traditional sociology possesses the theoretical insights or concepts with which to theorize the Internet, the self, and postmodernity, this book is not a jeremiad against sociology so much as an argument that we can find good sociology in surprising places, including the humanities and cultural disciplines. This book is a sociology, albeit one that broadens the discipline beyond its usual boundaries. I exercise selectivity where I don't tackle issues mapped out by the long omnibus sociology texts, not because these issues aren't important, but because I don't want to spend hundreds of pages rehashing what other introductory books do quite well. Mine is a different kind of sociology, one that addresses virtual selves living in postmodern worlds considerably different from the worlds of their parents or their teachers.

I have already used code words, such as **postmodernism**, that signal my approach to sociology. In what follows, I discuss Marxism and critical theory much more frequently than I discuss the latest edition of *American Sociological Review*, which may contain empirical articles on income, family, religion, region. Terms such as postmodernism and Marxism risk becoming slogans that do our thinking for us, whether we love or hate these traditions. I am much less interested in sloganeering (what Theodor Adorno, one of my intellectual heroes, called "ticket thinking") than in telling a good story that provides the reader with clues about what I read and considered in formulating my arguments. The older I get, the more I want to say things plainly, without artifice, and the less I care about hurting people's feelings by saying what I really think about shibboleths – sacred words that excite emotions. The older I get, the more I realize that there is no single "plain language" but only versions that compete for the reader's ear. For the record, I am not a postmodernist, although postmodern theory has much to say about our wired world. I am a Marxist, although I am closer to the interpretation of Marx offered by a group of theorists called western Marxists, including the **Frankfurt School**. People who have been exposed to these intellectual influences usually don't essay sociology for student readers or the public, as I am doing here. But I feel it is important to speak openly about virtual selves and virtual sociology, and to be honest about the lenses through which I view such matters.

Worldly Selves, Worldly Sociologies

I begin (and end) with the self, the person who lives in Arlington, Texas or Arlington, Virginia, Eugene, Oregon, Topeka, Kansas, Toronto, Canada. I do this both to emphasize that sociology is about people like us and that a postmodern sociology must deal with what I call the worldliness of selves – their ability to go anywhere/anytime, their saturation with popular culture, their penchant for travel, their tendency to change jobs, spouses, their bodies. You can read self-help books on weight loss, on picking a good plastic surgeon, on how to be more spiritual. You can find Web pages on your upcoming colonoscopy, an important check for the first signs of colon cancer – a rite of passage for people turning 50, as I recently did! By "worldly" I mean that selves in western and some eastern industrialized nations have unprecedented access to information and stimulation. They learn gossip, trends, fashions, lifestyles using electronic prostheses (extensions) such as television, the Web, cell phones, faxes. Yet the "more" people know about ephemera – things that come and go – the less they know about what really matters. Information and entertainment trade off against real depth of insight, the ability to reason, skeptical inquiry. People know more about the world than their parents, and certainly their parents' parents, but they accept the world at face value.

Some of the terms in this book will be unfamiliar, even to sociology instructors already steeped in theory. I will use these terms where necessary, but I will define them as I go along. There is nothing wrong with technical terms. Statisticians and methodologists use them, as do theorists. Technical terms are only forbidding and frustrating where they aren't easily translated into other languages; good writing, as I see it, recognizes its own blind spots and opens itself to other versions.

Postmodern and critical-theory terms can be scary both because they are different and because authors who use these terms are sometimes oblivious to their audiences. It is almost as if they are writing only for themselves, indulging what a French theorist named Roland Barthes (1975) called "the pleasure of the text." I remain convinced that the best sociologies challenge ordinary understandings and take the reader to a higher level, but, in order to do so, they must put themselves in the readers' shoes, anticipating where terms need to be defined and complicated concepts explained. Indeed, what makes for good writing – empathy with one's readers – also makes for good teaching. When I deliver these thoughts from a lectern (or, typically, pacing around the classroom trying to burn off my energy), I try to imagine how strange I must sound to 20-year-olds from Texas!

This is a book that introduces you to the abiding concerns of sociology, notably the concepts of self and social structure, within the social and historical context of the early twenty-first century, which has just dawned. When I took my first sociology course, at South Eugene High School in Oregon, the year was 1968. I couldn't see beyond the end of that turbulent decade, let alone to the end of my college years, or to adulthood, or to the end of the twentieth century. Like most around me who hailed from middle-class homes headed by fathers with professions (mine was a professor) and mothers who raised kids and tended the household, we were caught up in the moment of the sixties, which were so dangerous and yet full of promise. I skipped school to march against the war in Vietnam; I listened to the psychedelic rock music of the Jefferson Airplane amidst the pervasive smell of incense and (yes!) marijuana; I attended a purposively purposeless event called a Be-In, at which young people in tie-dyed t-shirts danced around a maypole and listened to music. (The philosopher Kant said that the unique characteristic of art is its purposive purposelessness, which might be another term for play.) People of my generation were searching for themselves and for community.

Much has changed in the meantime: The music is certainly different; it is less political and more about the self. I'm sick of classic rock stations, but so-called new music mostly leaves me cold. But much is the same: People still pursue careers, get married (and divorced), have children, drink too much, watch television, drive VW beetles. High-school kids are still pressured by parents to earn good grades in order to get into the best colleges and universities, in order to get into the best careers. If anything, the pressure to achieve is more intense than when I went to high school. Adolescents are still feeling their way through romantic relationships and friendships. They are still in pursuit of self and community, as I am calling them. As Simon and Garfunkel sang, they are looking for America.

This book can be read profitably by people outside of mainstream sociology, in disciplines in which the self and culture are at stake. As will become clear, I am mistrustful not only about a narrow conception of sociology as a hard science, but about the whole distinction between the empirical social sciences and the humanities. I seek to explain why sociology remains the most exciting discipline in university curricula, the discipline most suited to the discovery of selfhood and community. C. Wright Mills, a sociologist from Waco, Texas, which also gave us Dr. Pepper, wrote about the sociological imagination, which he characterized as the ability to relate personal problems to public issues, explaining them in terms of each other. Karl Marx, one of my intellectual inspirations, developed his own version of the relationship between self and community where he wrote that social being conditions consciousness but that consciousness, expressed in critique and action, can change social being, bringing into being a new society. You will hear a lot more from me about Marx, whom I regard as the most important sociologist ever. Charles Lemert (2002), a contemporary sociological theorist who borrows from postmodernism, has written that students above all want to live well, acquiring "the power to make and enjoy the worlds they imagine."

This book builds the conceptual arsenal of sociology from the ground up, beginning with the ordinary lives people lead. These lives involve activities of communication, experiences of identity, issues of the relationship between work and family, and people's use of time beyond the workday. I situate this discussion in a society connected by the Internet, World Wide Web, CNN, cellular telephones, pagers, fax machines, the many sinews of a wired society based on rapidly-evolving information technologies. Unlike certain theorists of postmodernity such as Jean Baudrillard, entrepreneurs such as Bill Gates, and politicians such as former Vice President Al Gore, I do not believe that virtual capitalism represents a new stage of civilization in which all social problems disappear (for a view similar to mine see Delanty 2000). Such optimism could be characterized as technological utopianism. Nor do I demonize these information technologies, as a Luddite might, as evil betrayals of people's humanity. (During the English industrial revolution, Luddites broke machines in order to protest human alienation.)

Rather, I view technology as a dense set of social relations defining the uses of machinery, electronics, media. I am interested in issues of virtuality, of being digital and of digital being, because these are familiar to you and me and, as such, they are a good place to begin to think sociologically about self and community, personal and public, consciousness and social being. Indeed, I am composing this book on my personal computer at home, producing pixels where, even ten years ago, many of us composed our manuscripts in longhand, using such ancient devices as fountain pens! I am also simultaneously listening to music on CD while I type, in this case the sounds of Terri Hendrix, an early-thirties Texas folk rocker. With a few keystrokes, if nostalgia strikes me, I can fire up Buffalo Springfield, which gave my generation several resonant 1960s anthems. Neil Young's autobiography, which I read last summer, has much to say about how sixties selves emerged from that tempestuous time with heavy baggage.

We need to think sociologically on the ground of our experience, which is what Neil Young does as he explores the intersection of his world and his self. Indeed, that is how I came to sociology at the end of the sixties, when the world was full of possibility, but no certainties. I have mentioned my first high-school sociology class. The next year, I took a college sociology class at the University of Oregon. The professor tried to make sense of the civil rights, antiwar, and emerging women's movements, which were hard to ignore given the protest marches snaking through the streets of Eugene, the 1968 Presidential campaign, and the hard-fought Oregon Democratic primary. I remember skipping school (again!) to attend a speech by Robert Kennedy, just days before he was assassinated in Los Angeles. I accompanied a girl named Karen, of whom I was fond. In retrospect, it's really hard to separate my motivations: To hang out with her, and to work for an antiwar candidate. Both strike me as valid. We leafletted for Eugene McCarthy and I remember rednecks telling us that if we didn't move on, they would come back and kill us. At the time, a hit song was Simon and Garfunkel's "Mrs. Robinson," from the movie *The Graduate*. My father was active in the civil rights movement, serving a term as the local President of the CORE (Congress of Racial Equality) chapter. He organized a benefit for CORE featuring the comedian and activist Dick Gregory, who visited our house. Other black leaders traipsed through our town and our home. My father became a close friend of Southern Christian Leadership Council leader Floyd McKissick, who told an audience at a local college basketball arena that my dad was the only white man he ever trusted. These were heady times, especially for the son of a left-wing professor active in movement politics.

My experiences of the New Left and counterculture formed my intellectual, social, and personal sensibilities. This influence blended with the antiwar music of Country Joe and the Fish, whose concert I remember attending. Before that, I watched the aftermath of President Kennedy's assassination on television, not only accelerating my political education but ensuring that I would acquire much of my social experience and values from the mass media. I became a professor and a critical social theorist largely because of these early experiences and somewhat later experiences in college, from 1969 to 1973, including ongoing national strife surrounding the bombing of Cambodia in 1970 and a course I took during my first year in college from a noted Marxist social theorist named John O'Neill, whose work I mention later. In the early 1970s, I studied Marxist-humanist philosophy and social theory in Tito's Yugoslavia, whose model of socialism significantly departed from Soviet Marxism.

My personal politics, lifestyle, and values were forged in this crucible of social change, cultural exposure, intellectual excitement, and travel. These experiences were hardly unique; many members of my generation, baby boomers born between about 1947 and 1960, came of age as young adults and citizens during the turbulence of social change. Sociology has much to say about the baby boom, when, at its height, women averaged as many as four children, compared to the previous and subsequent norm of just below two. (Brief sociological quiz: How can the US population grow if the fertility or birth rate falls below 2.0? Hint: Immigration.) Demographers (specialists in population dynamics) speculate that the baby boom was caused by a combination of post-World War II prosperity and the fact that people deferred having kids during the war years. Recall this vignette when I discuss a sex-crazed America later in the book!

For those of us who remember the JFK assassination, the murders of civil rights workers in the south, the televised Vietnam war, the first moon landing, the first time we heard the word "acid" to describe a mind-altering drug, epic concerts by The Doors, the decision about whether to go to Canada, to jail or to war, and, on top of all that, the many crises of adolescence, the notion of an "everyday life" seems somewhat misplaced. I don't exaggerate the uniqueness of the 1960s, although I have been heard to remark, ruefully, to my students that "1969 was the last good year"! (They just think "He's really old!") Many other interruptions in the ordinary lives people lead were similar in their intensity, wrenching them out of old habits and mindsets. People who lived through the French and Russian revolutions, the Battle of Britain, the Great Depression, the Holocaust above all, were similarly etched by a world that would never be the same again. All young men who have gone to war, especially the total wars conducted since World War I, were unavoidably damaged by their horrifying experiences and deeds, if they even made it out alive. Post-traumatic stress, the term given to describe the delayed effects of the Vietnam war on American soldiers, could be considered a generic condition of the postmodern epoch, although I will argue that our moment in civilization is perhaps less postmodern than meets the eye – I call it **fast capitalism**.

My contention is that it makes sociological sense to speak of everyday life or everydayness, describing people's ground-level experiences of themselves and society. But this everydayness can be jolted by the twists and turns of earth-shattering events that permanently redefine both social experience and the person's own sensibility. For most readers of this book, there is the world before and after September 11. Everyday life is always situated in a larger context of community, nation, race, class, gender, religion – the enveloping structures whose movement defines history. I suggest that sociology is a literary perspective on the relationship between people's experiences and actions in everyday life and larger institutions of civil society, politics, the economy, family, and media. Sociology composes (that is, writes about) our experiences of the world, and thus changes the world by its accounts. I pay particular attention to rapid changes in everyday life since World War II, and even in the past decade, that reflect and augur large-scale structural changes in communication and community, work and family, economy and entertainment. As such, this book is an exploration of the self, and its experiences, in a society in which people are now linked globally through nearly instantaneous electronic means in ways never before imagined, even by the proponents of a universal world history, such as Hegel and Marx.

This book is necessarily autobiographical, as are all sociologies, in that it traces my own path from childhood through high school, during which I participated in the antiwar movement and New Left, to college and my intellectual beginnings as a student of Marx, to my emerging career as a professor, author, father. My first memories of my childhood in Eugene have stayed with me: My father drove me around to poor and non-white neighborhoods explaining to me why America distributes life chances, Weber's evocative term, so unequally. Long before I took my first college sociology classes, these drives were my Sociology 101; they introduced me to a way of thinking about inequality and suffering as causes of social arrangements, to which, I later learned, we give names such as *capitalism* and *racism*. During my first year of college, I acquired some of these theoretical words with which to organize and enrich the experiences I had with my dad as he showed me the other America in Eugene. Sociology, thus, arises from experience, and the way we tell its story depends on how we remember who we were, and how we came to be the way we are. The autobiographical ground of sociology is nothing to be ashamed of; indeed, sociology is richer for arising from what an existentialist might call its ground in care. An exercise you might do is write a sociological autobiography in which you reflect on the parallels between your own development as a person and changes in the world around you. I remember exactly where I was and what I was doing on the day that President Kennedy was assassinated in 1963. I recall how I felt about it, and that my teacher, who gave us the news, was crying, which is why I couldn't understand her at first. What were you doing on September 11? How did you feel about it?

My dad was a liberal activist who was involved in the movements to end the Vietnam war and to promote black people's civil rights. He was an empirical political scientist who felt that Marxism was somewhat heavy-handed and ignored people's experience. I became a Marxist because I was taught by John O'Neill and Yugoslavian theorists that Marxism is humanism, at least judging by a reading of Marx's early writings, which grounded Marxist theory in people's experience of working and their **alienation** from their jobs, communities, colleagues, and nature. This version of Marx made sense to me inasmuch as it converged with reading I was doing in existentialism and phenomenology, philosophical perspectives suggesting that the truth is found not in the metaphysical heavens but in what Heidegger termed *existence*, the everyday experiences of selves who, like me, recollect their families, schooling, neighborhoods as they develop intellectual systems which explain themselves, and their worlds, to themselves. Mine is a Marxist sociology, because class is one of the most important structuring experiences of our lives, but it is also a sociology that drinks deeply of existence, experience, everyday life, requiring sociology to meet the test of relevance to those who read sociology in order to understand, and participate in, their worlds better. When I was 13, my parents took me and my sister to the Soviet Union. I couldn't believe my eyes as we drove by Red Square and then went to see the mummified remains of Lenin, who looked like a wax figure. I was taught by my dad that the Soviet Union was dictatorial and that its people lacked freedom, but that Lenin and the Bolsheviks were brave in trying to create a world different from capitalism.

Departing from Marx?

Today, the world seems very different from the world in which I came of age intellectually. I do not believe that the phenomena sometimes associated with the term **globalization** signal a departure from Marx, modernity having evolved into postmodernity with the mode of production being replaced by a mode of information (Poster 1990). These phenomena include just-in-time manufacturing around the world, the demise of the labor movement and the alleged eclipse of social class, the Internet, Web, cellular telephones, expanded leisure time, abundance reflected in both consumption and recreation activities. Nor do these trends suggest that our stage of civilization has segued smoothly into postindustrialism, as Daniel Bell (1973, 1976) predicted, class conflict having been abolished in the direction of general abundance and freedom from work. Middle-class Americans work more hours than they ever have since World War II; affluence has not liberated them from the workaday grind. People and their children lead harried existences on the treadmill of success, incurring back-breaking debt, a time bind especially for women who work, pressure to get good grades. My sixth-grade daughter does more homework than I did in high school. My young son attended a preschool in which he was clearly evaluated by adult criteria for demeanor, citizenship, academic skills. In his former school, his chastening teachers deemed his gross motor skills deficient; he was three. (He now beats older kids in tennis, his new first love.) The yuppie parents of my kids' classmates have their children tutored and lessoned on the side lest they fall behind. These parents also occupy many of their children's waking hours with activities – soccer, basketball, gymnastics, football, baseball, cheerleading. The boundary between childhood and adulthood is becoming perilously thin, with kids expected to do hours of homework and then hours of lessons and sports in order to leapfrog them into successful adulthood. Do we really want to abbreviate childhood?

There is still a working class and, beneath it, a desperately poor underclass, many of whom do not even show up on the radar screens of the census or official employment statistics. According to US Census Bureau statistics from the year 2000, nearly 25 percent of Americans are poor. Pestilence and plague, high infant mortality, despotic political regimes, genocide, protracted armed skirmishes in the Middle East, Asia, and Africa reflect what Lenin and Marx called uneven development. People in the third world suffer runaway population growth, malnutrition, inadequate health care, war – every conceivable variety of inhumanity. Postperestroika Russia and its former colonies are dangerously unstable, with an emerging capitalism not matched by mature democratic political institutions. Although the arms race between the US and USSR has apparently ended, the nuclear capability has spread dangerously throughout the premodern world, threatening everyone on the planet, and the planet itself.

I confess to a good deal of skepticism about the emancipating potential of new information technologies, although I agree with Kellner and Poster, authors I cited earlier, that members of the democratic left should not automatically concede these technologies to corporate America as transmission belts of capitalism and consumerism. Instant communication makes possible an electronic democracy that challenges the hegemony (dominance) of elites. "Distance education" can level the playing field for people in rural areas, underdeveloped countries, those who thirst for in-depth knowledge about all manner of subjects. Computers can enhance citizenship and contribute to rebuilding a public sphere in which people conduct fundamental dialogues about societal purposes. But in spanning distances electronically, the information superhighway can also contribute to what the German critical theorist Jurgen Habermas (1984, 1987) called the "colonization" of everyday life by system-serving imperatives to consume and conform. The French theorist Michel Foucault (1977) wrote of a society of ultimate surveillance, patterned on Jeremy Bentham's model of a prison, Panopticon, in which inmates' every activity would be scrutinized by the custodians of order. In Foucault's terms, this *disciplines* people, reducing the scope of what philosophers call people's **agency** – freedom to choose and to act. For a discussion of how sociology disciplines people, see my *Socio(onto)logy: A Disciplinary Reading* (1989b) and then my follow-up study, *Public Sociology* (2000), about how sociological writers compose what I call "secret writing."

I have just named a number of important, but difficult, European theorists, such as Habermas and Foucault. Look them up on the Web, and find summaries of their ideas. Think of them as sociologists. Also, look up Marx, the great bearded one. His economic ideas about capitalism are important in my virtual sociology, as is his vision of creative work. Pay attention to the ways in which subsequent theorists such as Habermas and Foucault interpret Marx. Both argue that Marx provides a useful framework, but that his framework needs to be rethought in light of twentieth-century changes in capitalism. Marx died in 1883. His last great book, *Capital* (1967), was published just after the American Civil War ended.

I introduce the themes of sociology by examining the ways in which enveloping structures of economy, politics, and culture have impact on people's daily lives – the lives most of us take for granted or at least experience as inescapable. Habermas' colleague Herbert Marcuse published an unsparing critique of the tendencies toward conformity in late capitalist society, tendencies that he characterized as **one-dimensional**. Published in 1964, *One-Dimensional Man* was read by college students and professors in America and Europe; he surely had impact on the college students who drafted the Port Huron Statement in 1962, the manifesto of the Students for a Democratic Society (SDS), who initiated the New Left and its protests against US racism, sexism, and the war in Vietnam (see Students for a Democratic Society 1999). Marcuse argued that middle-class affluence does not liberate people from the strictures of the prevailing capitalist ideology, which makes people unable to imagine a qualitatively different society in which they don't work 40 or 45 hours a week in return for brief annual vacations and weekends spent recuperating and shopping for entertainments and gadgets to soothe their anxieties and make them feel better about themselves – their selves, which they experience as objects. "One-dimensional" consciousness experiences the world as flattened, devoid of nuance and possibility, given. Hope is no longer world-historical in Hegel's terms, aiming at nothing less than millennial change; the prospect of the millennium was reduced to avoidance of a computer failure called Y2K. People hope for very little – promotions, better vacations, the avoidance of teenage suicide. What Nietzsche (2000) called *amor fati*, love of fate, prevails in a one-dimensional society.

Marcuse further suggests that we have lost the consciousness and discourse that would allow us to recognize and then talk about the inadequacy of this love of fate. The working class, Marx's harbinger of dramatic social change, has been integrated into middle-class consciousness and culture, now able to enjoy modest mobility and suburban lifestyles, thanks to the bargaining edge won for workers by unions. Marcuse was writing in the late 1950s and early 1960s. By the late 1970s, real incomes – what money will actually buy, in light of inflation – had begun to fall as American capitalism found itself positioned in a world market in which there was strong competition from Pacific Rim countries. But even the recessions of the 1970s and beyond were not matched by a critical consciousness, by theory, capable of explaining people's lives in compelling terms and then showing the way toward alternative political and economic institutions, culture, and values. This is because, by the 1950s, Eisenhower's America had closed off modes of consciousness and critique that raised fundamental questions about the social order. Instead, there was "euphoria in unhappiness," as Marcuse (1964) termed it, a narrow focus on goods, leisure, recreation, status symbols that displaces questioning about why people can't be liberated from the daily grind even as technology could provide for basic human needs the world over.

This was Marcuse's problem in his 1955 book, *Eros and Civilization*, in which he used Freud's psychoanalytic theory to explain how people willingly renounce pleasures and practices that the productive technology of post-World War II capitalism makes possible. People were, in Marcuse's terms, "surplus repressed," keeping themselves tightly in check, their noses to the grindstone and their political imaginations muted, in order to divert themselves from the prospect of liberation. With Freud, Marcuse accepted the fact that a degree of repression (basic repression) was necessary for people to cohabit the planet with others, accepting authority, making compromises, and inhibiting their egoistic, even infantile, aims. **Surplus repression** goes beyond what is necessary for peaceful coexistence; it bends people's creative energies in destructive and self-destructive directions, thus reproducing the existing social order. This surplus repression is imposed from above, by ideologists and advertisers, and self-imposed, by people whose "selves" have become so plastic that they do not have the will or psychic strength to resist. Conformity abounds.

Marcuse and his colleagues Horkheimer and Adorno attempted to explain how post-World War II capitalism has survived Marx's mid-nineteenth-century expectation of its demise. They contended that ideology, in Marx's era clear-cut claims about reality that purposely distorted it (e.g., liberation will only be found in the afterlife, capitalism involves a fair exchange of wages for labor power), has been deepened into what they termed **domination**, borrowing Weber's concept. Domination involves not only false claims but also a generalized mode of consciousness and experience steeled against liberating insights that jar everyday understandings of the goodness, rightness, and fairness of things. Domination is at once imposed and self-imposed as people's "subjectivity," as the Frankfurt theorists termed it, borrowing from German idealist philosophy, becomes little more than a transmission belt for system-serving imperatives that are now buried deep in the psyche. As such, these imperatives are not rendered as explicit doctrine but become subliminal. The Frankfurt theorists suggested that these imperatives to consume and conform have become "second nature," not exposed to clear thought and careful consideration but operating at an unconscious level shielded from the prying eyes of critical theory.

A one-dimensional society suffocates critical imagination about societal alternatives. For the first-generation Frankfurt theorists such as Marcuse and Adorno, this defeated the efforts of theorists, like Marx earlier, to explain to people how they are exploited and how they can burst through their bonds through critique and action. Tracts like *Communist Manifesto* (Marx and Engels 1967) are easily integrated into post-World War II society; they are sold as fast reads at Barnes & Noble or interpreted in doctoral dissertations. Having noted this, Marcuse's *One-Dimensional Man*, like a few other illuminating books aimed at an educated reading public not necessarily conversant with the works of European theory, led both to scholarly interpretation and civic action where it was read by New Leftists thirsting for social analysis explaining their changing world. Marcuse did not mean that society had become totally one-dimensional, completely closed off to critique and action. Marcuse knew the difference between a concentration camp and capitalist democracy. This was only a "tendency," as he called it; there remained "the chance of the alternatives," which could be kindled by theory and other cultural works that disturb people out of their doldrums and help them see themselves and their worlds in new and sometimes startling terms. Did Marcuse exaggerate his critique of capitalist democracy? Is it unpatriotic to have radical ideas? Are you willing to stand up and express views that are non-conformist and might subject you to ridicule by your classmates and friends?

One-Dimensional Man was just such a disturbing and illuminating book. Others included Michael Harrington's (1962) *The Other America*, which led President John Kennedy and after him President Lyndon Johnson to declare a war on poverty, and Betty Friedan's (1963) *Feminine Mystique*, which, in the early 1960s, helped middle-class women understand the roots of their own malaise in a sexist society, nearly single-handedly initiating the women's movement. Marcuse and Adorno came close to suggesting that the universe of discourse and critical reflection had been closed, leaving critical intellectuals no media other than very difficult theoretical writing and high-cultural forms such as classical music and opera. Adorno approached this sweeping indictment in books such as *Minima Moralia* (1978) and *Negative Dialectics* (1973). He declared that it was futile to write poetry after Auschwitz, suggesting total hopelessness. The Nazis' death camps suggested to a sensitive German Jewish intellectual with left-wing intentions such as Adorno that the project of the Enlightenment had gone disastrously wrong, making it impossible to uphold what Habermas called the project of modernity as a worthwhile goal. Paraphrasing and inverting Hegel, Adorno said that "the whole is the false." For an outstanding analysis of the work of the Frankfurt School, to which Adorno, Marcuse, Horkheimer, and Habermas belonged, see Rolf Wiggershaus' (1994) *The Frankfurt School: Its History, Theories and Political Significance*.

Ultimately, by the sheer act of writing about the eclipse of reason and of hope, the critical theorists expressed hope: Protest was resistance, even if they had no concrete blueprints of a better society, and how to get there. As Marcuse ended *One-Dimensional Man*: "It is only for the sake of those without hope that hope is given to us." Although orthodox Marxists (e.g., Slater 1975) criticize the Frankfurt theorists for stepping back from political action, almost disdaining class struggle from their rooms in what Lukàcs mockingly called "Grand Hotel Abyss," Marcuse, alone among the original generation of critical theorists, remained in the US after World War II and participated actively in the new social movements of the

1960s. Marcuse's thin 1969 book *An Essay on Liberation* theorized the "new sensibility" of the New Left and speculated about how Marxism is compatible with a new science and technology that do not dominate nature and that liberate people's imaginations and bodies. Although Marcuse recanted some of his initial optimism about the psychedelic sixties in his 1973 book *Counterrevolution and Revolt*, taking the New Left to task for abandoning reason and systematic social theorizing in favor of self-indulgence, the fact that he even bothered addressing the new social movements of the 1960s suggested that he was not immobilized by despair. Even Adorno in his esoteric, erudite philosophical works such as *Aesthetic Theory* found a refuge for critical reason in what he termed non-identity, which he said was the "ineradicable something" – mystery – remaining after the subject fails to explain fully, and thus dominate, the object. This philosophical remainder was Adorno's last, best hope that people, even in despair and servitude, would not be obliterated by a system of domination bent on total control – the project of the Nazis gone mad.

Sociology, in the hands of one of its founders, Emile Durkheim, although decidedly opposed to social problems of anomie and alienation, if not yet the domination of nature, also addressed people's subordination to social structures. In *Rules of Sociological Method* Durkheim (1950) argued that what makes sociology distinctive, demarcating it from the neighboring discipline of psychology, is its focus on "social facts," which he defined as instances of people's determination by the impinging social forces of economics, religion, culture, and nation. Although virtually everyone, on both sides of the ideological divide, would agree that sociologists usefully study the contexts in which people's actions are influenced and frequently hindered by social forces, Durkheim turned this into an ontology, a theory of social being. Selves are always to be dominated by societal objects, the foundational assumption of Comte (1975), Durkheim, Weber (1978) and Parsons (1937, 1951), in opposition to Marx, who argued that in a free society, which he called communism, people would imprint their sensibilities on the world without fearing what Hegel called "loss of the object," or alienation. This assumption by the founding sociologists was quite ahistorical, neglecting the possibility of radical social change which profoundly alters the balance of power between subjects and objects, selves and social structures.

Durkheim viewed all social behavior as caused by larger, impersonal social forces and social institutions. For example, instead of viewing suicide as an outcome of an internal mental state – despair, mental illness – Durkheim (1951) analyzed suicide as an extreme manifestation of anomie, or normlessness, caused by disintegrating social structures such as the feudal Catholic church in France. This approach divests the person of a purposive role in her suicide, even though, of course, Durkheim well understood that this was a heuristic device used to demonstrate the efficacy of the sociological apparatus and particularly of sociological method. He realized that suicide is a choice, even though, to people in despair, it may seem inevitable, inescapable. His sociological method, when used properly, would uncover people's social determination by the large institutions of class, nation, religion, habitat. Look up some research on suicide done by sociologists. Have Durkheim's ideas been overthrown? You might consider writing a term paper on the social causes of depression.

Weber went further where he described a three-dimensional model of social stratification, in opposition to Marx's unidimensional approach. Where Marx argued that a person's social class is a function of whether or not he owns the means of production in a capitalist society, Weber argued that there are three types of inequality, involving what he called class, status, and party. A person's class referred to his position in the labor market; a person's status referred to his "honor" or prestige in the community, which was largely a reflection of consumer behavior and lifestyle; a person's party standing referred to political party preference and to her possible participation in organized politics. Weber's tripartite approach to inequality allowed him to construct a complex topographical map on which people could be located. Where Marx argued that virtually everything about a person's life (or what Weber called life chances) was an outcome of his class position, Weber argued that a person could have class, status, and party positions inconsistent with each other, allowing a later sociologist named Gerhard Lenski (1966) to talk about status inconsistency. Priests experience status inconsistency because their honor or status is high, while their income is relatively low. Drug czars may command great wealth but they enjoy very low community prestige. These inconsistencies are conundrums for people, and should be studied. Class, status and party, in the hands of latter-day quantitative methodologists, became **variables** that can be analyzed statistically in order to determine the nature and direction of the social forces that, Durkheim and Weber agreed, could be said to cause people's behavior. Much of post-1970 American sociology involves the analysis of interactions among these carefully measured variables, which are linked in models or equations relating dependent to independent variables. To sample such equations, consult a recent sociological journal, such as *American Sociological Review* or *Social Forces*, in which you will probably find many articles with examples of these equations. Do you understand them? Do you think that you ever will? Exercise: Read an empirical article in one of these leading journals, really study it, and then, without reading the abstract that precedes it, summarize its argument in 100 words.

A dependent variable is a variable that, literally, depends on, or is caused by, another variable – an independent one. Durkheim theorized that the degree of a community's integration, afforded in his example by the Catholic or Protestant church, is an independent variable that, theoretically, has impact on the dependent variable, the rate of suicide. In simple terms, variation in the dependent variable "depends" on variations in the independent variable. Ideally, these variables admit of quantitative measurement so that statistical tests can be performed calculating the likelihood that co-variation in independent and dependent variables occurred by chance or because there is a causal relationship, of some strength, between them. By now, empirical sociologists have become very sophisticated at measurement, statistical inference, and the development of explanatory models (equations) that link a variety of independent variables to a dependent variable.

The main sections of empirical sociological journal articles contain rich and often obscure detail about the methods used in the reported study and devote considerable time and space to elaborate figural displays of both the data and the models (equations) used. This rhetorical strategy produces a **science aura**, reinforcing the legitimacy of sociology at a time when it faces an institutional crisis, with loss of majors and doctorates granted, diminished grant opportunities, a constrained faculty job market, and falling university prestige. These figural displays suggest that sociology is a science and allow the reader to "see the technology" underpinning the author's methodological activities.

This methods-driven sociology strays far from the matters occupying people's everyday lives such as having enough to eat and decent shelter, a problematic issue for the majority of the world's six billion, good health in an era of "managed care," schools for children that do more than just inculcate market-worthy and perhaps ephemeral skills, secure and even interesting work in the context of a global capitalism based on just-in-time manufacturing and Internet-routed information flows that destabilize work, education, and families.

As I explore in Chapter 3, I am not against methods (they can't be avoided in the sense that method is simply a route to knowledge), scientific journals, or grants. All have their place in the university. However, I question the hegemony (dominance) and exclusivity of quantitative, methods-driven sociology that disqualifies alternative versions of knowledge and discourse as illegitimate – qualitative sociology grounded in people's narratives about their lives, theoretical sociology that proceeds speculatively, politically-oriented sociologies stressing the urgency of sweeping social changes. This book explores an alternative framework for a narrative, literary sociology, rooted in a postmodern, post-Fordist capitalism of flexible accumulation and cybercommunications. I assess the relationship of self and social structure in this unprecedented stage of capitalism, not predicted by either bourgeois modernists such as Comte, Durkheim or Weber or by left-wing modernists such as Marx.

The Lives We Lead: From Marx to Ethnomethodology, Via Mills

I begin with the concept of everyday life – the experiences of people during their waking hours spent with families, friends, co-workers, salespeople, service providers, members of the anonymous public with whom one routinely rubs shoulders. Everyday life in the wired world has been accelerated, compressing time and leaving people scattered and restless. When most people go grocery shopping, they are in a rush and perhaps do not have a complete and legible list of what they need. They may have clipped discount coupons from the newspaper stuffed into an envelope that they thrust into their pockets or purses as they are leaving home. If they shop after work or on Saturday morning, as many do, they may have trouble finding a parking space. If they have children, they may plop one or more of them in the shopping cart, carefully avoiding the candy aisle or the displays of new and expensive Disney videos. (My daughter learned from television that the *Mulan* Disney video was due in stores on a certain day in February. She manufactured a grocery-shopping excursion – "We're out of milk!" – in order to induce her daddy down the aisle with the display of *Mulan* videos!)

We all know that it takes a good deal of social intelligence to navigate the swift and confusing currents of everyday life. Kant (1956, 1966), an important idealist philosopher, and Harold Garfinkel (1967), the founder of a sociological perspective called **ethnomethodology**, called this capacity **practical reason**, the ability to get things accomplished in a context of uncertainty and unpredictability. Little is more important for selves to survive the wired world. I am not a very practical person: I can't fix things, such as leaky faucets or my car; I can't fill out an income tax form accurately; I struggle to remember when to take out the garbage, and what sorts of detritus go in the recycling bin; my eyes glaze over when my wife, a quantitative sociologist who uses statistics in her research, tells me about our retirement funds. I know a few who have less pragmatic intelligence, and many who have more, such as my wife and daughter! As a sociologist, I explain my deficit of pragmatic intelligence, of practical reason, partly with reference to my privileged family background: My father wouldn't let me work during high school, arguing that this would take jobs, especially picking beans in the Willamette Valley of Oregon, away from migrant workers. Instead, he just gave me money when I said I needed it. I didn't have to be savvy in order to survive. I also explain my deficit of street smarts with reference to my penchant for the intellectual life, where people like me spend many hours, reading, thinking, apparently doing nothing, and many other hours writing books read by a few hundred, not a few hundred thousand.

I have often wondered whether I have an "everyday life" in the sense in which phenomenologically-oriented thinkers such as Edmund Husserl (1970a, 1970b) and Alfred Schutz (1967) intended the term – unreflected, taken-for-granted experience. I can make a trip to the supermarket or the dry cleaners a tortuous theoretical exercise, interrogating the rituals of interaction, salesmanship, and small-scale social organization surrounding me. My lack of practical intelligence corresponds with my insubordinate nature, leading me to protest the incidental injustices of everyday interaction. Recently, I took my daughter into a convenience store to buy her a drink for her sore throat, on route to her pediatrician's office. She picked a Sprite and gave it to me to take to the check-out area, while she browsed the merchandise. The salesperson, probably working at minimum wage, asked me if I wanted some Dorritos. I noticed a sign on her cash register telling her that she owes customers a dollar if she fails to ask them if they want to accompany their purchase with another unplanned purchase. I told her that I recognized that her suggestions of Dorritos was not her fault, that she was just following orders. But I told her gently that I really didn't like this because it treated customers as chumps and otherwise contributed to capitalism. It also sets a bad example for kids, who want to buy everything in the store. Similarly, at our local Sonic drive-in franchise, I sound impatient when asked if I want fries with my iced tea. I feel guilty after these exchanges, blaming the victim, the poor clerk or carhop, and my anger is redoubled at a system that pits all of us against each other. Describe your everyday life over the past week. Was it a typical week? What were your main activities? Was one day pretty much like the one before it? Did you eat regularly? Make a list of what you ate. How much quiet time did you give yourself in which to just think and reflect? How much time did you spend when there wasn't noise in the background, such as a radio or television? Did you have some fun? Are you happy with yourself?

The last thing the world needs is another grouchy intellectual who can't negotiate everyday life! I recognize that **everydayness** is a useful sociological category, but I resist, both in theory and practice, the compartmentalization of everydayness as a region of mute and dumb experience, in which people refuse to question and resist the quotidian, taken-for-granted, normative. My wife warns me that too much resistance makes me seem like a "jerk," which isn't, but probably should be, a sociological category, in counterpoint to everydayness! A jerk is someone who doesn't acknowledge that the cashier at the local convenience store is probably disempowered and shouldn't be taken to task for managerial directives designed to produce marginal profits by catering to customers' false needs – for Dorritos, french fries, sport utility vehicles, basketball shoes that zip instead of tie, makeup guaranteed to eliminate wrinkles. A jerk makes everyday life problematic by questioning its taken-for-granted routines that are, indeed, historical in that they rest on precedent and could be abandoned or changed. A jerk, in questioning everyday life, appears to assign responsibility for stupid decisions to people relatively low in the power hierarchies when, in fact, the jerk may know that the owners of 7-Eleven call the shots, even as they delegate minor authority to franchise managers who are not likely to be either rocket scientists or critical theorists.

The jerk is wrong to impute blame to the disempowered when, in fact, they are simply acting out the roles assigned to them. Not to play these roles will result in dismissal. But the jerk is correct when he implies that everyone is an agent, to use a philosophical term for possessing free will, and thus everyone can change her life and thus begin to change the world, albeit in small, halting ways. Everyday life, as Garfinkel reminds us, is transacted between practical reasoners, with pragmatic if not professional competence, who thus renew social structure by, in effect, "doing it." If we all quit our jobs and cease playing our other various roles, if we engaged in what Marcuse termed the Great Refusal, not only would capitalism screech to a halt, and with it the institutions of social control and discipline. We would also illuminate the possibility of different history by demonstrating that we are authors and agents of everything social. The jerk – the theorist! – is potentially an agent of change.

It's very difficult to orchestrate meaningful resistance and transformation at the level of everyday life among a billion, highly diverse selves. Even to approach agreement about what constitutes a good society seems impossible when people can't agree about which party should lead the country and states, how our schools should be run and financed, how expensive health care should be organized and delivered. But in his concept of the Great Refusal, Marcuse is suggesting, more eloquently than I, how people can seize authorship of their worlds, initially on a local scale. The environmental movement enshrined this basic plank of the New Left where it is said that people – jerks! – need to think globally and act locally. The western Marxists – Lukàcs (1971), Korsch (1970), Sartre (1976), Merleau-Ponty (1964a, 1964b), Marcuse, Adorno, Habermas, and I would include Marx himself, he of the 1843–4 manuscripts (1964) and the philosophy of praxis – argued that revolutionary change could not bypass selves. Indeed, the self, Marcuse's new sensibility and Merleau-Ponty's body subject, makes radical change possible, prefiguring, in Marcuse's term, the pacified society of the future in transformed everyday life.

In my sociology I examine the relationship between everyday life and enveloping social structure. Structure does not simply imprint itself on the blank slate of selves, playing out its supposed iron laws, but rather works through the self, who reproduces the dominant order. By the same token, the self can disobey social laws, overthrowing them through the force of will and leverage of social movements. This deviates little from Marx's original discussion of how the socialist revolution would only occur when the working class became a class "for itself," acting with desire and a plan, transcending its prior existence as a class merely "in itself." I depart from Marx where I address a capitalist world, now fully global in the present era of flexible accumulation and Internet connections, that Marx, even with his prescience and powerful theoretical imagination, simply could not have foreseen. There have been many changes since Marx published *Capital*, including the welfare state (inspired by Keynesian economic theory), which interposes government between capital and labor and thus forestalls class struggle; an equally efficacious culture industry which manufactures consciousness and diverts people harmlessly and profitably from their own misery; a permanent war economy; rapid population growth that prevents structural changes outside of the capitalist west; and the existence of nuclear weaponry. What has remained continuous since the Industrial Revolution is what Marx called the logic of capital. This is an irrational logic requiring the exploitation of labor for the sake of profit and subordinating labor in miserable, alienating jobs, threatening capitalism's undoing as working people grasp the structural nature of their exploitation and mobilize to change it. For an interesting and controversial discussion of globality, see *Empire* (Hardt and Negri 2000).

Marx understood everyday life simultaneously as a scene of domination and false consciousness and as a wellspring of revolutionary energy. The revolution, as Marx understood it, could not bypass everyday life, which in the nineteenth century was a hellish struggle for survival for almost everyone in emerging capitalist societies. Marx expected the contradictions of a capitalist society founded on a logic of capital that concentrates wealth in a few hands, impoverishing workers and at once depriving capital of workers' productive labor and diminishing consumption of the goods produced by their labor, to resolve themselves quickly in a socialist revolution, as "the expropriators are expropriated." As I explore further in Chapter 4, capitalism outlived Marx's expectation of its demise because capital found coping mechanisms, such as the welfare state, international imperialism, a permanently militarized society and economy, and the culture industries of Hollywood and Madison Avenue, that forestalled the imminent cataclysm Marx expected in the 1860s. But I maintain that capitalism has only displaced its contradictions and delayed its death throes by developing these defense mechanisms that, above all, depend on a quiescent, conformist self who performs the varied roles expected of citizens in the early twenty-first century. A wired capitalism is still only a depression away from its demise. Even if you aren't yet familiar with Marx's ideas, do you worry about the future? Does the current economic situation disturb you? Do unstable and unsafe global politics make you anxious? Do you find ways to ignore it all and carry on living? Do you think sociologists as a species worry a lot?

It is difficult to be a Marxist and avoid sounding like a determinist, who portrays a post-capitalist, perhaps postmodern future as inevitable. For someone who opposes positivism on both the left and right wings, the talk of predestination and iron necessity must be avoided at all costs. I am not certain that capitalism will collapse; but I am convinced that Marx's analysis of the deep-seated structural contradictions of capital make empirical sense, suggesting that capitalism is an impermanent, transitory social order that lurches from crisis to crisis, albeit with more self-sustaining resilience than Marx could have imagined in a relatively crude stage of nineteenth-century capitalist development. Many American sociologists disagree with me about the impermanence of capitalism. They suggest, on the evidence of failed socialist societies, that capitalism is the best social and economic order yet devised and that Marx's dream of a classless society is actually a hallucination. They go further and suggest, with many postmodernists, that the ideal of socialism has the status and social function of a myth, justifying short-term authoritarianism as a necessary expedient. But authoritarianism stretches into the long term, entrenching itself in a circulation of socialist elites, as the history of the Soviet Union amply demonstrates. Capitalism survives both because it is a preferable, more practical system and because socialism has proven to be a dismal failure.

How to rebut such good arguments? I am not attempting to persuade you to be socialists and Marxists! I am more interested in defending the concept of everyday life as the centerpiece of a wired sociology, and in people's actual everyday lives, in their diversity and commonality. However, the argument against Marxism raises an interesting question about history and evidence: Does the fact that socialism appears not to work or to endure, whereas capitalism does work, at least to some extent, and endures, mean that Marx was wrong in his claim that capitalism is a self-contradictory, flawed order bound to collapse of its own top-heavy weight? Marx may have been wrong about many things – the desirability of a classless society, the superiority of communism, his analysis of labor as a commodity, his contention that religion is merely the opiate of the masses. But he was not wrong in his prophesy of the overthrow of capitalism by virtue of its inherent flaws (contradictions) simply because the past, history, has not yet borne witness to capitalism's demise. The early twenty-first century does not end history, demonstrating capitalism's superiority over communism. There is plenty of evidence to suggest that capitalism is still crisis-bound and fundamentally irrational because private wealth depends on public misery and exploitation, with class conflicts now muted by the fragile social contract among big business, big labor, and big government and by people's diversion from public issues and their cynicism about politics. Indeed, I am composing the final revisions of this book as the American economy under President George Bush, Jr is in a nosedive and a depleting and destructive Iraq war has just ended.

Everyday life plays a crucial role in people's diversion from politics. People's routines appear untouched by the large structures of capitalism and colonialism, which are purposely shrouded in mystery. People are discouraged from theorizing their everyday lives, which are influenced by these powerful yet invisible structures, precisely because ideologies, which exist to protect this particular social order, portray society as governed by iron-clad necessities simply beyond the comprehension, let alone control, of ordinary citizens. Instead, people worry, understandably, about having enough to eat, decent shelter, their children's schooling and their futures, their own retirement. These are fundamental issues, but my point here, much as C. Wright Mills argued in *The Sociological Imagination* (1959) and as Marx argued in the mid-nineteenth century, is that we cannot understand these intimate issues without considering the larger historical and social contexts within which they are rooted. Will the Social Security fund be depleted by the time you retire? Will the quality of public schools continue to erode? Is the economy likely to produce enough jobs for most people to earn a decent living? These questions cannot be answered without theory, which seeks to comprehend what the philosopher Hegel called the totality – everything! This is not to pretend or attempt omniscience, which permits crystal-ball gazing. Rather, theory is not a specialized professional activity, but the capacity of people to understand what is happening around them, and to them, in sweeping historical and structural terms that are nowhere printed in a sacred text or taught as doctrine in schools and universities. Neither theory nor method can pretend to have unlocked the mysteries of the universe. What makes theory so vital is its attempt to seek the general in the particular, grand patterns in everyday things, that enable us to understand ourselves better both in our cosmic insignificance and in our capacity for building a more just and humane world. And then to write about it sociologically, with the vivid imagination and detail of a good novelist.

Mao Tse-Tung, the Chinese Communist revolutionary, portrayed the Chinese revolution as needing to traverse a long road, overcoming enemies and obstacles, including the industrial backwardness of China in the 1930s. The German New Leftist, "Red" Rudi Dutschke, borrowed liberally from Mao where he talked of the need for young German leftists to undertake a "long march through the institutions," boring from within in order to effect change. The role of consciousness in radical social change has been taken seriously since the early 1920s, when Georg Lukàcs, a Hungarian Marxist, wrote *History and Class Consciousness*, a treatise explaining why the revolution that Marx reasonably expected in the 1860s had not come to pass. Lukàcs' argument was that working-class consciousness had been manipulated by ideologists who pitted workers of different nations against each other in World War I instead of uniting international workers against their capitalist bondsman. He attempted to restore the role of class consciousness to Marxist theory, borrowing from Marx, Hegel, and Kant. Lukàcs argued that raising class consciousness was no simple matter but required working people to understand their own everyday lives, especially their jobs, not as predetermined outcomes of iron-clad capitalist laws of development but as fluid, subject to transformation.

The term **commodification** does not appear in many beginning sociology books, but it should. By commodification Marx and Lukàcs referred to the way in which all manner of human products and activities, especially labor, are bought and sold, taking on the appearance of natural things that have value only because the marketplace assigns them value, a price, through the ebb and flow of supply and demand. Marx invited us to view human labor much as we view a loaf of bread; when it is in abundant supply, its price is low, and when scarce its price is high. In reality, Marx argued, commodities have value because they contain congealed labor, or labor power, transferred to commodities by workers who renounce both ownership of the fruits of their labor and control of the working process in return for a frequently meager wage. In this context, the social relations of work played out between capitalist and worker that are imbedded in every product brought to market are concealed in capitalism; relations between people appear to be relations between things, taking on what Marx in volume I of *Capital* calls a "fetish" quality, indicating their mysterious origin in labor that is carefully covered over so that workers lose sight of their real stake in the economic system built on their backbreaking toil.

As capitalism advances, the activities and objects of everyday life become increasingly commodified, as virtually all aspects of human relations come under sway of market forces, which, as ever in capitalism, reflected deep-seated structural inequality between capitalists and workers, who have nothing but their labor power to sell. Adam Smith argued that workers should make less than their bosses because their bosses take all the risk by starting a business. Marx disagreed, maintaining that profit is only produced through the expenditure of human labor in the factory. Working people today are every bit as desperate as in Marx's time in the sense that they work and live at the mercy of their employers. Anyone who has been fired understands the desperation and degradation of this predicament, especially as we move from a Fordist mode of production, with manufacturing concentrated in large cities, strong labor unions, and large inventories of products that require large-scale bureaucracies, to a post-Fordist mode of decentralized, flexible production. **Fordism** is the name given to the system of mass production begun by Henry Ford, who understood that he would make more money by pricing his cars affordably because then more people would buy them. In this post-Fordist mode all sorts of enterprises "downsize" in order to save labor costs and dispense with inventory in favor of "just-in-time" production, where products and their components are FedExed and UPSed around the globe and where information flows in bits and bytes over the virtual pathways of the information superhighway.

FedEx, flexible production and accumulation, globalization, the World Wide Web do not set men and women free, as we shall see in this book. Self is dispersed, scattered, on the vectors of virtualization, as Tim Luke (forthcoming) calls them. Community is illusory if it is rooted in the instantaneity of e-mail, chat rooms, distance education. This is not to deny the potentially emancipating role of information technology, which, like all technology, needs to be understood in terms of the social relations imbedded in it and not celebrated uncritically nor dismissed as a tool of the oppressor. In order to assess the potentials of post-Fordist work, the postmodern family, as Stacey (1998) calls it, and the Internet we need to examine the lives people lead in their wired worlds. The powerful structures of work, family, education, and leisure are too often invisible even to well-educated people who dig no deeper than *Newsweek* or *ABC Nightline* for critical analysis of the world around them. We need a virtual sociology to make sense of our virtual selves.

One of the first sociologists to use the term "everyday life" was Henri Lefebvre (1984, 1991) a noted French sociologist of urban life. When I first read the term, I was reading one of Lefebvre's books. I quickly discovered that phenomenologists such as Husserl and Schutz used a related term, *Lebenswelt* or **lifeworld**, as it is usually translated. Husserl characterized people's mode of consciousness in everyday life as the **natural attitude**, suggesting an uncritical, unreflective orientation to taken-for-granted, familiar things, including other people, that clutter our lives. When we turn on the television, for example, we don't stop to consider the electrical circuits inside it or where it was manufactured, and whether workers were exploited. As such, everyday life implies an ordinariness corresponding to a mode of consciousness or natural attitude, contrasted with a **theoretical attitude** that views the taken-for-granted world as unfamiliar, strange. Husserl argued that we could penetrate to the essences of things only by experiencing things from the point of view of pure, untheorized experience which, in a way, is superior to theory in that it addresses things as they really are, not as philosophers imagine them to be. **Phenomenology** is a program of stripping away the philosophical and theoretical baggage that philosophers customarily bring to bear in their investigation of phenomena. Instead, philosophy needs to perceive things from the vantage of the natural attitude, thus learning from people's ordinary experiences of the world. Everyday life, for Husserl, was not stupefied, but a ground of powerful knowledge about things as they are. For an excellent and readable discussion of social phenomenology, see Berger and Luckmann's 1967 classic, *The Social Construction of*

Reality. Also consider an essay on sociology in the natural attitude, which influences much of this book and especially my argument in the concluding chapter, by my graduate-school mentor John O'Neill, called *Making Sense Together* (1974).

Cultural anthropologists have long argued that we should study people in their natural habitats, listening carefully to the stories natives tell us, in their own dialects and through their own lenses, which are often quite sophisticated. This has generated the program of ethnography, which describes behavior and discourse as they are perceived by the anthropologist who works at the ground level of everyday life. Within sociology, the ethnomethodological program, which I described above, develops a whole research agenda around this insight of Husserl's about the relevance of everyday experience and conversation to sociological knowledge. Far from being creatures of mindless habit, people living their lives in the natural attitude are effective practical reasoners who not only understand the traps and opportunities of their lifeworlds, but can speak persuasively about them, thus building a workable social order from the ground up. Harold Garfinkel urged ethnomethodology, by listening to everyday conversation, to document the ways in which people are not simply playing Parsonian roles prescribed from on high by the custodians of social order but transacting, literally "doing," social order through their everyday interactions. In this paragraph, I just used a key postmodern term, **discourse**, referring to all the ways we talk, write, and produce symbols. For a discussion of discourse-theoretic approaches to sociology and social theory, see my *Decline of Discourse* (1990).

This ethnographic, ethnomethodological agenda is quite populist, demonstrating the power of the people to live competently amidst the tremendous disorder of contemporary urban and suburban life. Some (Paci 1972; Piccone 1971) have even argued for a phenomenological Marxism. This Marxism grounds theoretical concepts in the creativity and contest of the lifeworld and thus makes way for a **dialectical** social theory that sees local in global and global in local, thus checking the left's tendency to view "subjects" in everyday life as ciphers to be manipulated by theorists and tacticians from above. Even the Frankfurt School theorists, in their understanding of the enveloping character of domination that chokes off critical insight at every level, portrayed the one-dimensional society too one-dimensionally, failing to notice nuances of resistance and difference that cut against the grain of the dominant ethos. In their cultural elitism and their despair over the continuities between fascism and late capitalism, they ironically converged with Soviet Marxists, beginning with Lenin, who prescribed truth to the proletariat "from without," making up for the masses' intellectual and political inexperience with the dialectical "laws" of an official Dialectical Materialism. (See Marcuse's book, *Soviet Marxism* (1958)). All of these theorists gave up on everyday life as a potential venue of critical insight and transforming practice. Were they elitist? Is it necessarily wrong to make judgments about other people, including judgments about the level of their consciousness? Do you have a right to tell your best friend not to take cocaine or drink too much? Is that different from social theorists deeming people "falsely conscious"?

For its part, mainstream American sociology has never adopted Lefebvre's or Husserl's notions of everyday life as a foundation of either theory or research. Parsons' (1951) discussions of the family as a female-tended haven in a heartless male world were the basis of his functionalist social psychology that viewed socialization as the seamless acquisition of social roles of instrumentality, expressiveness, industriousness, citizenship, and worship. In this context, the boundary between the public and private, between work and citizenship, on the one hand, and domesticity, leisure, and religion, on the other, was unproblematic: Parsons' unit actors, as he called them, dutifully played the roles assigned to them, with women primarily restricted to the private sphere, although, as Parsons acknowledged, this was important public activity – raising kids, cooking, ironing clothes, engaging in emotional labor (including sex) that allowed men to view the family as a retreat from the ordeal of work. For Parsons, there was no private sphere that didn't play a functional social role, although, paradoxically (I would say contradictorily) he deprived women's domestic roles of direct compensation and the social worth bestowed by the market.

Only with theorists such as Habermas, Lasch (1977), Sennett (1977), and Lefebvre and with the rise of feminist theory and queer theory, whose theorists wrote in the wake of the new social movements percolating to the societal surface in the 1960s, was the relationship between the public and private reappraised. American **feminism** arose out of the Movement politics of the male-dominated New Left, as Breines (1982, 1992), Zaretsky (1976), Gitlin (1987), and Hayden (1988) document. Movement women were no longer content to play public roles of protest against the war in Vietnam and against racism while being subordinated to their activist boyfriends. Critical social theorists wanted to assign value to a private sphere that, they theorized, was not private at all but "colonized," in Habermas' terms, by systemic imperatives – power, control, profit, the subjugation of women. Personal life, domestic labor, childhood were theorized as moments of reproduction and possible sites of resistance. In this context, Paul Piccone, who founded the journal of radical social theory, *Telos*, argued for a phenomenological Marxism that does not forsake everyday life, viewing it either as an apolitical remainder or as a functionalist safe haven for alienated men, but rather grounds critical theoretical categories in the lifeworld in which selves have agency, albeit often highly curtailed by colonizing systemic imperatives, to know and make their worlds.

This stress on agency and consciousness has remained the dominant theme in **western Marxism**, critical theory, and feminist theory since the early 1920s. For its part, American sociology awaited social phenomenology and Garfinkel's ethnomethodology in the 1960s before similar consideration was given to the effective self. The left needed to explain the failure of the European working classes to join an international socialist revolution, the emergent authoritarianism of Soviet socialism, especially after Lenin's death in 1924, the social-psychological continuity between fascism and post-World War II capitalism through the concept of authoritarian personality, the promises and impasses of the 1968 French May Movement, the Prague Spring in 1968, and the American New Left, which ended the Vietnam War and helped win important civil rights victories in the American South but failed to theorize a "new sensibility," as Marcuse called it. These are stories of both failure and success, a "dialectic of defeat," as Jacoby (1981) termed it, that hinge on the roles of subjectivity, consciousness, sexuality, domesticity in both everyday life and opposition politics. Although a struggling self has often been inadequately armed, politically and theoretically, to stave off discipline and system, the recognition of the importance of daily life, of reproduction, remains central to the theoretical left, whether Derridean, queer, Frankfurt-oriented, feminist, or influenced by Birmingham cultural studies, and to a critical sociology influenced by Husserl and Garfinkel.

This emphasis on everyday life has been paralleled, since Lukacs and the Frankfurt writings from the 1930s, by a concern with culture and cultural politics. Lukacs explained the failure of European revolutions largely with respect to the absence of class consciousness, which Marx, at least in *Capital*, treated more or less as a derivate from the crisis-prone economic base of society. This may have been reasonable for Marx in the mid-nineteenth century, when capitalism was still quite rudimentary and, absent the welfare state, prone to swing wildly from crisis to crisis, as early monopoly capital was plagued by problems of underconsumption. For

their part, the critical theorists argued that the failure of European socialism and the rise of fascism could only be explained by theorizing not only
problems of capitalism but problems of **the Enlightenment** itself, especially positivism, which, they contended, had become a new mythology,
ideology, and culture of domination. By the 1960s, cultural politics had
become central to the New Left and feminist theory, which recognized that
culture was no longer textual but involved all sorts of public discourses
from television to textbooks, music to movies. Ryan and Kellner's
1988 *Camera Politica* examines blockbuster Hollywood movies for both
ideology and critique; Willis' 1977 *Learning to Labour* documents the
cultural socialization of working-class "lads" in England; Walters' 1995
Material Girls points the way toward feminist cultural studies. The basic
contention of cultural studies people is that popular culture (think of
music videos or sitcoms) has become a political factor, suggesting values
and a lifestyle to people. Later on, I discuss a popular 1960s sitcom, *Leave
it to Beaver* from a political point of view, examining its images of men,
women and kids.

Do Positivists Have Everyday Lives?

American sociology, with a few prominent exceptions such as Garfinkel
and O'Neill, has been less affected by these themes of everyday life and
cultural politics than have humanities disciplines such as English, comparative literature, modern languages, even the relatively theory-averse
and male-dominated disciplines of history and philosophy. Many scholars
under 50 at the MLA (Modern Language Association) annual meetings,
which collects humanists from every discipline in paper giving and job
seeking, identify themselves as students of cultural studies. Even older
humanities faculty read and write widely in cultural studies and the
politics of subjectivity, using new faculty hiring to rebuild departments
that had formerly focused on canonical and textual studies in light of these
new theoretical and cultural developments in the humanities and social
sciences.

Since the 1970s, American sociologists have moved in the opposite
direction, away from personal politics and culture and toward science,
methodology and research grants. This is not to say that most American
sociologists are card-carrying Republicans who support the retrenchment
of sociology during an era of fiscal accountability and attacks on feather-
bedding academics. Most are liberals, aggrieved by rampant social

problems of modernity, supportive of the liberal arts, including sociology, firm believers in academic tenure and academic freedom. However, sociology's method is conservative in the sense that positivist writing freezes, by reflecting, the social world on the journal page, thus reinforcing the impression created by ideologists of modernization/modernity that this world is intractable, a plenitude of social being. Comte first wrote of sociological laws of progress, a refrain repeated by Durkheim, Weber, and Parsons. This notion of social laws was mixed up with Comte's claim that his sociology was a system of positivism (positive philosophy, as he termed it). On its face, positivism is merely an epistemology, a theory of knowledge stressing that the knower or scientist stands outside of the world he or she seeks to understand. More precisely, the knower is in the world, but can distance herself from the world using the cleansing procedures of method, a notion that originated philosophically with Descartes. But, with Comte, positivism became simultaneously a theory of knowledge and a narrative of progress grounded in the concept of social laws. This confusion was purposeful and, on its face, reasonable in that the natural sciences formulate laws of nature using the objectivist epistemology of positivism. A scientist who claims to stand outside of the world in order to know it typically views her inellectual purpose as the attainment of laws of cause and effect.

As American sociology has evolved, it has disconnected the discourse about social laws from the doctrine of positivism, which is now viewed purely as an epistemological posture. Most sociologists probably agree with Comte and Durkheim that a mature science describes laws. However, they do not believe that sociology has yet attained maturity and thus they restrict positivism to a theory of knowledge, or, more exactly, a methodological procedure designed to cleanse knowledge of bias and perspective. By now, even this aspect of positivism has been dropped from the rhetoric of scientific sociology as positivism has become less doctrine than discourse, a way of writing that relies heavily on representational figures and mathematical notation designed to produce the science aura and thus legitimize sociology at a time of its crisis. American sociologists gradually decoupled Comte, Durkheim, and Weber's theory of progress, on the one hand, and positivist method, on the other. Since 1970, American sociologists have gone a step further, dropping talk of positivism as an epistemological doctrine altogether in favor of a discursive positivism that stakes its claim to science on the basis not of explicit philosophical or methodological doctrine, but of literary gesture, the way science, to be science, writes.

Positivism, then, has become a literary agenda, taught to graduate students who read the journals and co-author articles and grant proposals with their faculty mentors. This literary agenda is deeply political, no matter how much it disavows politics as the scourge of the sixties, when certain sociologists such as C. Wright Mills and Alvin Gouldner championed an activist role for sociology. Graduate programs in sociology have become sites of "training" in the techniques and discourse of method. Faculty scramble to publish methods-driven articles in mainstream journals such as *American Sociological Review*, for which they are rewarded with jobs, tenure, and promotions. Sociology chairpeople attempt to convince higher administrators of the worthiness of their programs based on dubious national rankings of graduate departments that often combine perceived prestige with the number of mainstream journal publications and grants obtained by the department's faculty. Articles reproduce themselves as authors cite familiar literature and use standard quantitative methods in order to test narrow hypotheses about the interrelations among variables. Careers are staked on the primary and secondary analysis of large data sets that yield publishable nuggets treating a delimited literature, and the slender topics differentiating the author's work (or, more typically, co-authors' work) from prevailing wisdom in the field. Under what circumstances do elderly Hispanics rejoin their children's households? What variables predict church attendance among young families? Science, it is thought, inches forward incrementally, as research findings cumulate toward social laws that never seem to arrive.

The further sociologists plunge into this methods-driven journal discourse that sports the hieroglyphics of math and physics discourse, the further they get from the contested domains of everyday life and the structures that condition them. A problems-oriented critical sociology is viewed, in hindsight, as a relic of the sixties, which has been left behind by methodologists seeking legitimacy for their science, careers, grants, graduate programs, professional associations. The mainstream quantitative sociologists of former departments in which I worked mocked those few of us in critical theory as people who lacked numeracy, navel-gazers without data who did little to enhance departmental prestige given our paucity of mainstream journal publications, citations in mainstream journal publications, and grants. We are dismissed as too political, throwbacks to an earlier time when sociologists took to the streets in protest and studied street-corner behavior.

Returning sociology to everyday life is a return both to politics and to methods, including speculative theory, that understand themselves as discourse, necessarily perspective-ridden and self-limiting. As I explore in Chapter 3, these methods are not a royal road to truth but merely one version among many. This is not to decide against quantitative sociology; this approach can tell us much about large-scale phenomena such as domestic and global flows of wealth and population. It is simply to treat such methods as arguments for particular approaches to particular worlds. These methods have to make their case and not bury argument in the disinterested stance of the scientist. Science is already in the world and cannot be removed from it, no matter how hard sociologists work to cleanse their methodological protocols of contaminants such as passion and politics, that necessarily cling to methods as the unavoidable residue of science's inherence in the world. Sociology is a worldly pursuit that does its best work when it confesses this worldliness, not denying the interests of the scientist but making them plain for all to see. In no way does this forsake objectivity, at least for those of us who believe that science and social science inhabit a world extending beyond the pages of books and journals. Just because the text is a world involving politics and perspective, the world is not all text, nor sheer discourse. There are forests, oceans, cities, nation states, other people, other methods that do not cease to exist in the solitary imagination of the lonely scholar.

Having argued for a return to everyday life, I seek to view the concept of everydayness historically, contending that we need to view the mundane occurrences and patterns of daily life not as a timeless constant but as a particular outcome of a capitalist society that removes large institutions and structures from view. It does so because those with power want to hide their power, and its impact on "everyday" lives the world over, from ordinary people who are instead led to believe, and convince themselves, that fundamental social change is far less desirable than personal betterment, however that might be defined. I am not opposed to personal betterment – acquiring education, finding a better job, having children and raising them lovingly, getting fit. These are the desiderata of the good life, which give life meaning. I want to situate these pursuits, eminently reasonable though they may be, in a historical context that has blocked most people from achieving these goals, both today and for the past 2,000 years. I want to disentangle the personal, indeed the person, from an everyday life that has come to be marked by banality, routine, deprivation, meager expectations, absence of hope.

Even the adjective "everyday" suggests resignation to the ordinary, the ever-the-same. Ever-the-sameness is a crucial characteristic of the foreshortening of historical imagination, the flattening of history into a drab continuum of the "same ol', same ol'." Who among us does not view everyday life as so predictable, or, worse, so fraught with dangers, that we don't at least fantasize about winning the lottery, playing for the Chicago Bulls, or, if we are academics, receiving a grant for "geniuses"? My family lives in an upper-middle-class suburb between Dallas and Fort Worth. On the perimeter of our neighborhood is a poor transient area with flea-bag hotels that rent by the week for people who can't afford their own houses or apartments. A major train line runs nearby. At the 7-Eleven store, where I buy my children Slurpees, we regularly see poor people buying lottery tickets. Occasionally, we see people claiming their minor winnings. Some of the children of parents thus occupied have dirty bare feet, reflecting entrenched poverty. My daughter often asks me about these people, and after hearing my sociology lectures, she, in her analogical thinking, understands these down-and-out people living on the edge to be the people for whom Martin Luther King fought during the sixties. She remarks that we are "rich," by comparison, and live in a "mansion" (a house with just over 3,000 square feet). She is struggling to understand that the comforts and security she and her brother take for granted are not shared by everyone, especially these neighbors who waste precious dollars in order to purchase lottery tickets that never pay off with enough winnings to deliver them from poverty and hopelessness.

My wife, also a sociologist, and I want our children to understand the extraordinary variations in people's existences and levels of subsistence. People's life chances, to use Weber's term, are largely owed to the accidents of their parents' social class positions. These are, of course, not accidents: Class is produced by a certain social and economic system in which only a few fare very well. Social class reproduces itself across generations. My parents were comfortable, and stressed academic achievement. My wife's father, via college and dental school, rose from abject rural poverty, an exception to the general rule of inherited social class. Our children need to know that most of the world's other children are in desperate straits, and what causes that: Capitalism, Soviet-style socialism (a decade ago), various kinds of despotism in the Third World, religious dogma leading to holy wars, men's hatred of women, whites' hatred of people of color. Our son is Mexican-American and already it is obvious to us that he is positioned differently by the parents of his classmates. He is on the path to becoming white unless we are careful and reinforce his ethnicity as he gets old enough to understand these issues. He needs to understand why, in Texas, many construction teams, road crews, lawn-cutting services are composed of brown people, including many illegal aliens, who look just like him, but how these occupations do not exhaust his possibilities, with the right education, ability, and luck.

My son needs to be taught the importance of **historicity**, the fact that change is possible, but constrained by the powerful inertia of the past, both distant and recent. If my son does not learn this, he will not understand why his everyday life is so full of possibility whereas the lives of the little brown boys he sees at the store are probably over even before they started. If they beat the odds and escape the throes of poverty and racism, historicity will have made it possible – the possibility that people's lives can be improved through their own agency, hard work, saving, educational attainments, mentorship, and sponsorship, and that whole social structures can shift in ways that make it more likely that people's agency, as I am calling it, will pay off in substantially improved life chances. The real issue here is what will happen to the kids of the poor kids. Will poverty be passed down or will they somehow break the chain and bring up their kids differently from the ways they were brought up? Will learning replace lottery tickets?

People who used to be called liberals, stemming originally from the inspiration of the political philosophies of John Stuart Mill and John Locke, argue that people can be viewed as more or less separate individuals who, through perspiration and inspiration as well as assistance from a beneficent government, can ascend the ladders of success by doing battle successfully in the marketplace. When you think of this sort of liberalism think of the Presidencies of Franklin Roosevelt and John Kennedy. Today, liberals are usually called neo-liberals in order to signify a major rightward shift in the US Democratic Party since the Carter Presidency. The Democratic Party no longer defines itself as the party of big labor now that the social contract among business, labor, and the state or government has eroded. The ideological polarization and truncation of the welfare state began under Carter (zero-based budgeting) and gathered powerful momentum during Reagan's two terms in the White House, during which he decreased the taxes of the wealthy and corporations and reduced social welfare to the poor.

Since the mid-1970s, most Americans have agreed that the role of the government in civic affairs and even in the economic system should be reduced both because federal and state bureaucracies cost a lot of tax money and because people have been convinced that the United States has become a welfare state, a harbinger of creeping socialism. The so-called Proxmire Award, given by Senator William Proxmire, lampoons extravagant government spending and contracts in the spirit of both fiscal conservatism and greater government accountability. The 1990s became the proverbial decade of accountability, especially in education. Schoolchildren are subjected to standardized competency tests administered by a growing number of states suspicious of public school teachers, who now "teach to" these tests, piling on homework and administering a speed-up of the learning process. At my kids' school, classes that took a difficult standardized test yesterday were allowed to go Hawaiian today, wearing beach clothing and bringing blankets and pillows to their classrooms in order to de-stress – a virtual vacation from the job!

College faculty are also subject to accountability measures: Teaching loads are rising as administrative CEOs reduce the emphasis on research, largely, they claim, because external constituencies view faculty members' primary role as teaching, not doing irrelevant research that "no one" reads. Tenure is becoming a thing of the past as colleges and universities subject faculty to periodic post-tenure review (on top of annual evaluations done of all faculty), a mechanism whereby tenured faculty evaluate each other in a corrosive war of all against all. This erosion of tenure is the greatest threat to academic freedom since McCarthyism. Academic freedom is not the freedom from oversight but a freedom to live the life of the mind unencumbered by a clock, time-and-motion studies of one's efficiency and productivity, endless documentation of what one has accomplished over the past year or even semester, and administrative scrutiny of one's grade distribution and the student dropout rate in one's classes.

Although there is less government intervention in the economic system than before the Reagan Presidency, leading to even sharper disparities in wealth between the top and bottom earners, there is more institutional surveillance of people's lives. This surveillance is made possible by information technologies all the way from satellites to the Internet. We are increasingly being watched and tracked, in our personal and public lives. Our spending, working, telephoning, vacationing, charitable gift-giving are all subject to electronic scrutiny by credit-card companies, credit agencies, social-welfare bureaus, the police, military intelligence, the Internal Revenue Service, our bosses. Privacy has eroded under the all-seeing electronic eyes of a surveillance society, which subjects us to discipline in order to produce and reproduce disciplined selves.

There are paradoxes here: Big government is unpopular, especially in its welfare-giving role. Reagan dismantled the safety nets first put in place by Franklin Roosevelt to cushion the poor. Think of welfare and food stamps. But information technology, which connects people in a global village, permits total surveillance that runs counter to the trend toward smaller and less invasive government. Computer hackers can gain access to our histories of personal debt. We receive unwanted e-mail that, if we reply, allows companies to send us promotional messages. The freedom to shop online, simply by entering our credit card numbers, is balanced against electronic surveillance of our electronic conversations with colleagues and friends. We shrink government but enact open-records laws allowing people to snoop into each others' lives. Although it could be argued, especially by one who views knowledge as power, that an open society shares information freely, the democratization of knowledge slides into authoritarianism where secrecy is replaced by surveillance. Since McCarthyism during the 1950s, when a "red scare" licensed the paranoid right to launch a witch hunt against people in politics, academia, and entertainment only suspected or accused of being Communist subversives, without evidence, surveillance has become a powerful tool of the religious right. This born-again right no longer sees Soviet sympathizers under every bed, the Soviet Union having collapsed of its own top-heavy weight during the 1980s, but imagines that civic morality and the American way of life are imperiled by latter-day demons – gays and lesbians who proudly call themselves queer, rock musicians who script satanic lyrics, useless university professors who teach and write postmodern philosophy instead of transmitting job-worthy skills.

These are curious times: Big government and big labor are viewed as obstacles to social progress. Big business receives give-backs from organized labor and tax concessions from government. Information technology allows global shopping, global coordination of the flexible accumulation of capital, global military defense, global news and popular culture, global surveillance of individuals. What are the costs and benefits of these sorts of globalization? Can we still speak meaningfully of capitalism, using Marx's or Weber's nineteenth- and early twentieth-century categories of analysis? Does information technology set us free or further enslave us? Do e-mail and chat rooms create vital electronic community, mitigating the isolation that most people experience? Is everyday life better, and more promising, for those of us with jobs, VCRs, and home computers? What is the future of democratic politics?

This book will answer these questions. To preview my overall perspective, I believe that information technologies have the potential to enhance people's lives by joining them in democratic communities that can challenge existing monopolies of power, wealth, and information but that, frequently, these technologies are used to render citizens disciplined and docile. I disagree with liberals who view electronic prostheses such as the Internet as good in themselves because they help people "connect" with each other, surfing the world from their offices and homes – "go anywhere you want today," as the Microsoft advertisement suggests. It is an open question whether these electronic connections empower people who otherwise play dutiful, disempowered roles in capitalism, the patriarchal family, traditional religion, the nation state. Although knowledge is power, and communication too, power also involves other sources of leverage – wealth, monopoly of armaments and armies, cultural influence (I almost wrote the pejorative term "propaganda"). Using search engines like Yahoo or Lycos in order to plan vacations, read *The New York Times* online, apply to college, find out late-night basketball scores, or learn more about how to groom your long-haired cat does not signal a major social change. Using electronic mail and chat rooms to connect almost instantaneously with like-minded bass fishermen, Young Republicans, or horny members of the opposite, or same, sex between the ages of 18 and 24 does not elevate the culture or liberate the imagination.

It could be said that we have access to more information and stimulation than ever before in world history, and yet that most people are less well educated than their counterparts a generation ago, who were not inundated with television and the World Wide Web. Are people getting smarter and stupider at the same time?! I view information technology as having a "dialectical" potential, making way for possible progress and regress at once. The Internet could allow people to become even more manipulated and simultaneously allow capital to disperse itself globally in ways that increase its profits. Amazon.Com, the online bookseller, advertises itself as having the biggest book inventory in the world. Actually, it has no inventory at all, instead buying its books from wholesalers who warehouse the books. For academic readers who live in the suburbs, like Arlington, Texas, which boast only Barnes & Noble outlets and not serious academic bookstores, or in small towns, which have no bookstores at all, vendors such as Amazon.Com are the only game in town. In this sense, Amazon.Com is a mixed blessing.

Or the Internet could make possible virtual democracy, allowing instantaneous plebiscites on issues of the day and joining citizens in town meeting-like chat rooms. Public-access television could be a model of this public empowering, challenging the domination of the networks with vital, self-made cultural products and practices. E-mail enhances discursive competence, allowing everyone to be a writer. And e-journals and e-"book" publications begin to break the monopoly over print enjoyed by the mainstream publishing cartels, which are often vertically-integrated corporations that own mass-market magazines, trade-book imprints, television networks, and baseball teams. Although it has been noted that e-communication makes for rough-hewn, careless literary products, the cultural hallmark of a fast capitalism based on planned obsolescence and junk food, e-communication also empowers and unites, challenging domination at its roots: Readers become writers, an issue I pursue in Chapter 6.

And readers not only become writers; they become active citizens who no longer accept the ordinariness of their everyday lives, working toward something more. If, as western Marxists, feminists, and the Freudian left have always maintained, sweeping social change cannot bypass consciousness, the body, values, the household – everyday life writ large – then issues of self and community, as I am calling them here, are uppermost on the critical agenda. Sociology as a discipline has always dealt with self and community, although, with Durkheim and Weber and then Parsons, most sociologists have accepted domination as the essential condition of humanity. Members of the left, diversely understood, believe that we can overthrow domination as people begin to change their lives in the here and now, thus changing larger institutions whose transformation conditions further changes at the level of the lifeworld. The personal is political, just as the political is personal. The personal must also be defended as a realm of experience inviolable by political and ideological imperatives, a private space off limits to advertising and unwanted Web sites. But we are far from that point inasmuch as our everyday lives are administered by external forces of consumption, control, and conformity. We are perhaps most manipulated where we do not recognize the constraining influences of social structures on the ways we think and behave, on our very sensibilities, which we are accustomed to viewing as unproblematic, apolitical.

In this opening chapter, I have discussed the relationship between people's everyday lives and what sociologists typically call social structure. Structures are things you can't easily see or discern. But they make their presence felt. Think of religion and churches. Think of the economy and money. And, now, think of the Internet and other electronic connections that alter the distinction between self and society, inside and outside. In the next chapter, I will talk more about what sociology already knows about social structures, and how it conducts its business of investigating them. We won't stray far from selves, and their experiences. In the third chapter, I will explore methodologies – how people, including sociologists, know, and how they express their knowledge.

CHAPTER TWO

Sociology's Encyclopedia

Sociological theorists have conceptualized the self as an outcome of social forces, which impinge on the person. Positivist sociologists model their work on the sciences of the Enlightenment, seeking to describe social laws. Alternative traditions like Marxism and ethnomethodology view social structures as products of human interaction, work, and language.

Where did sociology come from? Is it a science? If not, is it fiction? In this chapter, I explore the history and present of sociology, asking what it knows about the world. I discuss its key assumptions, especially its intent to be a science. What I call the science question is central to this book. Most postmodernists mistrust the claim that social studies and cultural studies can be sciences in the same sense that physics and chemistry are. I am a big fan of science if by that we mean a systematic approach to knowledge. But there are different ways of doing science, which rest on differing assumptions about the nature of reality. I am not among those who believe that sociology should liken itself to science, although I am not anti-science, as some postmodernists are. We need to know about the empirical world, but we can't know anything without looking through lenses that necessarily distort what we see. Those lenses are called theories. In this chapter, I discuss the various ways in which different theories see the same world differently, and I address implications of these different ways of seeing. Throughout, keep in mind that an excellent term paper would involve taking an empirical topic, say the impact of divorce on children, and discussing how different theories would analyze the same problem differently.

Most introductory-sociology textbooks spend hundreds of pages distilling the many facts, concepts, theories, and methods that represent the discipline's stock of knowledge. I admire the patience and erudition of those authors, who write massive manuscripts and send them off to publishers in the hope that instructors will adopt these textbooks in their own introductory courses. But I am not as patient as they are, and I want to get on with this story, which is about my life and yours in the Internetworked world of the early twenty-first century. I want to write about our lives today, amidst computers, the Web, Napster, cell phones, globality, CNN, FedEx, Generation X, Ecstasy, dual-career families, children of divorce, media culture, and media spectacles. But let me pause and see if I can tell you the story of society often told by textbook writers who spend many pages telling you about Emile Durkheim, socialization, deviance and crime, social stratification, objectivity in science, life expectancy and the birth rate – what I call sociology's encyclopedia, what it knows about the world. Given that I am limiting myself to a single chapter, I am going to omit certain details and just give you the high points, equipping you to read further as I explore life in the twenty-first century. As I tell my students gently when I lecture, "You can write this down," hinting that they might want to take a few notes. I know that I will repeat myself anyway, given my non-linear thought processes, but I don't need to tell them that!

In a sense, the self is a project. People come into the world utterly helpless. They are infantile. It takes many years – far longer than for any other animal species – for people to become self-sufficient. Freud said that people don't actually have a self, or what he called an **ego**, until they are into their adolescent years, and even then their budding selves, egos, or identities are in flux. Growing up, as we all know, is turbulent as we try to juggle the expectations of adults, especially parents and teachers, and peer-group pressures and influences, not to mention what we see on television and on the Internet. There is no magic moment when we know that we have arrived, having secured a safe psychological harbor. This only occurs to us gradually, during and after college, and sometimes much later.

Sociology, Not Psychology

Sociology's great intellectual contribution is to have recognized that the self is very much a social product. Although people have instincts, dreams, private thoughts, human experience is heavily influenced by our membership in important social groups such as family, church, school, neighborhood, class, race, gender, generation, nation. There is a raging debate within sociology, especially between Marx and his opponents, about whether it is fair to depict people as inevitably determined by these impinging influences or whether people are free to make choices. Marx spent most of his career explaining how people who are poor are unable to exercise significant influence over their lives. They would only taste self-determination once capitalism was overthrown. Other sociologists, such as the group of thinkers I am about to discuss including Comte, Durkheim, and Weber, argued that people could never be free of social structure, contending that our social experience is always the experience of being unfree. In any case, the self, for every sociologist, is largely, but perhaps not entirely, an outcome of what I am calling social structure – the enduring, but sometimes changing, ways in which we organize our economies, political systems, cultures, media, religions, military, policing, education. To ignore all of these external influences is to be a psychologist!

Sociology was invented by Auguste Comte in the late nineteenth century. As a discipline, it is only just over 100 years old. Philosophy, by contrast, has been with us since Plato, who wrote hundreds of years before the birth of Christ. Physics dates from the seventeenth century, when the Enlightenment began to occur. The philosophers of the Enlightenment, or age of reason, decided that the best way to know the world is using empirical science, collecting facts and testing theories, in order to control nature and society. Before the year 1600, people such as Plato believed that all of what you could know resided in the mind already, and could be accessed simply by sitting in a comfortable chair and thinking about it. Plato believed he knew the nature of the good society, of justice, of eternal truths. After the Roman Empire, when Christianity swept over Europe, medieval philosophers such as Augustine and Aquinas decided that all of what we could know was to be found in the Bible, which had to be interpreted correctly. Toiling over Biblical interpretation was a primary intellectual activity for monks and other learned men during the long and dreary middle ages. Charles Lemert has argued that sociologies existed long before Comte, as early as ancient Greece. Philosophers have been theorizing about society and the self from the dawn of civilization. Do some reading in Greek and Roman philosophy and medieval Catholic theology, including the Bible, and see if you can detect sociological claims and assumptions in these works.

Sociology is usually considered an Enlightenment project, an outcome of the Frenchman Auguste Comte's attempt to create a science of society that would rival the sophistication and methodologies of Newton's physics. Comte went as far as to term sociology "social physics." Before sociology, people thought that they knew a good deal about social things, but they did not use scientific methods of observation, investigation, and generalization to arrive at these truths. They either thought them up (we call that speculative knowledge) or they found them in the Bible, especially advice about how to live a moral life. Comte began to change all that and he was followed soon by Emile Durkheim and Max Weber, all of them believing that sociology should be developed as a science, a rigorous field of study that used direct observation, surveys, and statistics in describing and mapping society. This move to develop sociology as a science relying heavily on mathematical methods was fully consistent with the Enlightenment's vigorous development of the natural sciences such as physics and chemistry.

The first sociologists, Comte, Durkheim, and Weber, wrote long essays and books. For the most part, they did not use mathematics in their own writings. From the perspective of sociological writing today, especially found in mainstream sociology journals such as *American Sociological Review*, the early sociologists, who lived and wrote during the nineteenth and early twentieth centuries, were quite philosophical and theoretical in their approaches to social questions. Although they wanted to integrate mathematical methods into sociology, neither statistics for the social sciences nor computers had developed far enough to make sociological computation possible. Weber even wrote that good sociologists needed to be able to do thousands of calculations in their heads! This created the curious impression of early sociologists who valued mathematics and wanted sociology to resemble physics in its "hardness," predictability, rigor, reliance on math and method, but who wrote sprawling, speculative essays that did not present systematic data or test scientific hypotheses.

The early sociologists were positivists (a theory of scientific knowledge) because the wanted sociology to seek cause-and-effect laws and because they prized objectivity, or value freedom, as Weber termed it. Positivism was a doctrine, an intellectual game plan, and not yet a discourse – a way of talking, teaching, and writing heavily reliant on mathematics. Today, as I noted in the preceding chapter, positivism is less an overt doctrine that models sociology on physics than a literary strategy, a habit of writing that lards sociological articles and monographs with dense figural displays, equations, statistics, and discussion of methodological fine points.

As a result, many sociologists appear preoccupied with methodological matters such as how to study and measure things, and how to interpret data. This has obscured the founders' concerns with large issues such as the nature and cause of inequality (sociologists term this **stratification**) and of social change, the tendencies towards bureaucracy, the shifting nature of families and friendship, trends in education, the role of the media in politics and culture. Of special concern to Durkheim, Weber, and Marx was alienation – the loss or lack of meaning in everyday life. This loss of meaning is caused by industrialization, which tends to divide jobs and tasks (sociologists, following Durkheim's (1956) lead, call that the **division of labor**) and reduces people's senses of meaning and of community. Human alienation was especially problematic at a time when religion, Catholicism in particular, was in decline, denying Europeans the comfort and closeness of Christian community. Durkheim, in the first sociological study employing the systematic analysis of data, entitled *Suicide*, concluded that people tend to commit suicide when they exist in a state of what he termed "anomie," or normlessness. Anomie exists when meaning, norms, values, traditions, habits disappear, one of the consequences of industrialism, materialism, and individualism, all of which were sweeping Europe and the Americas during the late nineteenth century, when Durkheim wrote. There are other approaches to methodology, as I discuss in the next chapter.

The first sociologists were animated by the problem of anomie or alienation, which they saw as the most pressing social problem of the day. I will argue that anomie is still a leading human problem, although it takes somewhat different forms, given advances in communications, technology, media, and culture since the late nineteenth century. One of my main questions in this book is whether we should view the solitary Web surfer, alone in her darkened study staring at the illuminated screen, as anomic and lonely or plugged-in and connected. This depends on perspective, as I will explain. Where in the nineteenth century, when Durkheim theorized about the causes of suicide, the person or self was more or less intact, albeit troubled, today selves risk disintegrating and dispersing into cyberspace, connecting with others over the Internet and cell phones but losing themselves in the process. This was termed **self-alienation** by the German philosopher Hegel, who inspired Karl Marx to theorize about social and economic alienation in capitalism. Hegel suggested that it is in our nature as productive and creative beings to externalize our inner spirits through our various work projects – painting pictures, fixing cars, teaching school, writing articles and books. But there is a certain distance, he contended, between people and the world – between **subject** and **object**, in his language – that requires "loss of the object" to occur when we externalize ourselves through our creative activities. Durkheim and Weber felt much the same way about the character of work in industrial society. Karl Marx disagreed with Hegel, Durkheim, and Weber that this loss of the object is inevitable; Marx believed that in a just and humane society, which he called communism, people's work would not be "lost," taking on a life of its own, but would remain organically connected to the person, who would own and control the product and process of working. One of the most telling disagreements in sociology is over whether we can create a society in which there is no alienation, anomie, loss of the object, loss of meaning. What do you think?

What I term the virtual self is a good example of what Hegel was talking about, as we attempt to fill our lives with meaning by connecting with others and with the world electronically, achieving what computer-speakers call **virtuality** – the appearance of the world and of spoken language on the computer screen. The virtual world cannot exactly be touched or manipulated, except through the manipulation of characters and images that stand at one remove from reality. Virtual selves are people, with whom you communicate electronically, whether in real time or with interruptions and delays, whom you cannot see or touch. But you feel their presence in your room, perhaps even in your head. Virtual selves seek meaning, community and love not face-to-face – F2F, in Internet language – but through the computer screen, cell phones, pagers, fax machines that connect us globally, and nearly instantaneously, because we have become so physically and socially distant from one another. The postmodern condition is communicating with people whom you can't see, but can imagine.

Sociology, Modernity, Social Problems

The founders of sociology confronted a rapidly changing world in which industrialization and the growth of cities, beginning in the eighteenth century, jeopardized the traditions and order of feudal Europe. Imagine French life in the year 1400. If you were alive then, you probably lived in a small rural village. You were part of a large family in which everyone toiled in agricultural work. You did not own much beyond your tools and clothing. Your diet was meager, although it was low in cholesterol and fat. You ate regularly only if crops survived bad weather and pestilence and you could catch animals, who were lean. There were many wars and violent crimes, as well as plagues spread by rats for which there were no cures. As a result, people lived only an average of 28 years. Many infants died during, or just after, childbirth, given the absence of sophisticated medical care and basic medicines. There were no organized schools; what you learned about the world you probably learned in church, from various interpretations of the Bible, and from your parents and village elders. If you didn't live in Paris, you probably never traveled there, given the absence of mechanical conveyances such as trains and cars. You never went on vacation, and you didn't have what we call "fun" on the weekends, which were given over to toil and sheer survival. Time was measured by the passing of seasons, which had significant impact on whether you had enough to eat. A group of imaginative French social historians called the Annales School, including Fernand Braudel and Marc Bloch, devoted their attention to describing everyday life in France and Europe during this late-medieval and coming early-modern epochs.

This world as I describe it wasn't to change, even slowly, until about 1600, when Europe began to awaken from the middle ages. By the eighteenth century, people were exploring the world with sailing ships and engaging in commerce and trade that would lay the foundation for later capitalism. Although life for most Europeans and Britons in the year 1700 was not appreciably less difficult than it was 300 years earlier, wheels were set in motion that led Europe and England toward the dawn of industrialism and the growth of cities, which fundamentally revolutionized work, family life, national and regional identity, diet, transportation, education, medicine, and science. The term often given to this new social order, which involved both the Enlightenment and Industrial Revolution, is **modernity**, and the process of achieving it is termed **modernization** by sociologists. Theorists such as Comte, Durkheim, Weber, and Marx felt that there was a certain inevitability about the arrival of modernity, which they viewed as the end or apex of history, beyond which lies a perfect world in which people don't want for anything.

Sociology was the social-science discipline that theorized most vigorously about modernity. Of primary concern to the discipline's founders was how to expedite and improve modernity, eliminating obstacles to progress and smoothing over the social problems of anomie and alienation that progress temporarily creates. Progress created problems unintentionally because the engine of industrial growth was the unplanned, largely unregulated market economy of capitalism. Social and economic development as a result was uneven, benefiting some but ignoring others, such as the poor. Sociologists sought to identify and diagnose social problems associated with cities, health care, transportation, factories, national and religious conflicts, human alienation – the loss of meaning, as Weber termed it. The founders believed that modernity was good and inevitable, "progress," as it was then termed. Modernity would end the darkness of life in the middle ages, as I just described it in the year 1400. Reason, industry, science, and medicine would reign, framed by political democracy which establishes the rights of men, as Tom Paine urged. The Enlightenment leads to industrialization, which in turn requires democracy, culminating in the French and American revolutions. These revolutions were against the *ancien régime*, the old feudal order, and they were carried out on behalf of the new middle class of entrepreneurs who were bringing capitalism into being in Europe and America through their industrious striving.

The founding sociologists thus assumed progress as an inevitable, lawful process. But they were troubled that progress bore certain human costs, notably a feeling of disconnection from the human community, from the church, from families, even from nature. This feeling of disconnection is caused by a number of related developments – the decline of religion and the subsequent "disenchantment of the world," as Weber called it, referring to the way that the world and human affairs are subject to mathematical analysis and calculation; the growing division of labor, which fragments work and divides workers from each other; the growth of anonymous and crowded cities, with poor public transportation, schooling, health care; the decline of the family, which begins to lose its functions as people eat at restaurants and entertain themselves outside the home; the breach between the city and the countryside, accompanied by the growth of suburbs, making it difficult to commune with nature and participate in the vitality and diversity of neighborhoods except in theme parks, such as Disney's recreations of bucolic small-town life on Main Street. Is Disney's world realistic? If you have been to one of the Disney parks, consider writing a paper on how valid its sociological depiction of small-town life is.

These problems were conceptualized by the first sociologists as unfortunate byproducts of modernity, prices to be paid for progress. Durkheim and Weber worked overtime to think up remedies for these ills, which later sociologists beginning with Robert Merton (1957) called **social problems**, implying that they could be minimized or altogether eliminated without changing society's basic structure. Herbert Spencer likened society to a living body, providing an organismic analogy and suggesting "cures" for societal ailments. The first sociologists thus tried to fine-tune society, tinkering with it by making minor reforms that would restore heart and meaning where factories, cities and the decline of religion threatened them with the machine-like forward march of progress.

Karl Marx, it should be said here, did not believe that we could eliminate disconnection, alienation, and anomie without replacing capitalism with communism. This is why we consider him a revolutionary, not an evolutionary, theorist. There is an unfortunate tendency within sociology to assimilate Marx to early sociology by reading him not as a revolutionary thinker but as a "conflict theorist," someone who argues that society is marked not by consensus, as Durkheim, Weber, and Parsons (one of their later American followers, translators, and interpreters) believed, but by conflict, which would be everlasting. Actually, Marx, a utopian, believed that one day conflict would end, with the arrival of communism, an economic system in which private property such as businesses is abolished and the workers own wealth and the means of production and control the working process. Marx is misread purposely by many mainstream sociologists who want to narrow the distance between Marx, on the one hand, and Durkheim and Weber, on the other, portraying a textbook version of general agreement among sociology's founders about the inevitability and even goodness of capitalism and modernity.

The first sociologies addressed remediable problems such as anxiety, poverty, and pollution, conceptualizing these as the cost of doing business in modernity. This is not to say that Durkheim and Weber were heartless or callous. If they lived today, they would probably be regarded as liberals and they might have voted for Franklin Roosevelt during the 1930s or for Bill Clinton during the 1990s. The first sociologists wanted modernity to have a conscience, to be caring and compassionate, refusing to sacrifice people to the juggernaut of progress. They would have approved of the welfare state, the new role of government conceived by Roosevelt as it stepped into the economic arena in order to prime the pump by investing, deficit spending, and creating jobs. In this regard they would have disregarded the economic theories of the Scottish economist Adam Smith who urged that government should stay out of the marketplace and let buyers and sellers ply their trade unconstrained by taxation and other government regulations. The welfare state plays a Robin Hood role by taking from the rich and giving to the poor in order to protect all of us against the economic and human costs of too much poverty. Roosevelt realized that the US needed to have full employment so that people could contribute economically through their work, enhancing overall wealth (sometimes measured as GNP or gross national product) and having the means to shop and spend. Roosevelt studied the economic writings of John Maynard Keynes, an English economist who made certain crucial revisions to Adam Smith's defense of the marketplace found in his classic treatise *The Wealth of Nations* (1976), first published in 1776, a fateful year for Americans.

As liberals, Durkheim and Weber wanted to see humane social reforms such as a minimum wage, anti-pollution measures, occupational health and safety guidelines, welfare delivered to the very poor. Their successors advocated these measures, and more, within the framework of the existing capitalist society, which, they felt, could not and should not be tampered with. Modernity has a relentless forward march; it is inevitable, although its more unfortunate byproducts such as anomie and air pollution can be eliminated, or at least minimized. And modernity, according to the first sociologists, is necessarily capitalist, built on the free market and on private ownership of wealth and capital. The great debate within social theory is between Durkheim and Weber, who felt that modernity must be capitalist, and Marx, who argued that capitalism was simply a stage in modernity, eventually to be surpassed by socialism and finally communism. All three theorists agreed that modernity is inevitable and rational, by comparison to which early forms of society and economy such as antiquity (before the birth of Christ), the Roman Empire and the middle ages, ending roughly in the seventeenth and eighteenth centuries, were downright miserable, given poverty, scarcity, agrarianism, plague, warfare, illiteracy, violence, and the absence of civil and political liberties. The middle ages ended with the Enlightenment, which liberated reason, science, and mathematics to know the world and thus to solve problems such as the need for energy, better crops, mass-produced clothing and housing, transportation.

Let me summarize the assumptions made by the first sociologists:

1 *Modernization*: Modernity, especially industrialization, cities, democracy, transportation, universal literacy, and global consciousness and culture, is inevitable and welcome.
2 *Social problems*: Accompanying modernity are various social problems such as alienation and economic inequality, which sociologists and policy makers must minimize, notably by providing people with meaning (in the absence of religion) and providing poor people with a

measure of welfare. Meaning was to be delivered by culture, which both elevates and entertains.

3 *Positivism*: Sociology is a science, much like physics, which seeks lawful statements about cause and effect. The scientist stands outside of the world in order to know it objectively. His or her mind is free of preconceptions and wishful thinking.

4 *Methodology*: Sociology's major methodology is observation and surveys, and its basic interpretive tool is statistics. Sociology is to be mathematical in order to eliminate bias and fuzzy thinking.

5 *Professionalism*: Sociology is a profession, which is organized as an academic discipline. Professional sociologists earn advanced degrees in sociology, enabling them to teach college students and conduct research. They publish their research in refereed journals, which use outside readers, who are other academics, in order to evaluate the quality of submitted writing.

6 *Value freedom*: Sociological writing is dispassionate, avoiding the first person, autobiography, and polemics. Weber urged sociologists strictly to separate facts and values, refusing to use the journal article and lectern as venues for persuasion and politics.

These six points were akin to the professional credo of sociologists, their Hippocratic Oath. Virtually everyone in the new discipline agreed with these themes of modernization, social problems, positivism, methodology, professionalism, value freedom, everyone except Karl Marx. Although most sociology textbooks that recount the history of the discipline and discuss its contemporary theoretical schools, as they are often called, insert Marx into the sociological tradition, this is not exactly accurate, given his training as a philosopher and self-training as an economist, and given his message, which was a clarion call for communist revolution. Marx did not agree with many of the six themes above, although he certainly believed that there were serious social problems of poverty and inequality that needed to be eliminated. He also believed that the world could be known empirically, through observation and analysis. He felt that problems, which in his Hegelian language he called "contradictions," could only be eliminated if capitalism were abolished. But the first sociologists maintained that capitalism was a central feature of modernity, which they generalized to include all societies and cultures. Where Weber, Durkheim, and Comte ended history with capitalism, to them the perfect society, Marx ended history with communism, preceded by socialism and capitalism.

Whether Marx should be considered a sociologist at all depends entirely on how one views the contemporary discipline of sociology. If one is a die-hard positivist and endorses value freedom and the other core assumptions outlined just above, then one is likely to view Marx either as an intellectual and political renegade who doesn't belong to the discipline or to reinterpret Marx as a tame, essentially positivist sociologist who, like the other founders, sought objective laws of social motion. From my vantage as a student of Marx, Marx is neither a positivist sociologist nor a conflict theorist but someone who rejects most of the core tenets of the founders, instead proposing a dialectical and revolutionary view of history. The word *dialectical* is key here; it refers to a theory that views people as *both* subject to powerful social and economic forces, such as capitalism, racism, and sexism, *and* as agents and authors of their own destiny. Dialectical theorists oppose the positivist pursuit of social laws that can perfectly predict people's behavior, preferring to portray history as an open book of possibilities that can only be understood if we simultaneously address people's powerlessness before large-scale social structures and people's essential powers to redirect the course of history as they build a new future.

I just used a term that is central to the sociological founders, and to subsequent students of society, including both Marx and his opponents. **Social structures** are the basic raw material of sociologists, their most important conceptual tool. Social structures are social arrangements, such as the economy, polity, culture, religion, the media, entertainment, education, race, gender, within which people act. Social structures tend to endure over time, although how long they endure is an empirical question that can only be answered with careful research. When I say that something is an empirical question, I mean that we can only answer a question with data, or what Durkheim called "social facts"; it cannot be answered from the armchair, although, having said that, I as a non-positivist also believe that the sociologist cannot just go out in the world naively and take snapshots of social facts but must actively theorize about their existence, meaning, and how to study them, using particular research methods. Social structures do not present themselves to the naked eye but must be developed theoretically so that others can study them, once they decide how to identify and even measure them. The concept of social structure is a convenient fiction, what Weber called an "ideal type."

Examples of social structures include capitalism, a particular type of economic system. If you travel to New York City to the see the Stock Exchange, you are visiting a shrine of capitalism. But if on your return home, you stop at a local Wal-Mart to pick up a can of tennis balls, you are also participating in capitalism. If you order a sweater online from L. L. Bean, you are contributing to capitalism. As I said, "capitalism" is not something that you can exactly see, but it is the way you organize your theoretical thoughts about varieties of economic activity, and an economic infrastructure, that could be called other things. For example, you could talk about Wal-Mart as a chain store, the colossus of all chain stores! Or you could analyze the Stock Exchange architecturally. Or discuss the social circuits involved in ordering a sweater online or using an 800 number under the concept of "telework," which I discuss later.

Social structures, these immensely powerful arrangements that condition how we act and what we experience, must be carefully defined and described by the sociologist before we study them in rich detail. Durkheim, for example, wrote about the division of labor, one of his key social structures that, he contended, influences people's behavior, both limiting and enlarging their social possibilities. Given his investment in a view of modernization, mentioned above, he contrasted the division of labor, which was only recognized at the beginning of the Industrial Revolution and factory system in Europe and England, with a prior social arrangement that could be characterized as organic or craft work.

You can see office towers, bridges, schools, ballparks, farms, airports, suburban houses, urban apartments, churches. All of these are fair game for sociological studies, but only as they illuminate the larger issue of "social structure" – the organized ways in which people live and, over time, the impact these ways have on contemporary people and future generations. Social structure, thus, is a concept, almost a hypothesis that explains all manner of social outcomes, from the crime rate, to income inequality, to the impact of divorce on children. Structure is a huge but invisible force, a type of sociological gravity, acting on people, influencing their behavior, emotions, identity, feelings. The study of social structures is the lifeblood of sociology, although sociologists differ about which ones are the most important, and they frequently disagree about the effects they have on human action and experience.

One of the most important disagreements among sociologists is over whether social structures bear down on people so heavily that they cannot be changed. Indeed, these sociologists, inspired by Comte's social physics, by Durkheim and Weber, and later by Talcott Parsons, view such structures – economy, race, gender – as virtual forces of nature which cannot be altered. Think of my analogy to gravity just above. Theorists inspired by Marx believe that such structures can be changed through concerted effort because they were built by people, sometimes a long time ago, and thus can be rebuilt. Marxists do not exaggerate the ease with which change can be brought about, recognizing that institutions such as capitalism have become inertial, reproduced by many generations of people who, like Comte and Parsons, thought that they were intractable or inevitable. Although both traditions of social-structural analysis have produced rich empirical studies, there is little consensus among sociologists about which view is correct. Indeed, perhaps there is little consensus because there is abundant evidence both of structures' change and enduring quality.

As I explore in my following chapter on methods, there is also disagreement among sociologists about the role played by what I just called "evidence" in resolving such disputes. Positivists, who believe that sociology can be a science like physics and the other natural sciences, believe that evidence in and of itself can resolve theoretical disputes, for example concerning the tendency of social structures to endure or dissolve. Antipositivist critical sociologists maintain that evidence cannot simply be placed on the table and used to arbitrate disputes because, they contend, evidence must always be interpreted, and the act of interpretation is freighted with theoretical and value assumptions. In other words, certain sociologists believe that you can point to facts that, to all views, resolve intellectual disputes, whereas other sociologists believe that facts are theoretical artifacts that can be constructed and interpreted to support any argument. As a critical sociologist, I believe that "facts" *can* resolve disputes once you agree how they are to be defined, observed, measured, evaluated. But this methodological process of what my empirical colleagues call "operationalization" (deciding how to observe and/or measure your variables, the things you are interested in) is bound to produce theoretical disagreement between sociologists who use different intellectual and political lenses. A feminist is not likely to define marital equity (fairness) in the same way as a die-hard conservative. Some of the most interesting debates within sociology, thus, are about how to define, observe, measure, and evaluate "facts," which don't speak for themselves but must be "constructed," a key term in the phenomenological and ethnomethodological traditions.

People who emphasize that facts, and indeed the world itself, must be constructed by the analyst or theorist are sometimes accused of ignoring reality altogether, an issue I take up explicitly in my following chapter on methodologies. But they are not ignoring an external reality – the Stock Exchange, Wal-Mart, the distribution of household income – so much as saying that "reality" does not simply imprint itself on the scientist's mind but must be filtered or "mediated" (Hegel's word) by thought, theory, argument. This mediation or construction (a word I prefer because it connotes the "building" of theory, of concepts) doesn't ignore reality but engages in selectivity, focusing on certain issues and thereby ignoring other issues. If you want to study social stratification, you can focus on inequalities of household income, of years of formal education, of personal savings and investments, of the cost of real estate in one's neighborhood, of life expectancy, of job type, of length of annual vacation . . . the list is endless. How we define "stratification" is an exercise in social construction, in theory by another name, even though no critical sociologist believes that stratification is simply in the eye of the beholder; it is not anything you want it to be. Stratification is not the time it takes to travel to planet Pluto; it is not the winner of last year's Super Bowl; it is not a novel by Toni Morrison. It is the pattern of household incomes, differing levels of education by race, the impact of gender on lifetime earnings.

Thus, resolving the matter of whether social structures have a tendency to endure and be highly constraining or to be subject to transformation is actually an exercise in theoretical argument. Whether "facts" can decide debates – or, better, under what condition facts can decide debates – is one of the most interesting questions debated by theorists. People who believe that facts can be definitive are usually called positivists, whereas people who demur are usually viewed as opponents of positivism. Terms such as **positivism** shouldn't be allowed to do our thinking for us, and so I don't want to get caught up in splitting terminological hairs. But, as a general intellectual stance, the term "positivism" is useful because it summarizes the dominant position taken by empirical sociologists and social scientists on the epistemological (theory of knowledge) issue of how, and how much, we can know.

When surveying the findings of sociology, as I am doing briefly here, one cannot cleanly separate the how and the what of sociological research – methodology (including the formation and definition of concepts) and findings. How people conduct their studies frames their findings, drawing attention to what is important and ignoring what is not – a process one might call "selectivity" or, in phenomenological talk, "perspectivity." The study of social and economic inequality is carried out within two opposing frameworks, inspired by Weber and Marx. Weberians count income and wealth to determine social class, whereas Marxists identify people's structural class position, determining whether they own the means of production (capital, or productive wealth) or whether they merely work for those who do. As I said earlier, one's "findings" about inequality, poverty, class are to a large extent already determined by how one defines one's terms and conducts one's study in that light.

Modernization

Most sociologists, and sociologies, agree that world civilization has moved, albeit in fits and starts and often quite unevenly, from a period roughly called the pre-modern to modernity. Some, influenced by French theorists such as Foucault and Derrida, even contend that we have entered a distinctively new stage called **postmodernity**. Even Marx agreed that modernity – capitalism, industrialization, the growth of cities, the decline of European Catholicism, the flourishing of science – is a useful way to periodize, or put boundaries around, a stage of history qualitatively different from what went before, during antiquity (ancient Greece and the Roman Empire) and during feudalism or the middle ages.

Theorists such as Comte, Durkheim, Weber, Marx, and later Talcott Parsons (the father of structural functionalism) contend that most societies tend to evolve into "modern" ones. Comte said that this is a virtual law, a law of progress. And modernity is often deemed to be the end or pinnacle of history, the final destination of social evolution. Although there is disagreement between Marx and the other sociological founders, and among present-day sociologists of development, about what exactly "the modern" contains, and whether all of it is welcome and worthwhile, they all agree that societies possess an inner dynamic causing them to emerge from primitive hunting-gathering economies, to agricultural economies, to industrial and even post-industrial economies. By post-industrial, theorists usually refer to the gradual replacement of blue-collar manual labor with white-collar mental labor, or office work, organized bureaucratically. Max Weber wrote about how **bureaucracies**, with top-to-bottom chain of command and highly specialized tasks, are the most rational way of organizing human activity, whether in the public or private sectors.

Modernity is said by theorists such as Weber and Parsons to be "rational," meaning that modern societies are both inevitable as evolutionary outcomes of an inner dynamic of progress and well-ordered, reflecting the best of human reason and design. Marx, too, supported rationality (as opposed to a divine or cosmological plan), but he felt that capitalist rationality was actually quite irrational, given the large number of poor people and the tendencies for capital (productive wealth) to be amassed in a few hands. As the rich get richer, according to him, it would be more difficult for them to invest their wealth productively, in a way that creates jobs and allows workers to spend. But Marx agreed with Durkheim and Weber that we could design and then implement the good society, applying human design to nature and society in creating the most viable social institutions. Marx disagreed with them on the issue of inevitability, contending that capitalism is a necessary and unavoidable stage of social history but that there are higher stages which necessarily surpass it, namely socialism and, finally, communism.

How do we recognize modernity when we see it? This is an important question because societies and culture fall along a continuum, or path of development, ranging from the most primitive to the most developed. Sociologists generally agree that modern societies are industrialized (or, now, post-industrial), democratic, highly technological, global in consciousness and culture. Furthermore, these societies have nearly universal literacy, available public education, accessible mass media and electronic culture, organized health care, far-reaching transportation systems, large cities and suburbs. One could take a snapshot of "modernity" in various urban centers, such as Zurich, Stockholm, Chicago, San Francisco, Toronto, Tokyo.

By comparison, less fully developed but still modern societies, and even pre-modern ones, are evaluated according to the model of modernity captured in the cityscapes and nation states of the industrialized capitalist west and east. Sociologists and economists reduce these comparisons to sheer numbers, with various quantitative indicators used to measure degree of modernization: level of education, income, gross national product, infant mortality, population, and many more. These quantitative indicators of development serve as yardsticks by which societies and regions can be measured and compared. More qualitative indicators, such as happiness and justice, are cast aside, even though the original theorists of modernity such as Rousseau (1968) stressed the importance of existential and political modernization, notably embracing the fulfillment of the self and democracy as important goals of modernity.

Perhaps the two key features of modernity are secularism and capitalism, representing the major ways in which modern societies break from the feudal and primitive past. The secular worldview, according to which nature can be explained not magically or religiously but with reference to physical cause and effect, began to prevail in the seventeenth century. It was ushered in by the Enlightenment, whose very name connotes a break with the dismal, dogmatic past of antiquity and feudalism. Thinkers such as Descartes, Condorcet, Newton, and Kant replaced religious with scientific explanations and thus freed Europeans to master nature in order to improve life on earth – locomotion, medicine, printing and publishing, iron foundries, scientific farming and animal husbandry. Kant, one of the Enlightenment's most articulate spokesmen, said "dare to know!" and thus emphasized an element of risk involved in giving up the comfortable certainties of religion in favor of science, which, in itself, offers no cosmic guarantees of meaning, morality, or an afterlife.

Max Weber has convincingly shown that secularism in general and the Protestant Reformation in particular laid the ground for subsequent capitalism. The Enlightenment enabled a view of the self as an efficacious actor who could dominate his or her world, especially nature, using the scientific method and various technological prostheses. The Enlightenment – Descartes' (1956) "I think, therefore I am" – was an intellectual revolution that made possible the eventual Industrial Revolution, which began to emerge 100 years after the dawn of enlightenment. Weber, like other important theorists of modernity, defends modernity as an improvement over what came before, during antiquity and feudalism. With modernity, people can think freely, unbound to mythology and deities. And intellectual liberation spells political freedom and economic freedom from misery and scarcity. However, Weber, like Durkheim, Freud and Marx, notes that modernity, which makes man the measure of all things, loses the enchantment and mystery of earlier worlds, which refused the self enormous powers properly reserved for gods and legends. Weber argued that reason disenchants the world, requiring people who now enjoy a measure of material comfort and political liberty to find substitute sources of meaning now that the church has been eclipsed in importance. Durkheim, in the very first empirical sociological study, observed that Protestants commit suicide more frequently than do Catholics because, he explained, they are less tied to the church and religious community, denied the *Gemeinschaft* (intimate rural community) of the feudal village and parish. Interestingly, the early sociologists were quite religious in their private lives, even though they noticed the decline of organized religion. Is believing in God inconsistent with being a sociologist?

Social problems

This leads directly to the second assumption made by the founding sociologists. Modernity, although inevitable and necessary in the large scheme of things, brings with it certain social problems such as alienation, estrangement, economic inequality, crowded cities, a despoiled environment, which sociologists and policy makers need to minimize. The cost of progress is the self alone, no longer sheltered by the church, gods, religions, collective belief systems. The underlying issue in this book is whether the Internet can replace churches and synagogues as sites of meaning, intimacy, community. Selves lack meaning and often they lack sufficient material resources. In capitalism, selves, especially Protestant ones, are set free in the marketplace to succeed or fail, without strong safety nets to cushion their fall. Since Reagan and the two Bushes in the White House, the safety nets first put up by Roosevelt have become more porous and flimsy.

For Weber, like Freud an ambivalent proponent of modernity, progress produces benefits and incurs costs. The main benefit is material, pried from nature as people organize themselves rationally in factories and parliaments. Thomas Hobbes had already noticed that a strong government delivers people from a state of nature that resembles a war of all against all, as he explained in *Leviathan* (1996), the first text of democratic theory. But government constrains people by limiting their liberty, requiring them to obey laws, police, and armies. Rousseau later theorized a "social contract" between people and government according to which we voluntarily curtail our freedoms in return for protection and security. Durkheim in a different vein suggested that factories are organized most rationally where there is a certain division of labor that slots people into narrow roles coordinated by management. By the early twentieth century, the classic manifestation of this division of labor was found in Henry Ford's first Michigan automobile factory, where cars were assembled by scores of workers connected and coordinated on the assembly line. The problem for modernity theorists is that such work is often routine, devoid of skill and craft. For imaginative, and somewhat contrasting, discussions of the history and theory of work see Reinhard Bendix's *Work and Authority in Industry* (1956) and Harry Braverman's *Labor and Monopoly Capital* (1974).

A related problem of modernity, identified by Marx, is that the industrial division of labor involves, and exacerbates, inequalities between the people who own and manage the factories and those who merely work for a wage. Marx argued passionately that the real source of wealth and profit is the sweat and ingenuity of labor, not the grand designs of capitalists, who merely live off the spoils produced by underpaid workers. As such, Marx offered a moral critique of capitalist modernity. Indeed, for Marx, capitalism and modernity were one and the same thing, although he believed that we could create a modern society without class inequalities. (He might have termed this stage "postmodern," had he thought of the term.)

Durkheim, Weber, and Marx agreed that assembly-line work was frequently numbing and meaningless. Durkheim and Weber disagreed with Marx about whether workers are fairly compensated. They agreed with Adam Smith, the architect of capitalism, where Smith said that the worker is paid fairly because the worker is compensated for his stint of daily labor, whereas the capitalist deserves extra recompense in the way of profit for his risk and initiative. All three theorists agreed that capitalism (or modernity) tends to create certain social and human problems of meaninglessness and loss of community and sometimes even poverty, where the distributive mechanisms of the market economy fail to function properly. They all acknowledged that capitalism is imperfect, although Durkheim and Weber believed that capitalism could smooth out its wrinkles, such as alienation and poverty, whereas Marx felt that capitalism would eventually implode and become socialism and then communism because it cannot remedy its shortcomings within the framework of the market economy.

"Social problems" are conceptualized by non-Marxist sociologists as remediable – things that can be fixed. The divorce rate can be lowered through family counseling, poverty can be buffered by welfare, the environment can be protected and cleansed by government agencies. The main mechanism for non-Marxist social reform is what Marxists call the **state**, or government, which, since President Franklin Roosevelt, has taken the lead in redressing the shortcomings of the market economy in the US. The state stimulates the economy and redistributes modest amounts of wealth in order to keep the poor shopping. This is especially crucial where nearly a quarter of all American households fall below the poverty line, with an average yearly income of less than $17,000. For neo-Marxist discussions of the state, see Nicos Poulantzas' *Political Power and Social Classes* (1973) and Ernest Mandel's *Late Capitalism* (1978).

The other mechanism for non-Marxist social reform is culture, or, as leftists term it, the **culture industry**. The culture industry – actually, industries, plural – includes radio, television, journalism, advertising, movies, videos, music, art, the Web. Culture, especially after World War II, intervenes in everyday life to minimize people's psychic crises, which involve a deficit of meaning in our godless, materialistic world. This argument was first made by Horkheimer and Adorno in their *Dialectic of Enlightenment* (1972). Whereas Roosevelt's state intervenes to forestall economic crisis both by stimulating growth and spending and by offering meager welfare handouts, the culture industries forestall existential crises that would result if people really reflected on what their lives mean, how powerless they are, how empty shopping is, how manipulated they are by advertisers, government, and corporations.

Non-Marxist sociologists such as Daniel Bell argue that middle-class people today are largely free from earlier economic anxieties about subsistence. Now, people experience "affluence," as Galbraith called it in *The Affluent Society* (1958); their lives are spent not in desperate poverty but in finding meaning and solace in "leisure time." Theorists of modernity, both Marxist and non-Marxist, generally agree that the Enlightenment and then the Industrial Revolution eroded feudal, agricultural communities and weakened the Catholic Church, throwing people into a state of what Durkheim called anomie or normlessness. The Enlightenment in this sense gave birth to the concept of the self, the unique individual who can determine her own needs and choices of action. The self is necessarily reflexive, capable of thinking things through. But the self, with the weakening hold of custom and religion, experiences the inherent meaninglessness of the universe, an occasion for the later philosophical tradition called existentialism, developed by Heidegger (1962) and Sartre (1956), which acknowledges the erosion of certainty and the inevitability of death as the first insight of philosophy and the ground of all existence.

The self is inherently, sometimes ineffably, alone, unconnected to the body politic and to other bodies. The age of reason freed people to conquer the world and nature, moving societies forward in a material and technological sense. But the self experiences a certain mortal aloneness, which is confronted in post-World War II societies as the predicament termed "affluence" – having too much time on one's hands, too many technological prostheses of entertainment, sleeplessness, loneliness, a general lack of direction. This existential condition is precisely what gave rise to postmodernism, which declares the grand narrative or big story of modernity and modernism obsolete, having been transcended by the plural narratives borne of gender, race, region, religion. Non-Marxist sociologists beginning with Durkheim and Weber consider anomie or the loss of meaning as one of the central social problems of the age, of modernity, to be redressed in secular times by hobbies, self-help manuals, fitness and diet routines. In a sense, then, non-Marxist sociologists argue that a mature capitalism does away with poverty and economic inequality, at least in western nations, but introduces a reduction in purpose and social connection that stems from being materially comfortable but bored.

For their part, Marxists also identify the damaged self as a casualty of capitalism, but they conceptualize the causes and consequences of this alienation differently from Weberians and Durkheimians. They remain more concerned with poverty than boredom! Marxists stress that the capitalist division of labor results in both economic inequality (as society is divided between capitalists and workers) and what early Marx termed alienation, loss of connection to the self, body, nature, community, the species as a whole. According to Marx, the traditional capitalist/modernist cure for social ailments, notably modest transfer payments doled out by the state in the form of welfare and meaningful leisure time, is but a palliative that does not address the real problem, which is the capitalist economy. Only a socialist revolution would level class differences and overcome people's alienation.

Marxists and Weberians disagree fundamentally about whether "social problems" can be resolved within the framework of capitalism. Weber, Durkheim, Parsons, and Merton believed that they could, whereas Marx and later Marxists contend that capitalism itself is the problem, and must be overthrown. Weber and Durkheim theorized that all societies require a certain degree of economic inequality and incur inevitable alienation, anomie, the loss of meaning. They argue that we can reduce the levels of inequality and alienation, but not eliminate them entirely. Many twenty-first-century sociologists who disagree with Marx's idealism and optimism contend that Marx is not supported by the empirical facts of history inasmuch as all societies up to now, including our present one, have had social problems, including poverty and alienation. They conclude from this that all future societies will also contain social problems, which can be lessened but not totally eliminated. Marxists respond by saying that just because the past has seen social problems, we cannot conclude that the future will necessarily follow suit, especially if we work hard to change things in radical ways, such as overthrowing capitalism.

Positivism

All of the founding sociologists, and virtually all contemporary sociologists except for a few of us who occupy a postmodern fringe of, or beyond, the discipline, place their faith in science. Drinking deeply of the Enlightenment, Durkheim, Weber, and even Marx wanted to replace religious certainties and dogma with the open-minded skepticism and empiricism of scientific method. By the beginning of the seventeenth century, the interpretation of sacred religious texts was to be replaced by science, especially mathematics and natural sciences like physics and chemistry, as the royal road to truth. The a priori reasoning of the Greeks during antiquity and the Biblical interpretations of Catholic theologians during the middle ages were overthrown by direct observation, experimentation, and survey research as Descartes and Newton empowered thinkers to know the world empirically, gathering sense data.

As I have discussed already, this liberated Europe and eventually many parts of the world from mythology and tyranny, installing science and democracy and principles of epistemology (theory of knowledge) and political theory. By the nineteenth century, especially in England, science had been harnessed to technology as the Industrial Revolution accelerated the growth of cities and led to industrial mass production. This increased life expectancy as people ate more and better food, lived in more habitable dwellings, gained access to health care and education. It also liberated people from the local confines of the village and town as they traveled to other towns and regions, even nations, replacing parochialism with cosmopolitanism, a process that is still underway. Overall, the Enlightenment triggered industrialization, greatly alleviating people's material deprivation, which, until the nineteenth and twentieth centuries, had appeared to be an inescapable part of the human condition, a virtual iron law.

Advances in technology and industry were caused by advances in intellectual methodologies, notably science, which threw out the old certainties of Plato and Thomas Aquinas, neither of whom had use for empiricism, an approach to knowing relying on the collection of systematic data or information. I want to distinguish here between **empiricism**, an intellectual method grounded in sense data, and positivism, a particular type of empiricism that rules out alternative, non-empirical methodologies such as intuition, speculation, theorizing. Positivism is a type of empiricism, but there are empiricisms that aren't positivist. To be a positivist requires that one make these assumptions:

1 The knower can stand outside of the world and see it objectively, for what it is, without his or her perspective muddying what is known.
2 If one collects enough facts or data, one can formulate laws of natural and social behavior – cause-and-effect statements about the relationships between things (or variables).
3 The best way to express one's knowledge is mathematically, in order to remove the distorting effects of language. The highest form of knowledge is mathematics.

Other empiricisms do not require any of these assumptions. To be a non-positivist empiricist simply requires one to ground one's knowledge in sense experience, in the examination and analysis of observable phenomena. For example, in order to study crime, an empiricist would collect facts (or analyze someone else's facts) about the incidence of crime. A positivist criminologist would require that these data be quantitative; she would attempt to formulate laws of criminal behavior; and she would accept that one can analyze criminality from the outside, as it were, not worrying about the distorting effects of the criminologist's value positions, gender, race, social class, country of origin, etc.

This distinction between empiricism and positivism is crucial for understanding the Enlightenment and the subsequent sociologies, especially that of Comte, following from it. For the most part, sociologists both then and now have tended to be positivist, not only empiricist, embracing the doctrine of value freedom which suggests an unproblematic objectivity and freedom from bias as well as a penchant for quantification. Although a significant minority of US sociologists conduct empirical research using non-quantitative methodologies (and reject the explicit strictures of positivism, such as the notion that the mind is a blank slate), for the most part these are faculty at fringe colleges and universities, in sociology departments that don't have doctoral programs. They are not opinion makers in the discipline, and they don't edit the mainstream journals.

The postmodern turn has enabled critical scholars to read science not as a rigorous methodological protocol but as rhetoric, a way of making an argument. What is scientific sociology's argument? How could sociology even "argue," given its commitment purely to describe and represent? I contend that interrogating science deconstructively, unraveling its hidden meanings and inconsistencies, does not negate science but democratizes it, putting it on the same epistemological footing as other versions of the world – editorials, fiction, music, philosophy. Although postmodernism sometimes makes itself available to be read as nihilist and anti-science, these are readings that spring from a certain irrationalist version of Nietzsche, not he of happy science but he of the rejection of all values. Just as there are many versions of the text, so there are many Nietzsches, he who inspired both postmodernism and critical theory. The misreading of deconstruction as anti-science is also frequently facilitated by deconstruction's own literary and philosophical emphases. For example, Derrida writes voluminously about culture and philosophy but rarely about science and technology, which is only to observe that postmodernism was not originally grounded in the social sciences, although it could be (see Rosenau 1992). As I discuss further in the following chapter, deconstruction is Derrida's technique of literary interpretation for demonstrating that all writings in fact contain contradictions, lapses, blind spots and are not seamless unities of meaning. To make sense of these elliptical, unfinished texts (that don't simply reflect the world out there), readers must, in effect, write their own versions of them, blurring the boundary between reading and writing.

The issue of positivism, then, is really the issue of science: How are we to know, and then write about, the world? Virtually all sociologists, indeed all social scientists, are empiricists in the sense that they base their knowledge on observation, experimentation, fieldwork, surveys. Positivists are empiricists who impose additional conditions on knowledge, such as that it be quantitative, totally free of bias and context, and aim toward laws. It is in this sense that positivism today is less a doctrine than a discourse, a way of writing, which, by its example, reproduces itself as "normal science," as Kuhn (1970) termed it. Whether this version of science should be normal is hotly debated, especially outside of empiricist and positivist circles. Some of us who do interdisciplinary work in critical theory and cultural studies believe that empiricism is valuable and necessary, although we maintain that there are many legitimate ways of scripting science. Indeed, we argue that science is best regarded as a type of fiction, a made-up story or narrative about the world that, through authorial selectivity, perspective, and voice, is no less "literary" than novels and poetry. As I explore in my concluding chapter, this self-consciously literary approach is embraced by a virtual sociology.

Methodology

As I just indicated, mainstream sociologists require empirical data, typically collected through surveys. These data are quantitative, permitting their statistical manipulation and elaborate figural display in journal articles. Quantitative methods are closely tied to the rhetoric of journal science, as I have called it, which reduces prose in favor of "gesture" – numbers, equations, correlations, graphs, and even highly technical prose read as gestural. By **gesture**, I am referring to the ways in which authorial markings appear on the page, especially where they are de-authorized in order to conceal their literariness – their having-been-written – altogether. John Locke's blank slate of mind, the centerpiece of the positivist theory of knowledge, is nearly achieved by the journal page which relies on quantitative methods to purge the text of textuality, of the author's scribbling, in order to suppress the author's presence as a passionate, even political actor. Sociologists affix the epistemological Good Housekeeping Seal of Approval to their work by ensuring that their work is methods-driven, with great attention to how the study was conducted, the data sources used, and the actual statistical analyses themselves. Methodology prevails both through the preponderance of what I am calling gesture and by the sheer volume of methodological preoccupations found in the article's title, abstract, literature review, methods section, and in technical footnotes and appendices. Methodology is in the saddle, both rhetorically and in emphasis.

This emphasis on method – and the way in which prose is transformed into methodological gesture – is found in the journals themselves and in article reviews written anonymously by experts in the field, as I reported in *Public Sociology* (2000). It is also found in graduate-school curricula in sociology, where doctoral students are often required to take several courses in quantitative methodology and social statistics and perhaps a preliminary examination in methods and "stats." The overhaul of US sociology as a science discipline has had rhetorical impact on the way sociologists compose, review, edit, and publish their work. It has had institutional impact on the structure and nature of undergraduate and graduate curricula, which, with few exceptions, presume that all sociology degree holders must have been trained intensively in quantitative methods and statistics, even if they don't do, or intend to do, quantitative work. This curricular bias in undergraduate and graduate training reproduces the quantitative orientation of the discipline inasmuch as it predisposes students to learn SPSS and obtain data sets with which to churn out term papers, theses, dissertations, and conference papers.

Quantitative sociology curricula are found in most of the leading graduate programs, from which doctoral students obtain the best faculty job placements. This also reproduces the discipline's orientation to methodology, in effect replicating and reinforcing the work styles and methodological orientations of senior faculty who mentor and supervise graduate students. This emphasis on quantitative method is not the outcome of an original conspiracy, where the opinion makers of the discipline congregated in a smoke-filled room, perhaps at the American Sociological Association annual meetings. It is an outcome of gradual shifts in the discipline that built on each other, gaining momentum and entrenching themselves as the conventional wisdom about what constitutes good sociology (and by implication bad sociology and, even worse, non-sociology). The turn toward sober science strengthened Comte's vision of sociology as social physics, but it differed with Comte, who established positivism as epistemological doctrine but not as methodological and literary protocols for how people conduct, and then write up, their research.

Comte was writing in the nineteenth century, before computers, data sets, inferential social statistics, journals, conferences, PhD programs, faculty hiring networks. When Comte said "positivism," he was referring to John Locke, Newton, the natural sciences and their assumptions about objective knowledge, truth, laws. When post-1970s sociologists developed their positivism, even where they didn't use that explicit word to describe their philosophical underpinnings, they built positivism into the machinery of methods and of computing machines themselves, out of which spew methodologically-compulsive sociological journal articles on slender topics that avoid public issues and social problems. There is another irony here: Comte, Durkheim, Weber, and Marx wanted social science to improve the world, not simply advance methodology, let alone academic careers. Although a self-styled positivist, Comte meant for positivism to be what he termed a "philosophy," a veritable value framework foretelling social progress.

Professionalism

Alas, Comte, Durkheim, and Weber weren't professional sociologists but public intellectuals who happened to call themselves sociologists. They wrote big books, on broad topics, for a general public, including but not limited to other academicians. Their theories were of modernity, not divorce, crime, migration. Aiming high, they tethered their empirical analyses to broad-gauged analyses of Europe, of industrialization, indeed of civilization, albeit in a way that omitted parts of the globe taking different paths toward development and ignored women, people of color, much of the working class, especially the segment that Marx termed the lumpenproletariat – the desperately poor, the unwaged, the mentally ill, people about whom Barbara Ehrenreich writes in her *Nickel and Dimed* (2001), an account of working as a maid and at Wal-Mart in minimum-wage jobs. But we all have blind spots, topics, and subjects about which we are silent. I am not excusing the sociological founders' "Eurocentrism," an "eighties" term for the worldview restricted to Germany, France, Italy, the Benelux countries, and England, but only noticing that Comte, Durkheim, and Weber would have viewed quantitatively-driven journal sociology as a betrayal of their sweeping theories of modernity.

Most global sociologists today, especially Americans, view themselves as **professionals**, people who have advanced degrees, regular university salaries, who belong to professional associations, purvey specialized knowledge, build careers, and network. In these respects, they are like dentists, social workers, lawyers, physicians, physicists. Sociology is not only a science, it is a profession, and a career, with its own institutions, discourse, norms, and values. Entry into the profession is regulated by universities, which grant doctoral degrees, and which hire younger faculty and thus replenish the professoriate with new professionals. Graduate school and the first years toward tenure, spent on the tenure "track," are given over to busy teaching, writing, conferencing, and now grant writing; they are especially devoted to what sociologists themselves call "socialization," instilling values, a code of conduct, and discourse in young scholars who would be professors, and professionals. In this sense, as in medieval guilds and the helping professions today, a crucial aspect of the training process is apprenticing to a mentor – here, the head of one's doctoral dissertation committee and, later, one's department chair and senior colleagues.

Professionalism is to be prized, by comparison to what came before it. If you have a bacterial infection, you want an antibiotic dispensed by a competent and qualified medical professional. If you want your taxes prepared, you want to go to a certified accountant who can save you money. If you want a sociologist, you want one trained at Wisconsin or Princeton! But why *would* you want a sociologist? Sociological professionals don't dispense services in the usual way that professionals do. They dispense knowledge, only some of which can be "used" in everyday life. One of my arguments is that a public sociology, written accessibly about social and political topics that matter, could make a difference in people's lives, helping them think clearly about their circumstances and perhaps even motivating them to change those circumstances, with the aid of others. Sociology should make people mad, and make them think. But you don't need a PhD from Wisconsin or Princeton to dispense that sort of knowledge. Indeed, if your graduate training has emphasized quantitative methods and statistics that obstruct accessible writing and an engagement with social problems, one might well want to avoid such professionalism and "hire" a sociologist from a school off the beaten path, such as CUNY-Graduate Center (in New York City), or Wesleyan, or perhaps even someone from outside of sociology, indeed from outside of academia.

Professionalizing academic life has been inseparable from the growth, role and scope of American universities, especially in the post-Sputnik era, when universities became more closely linked with the initiatives of government and business. This has produced a practical or "applied" emphasis in academic life, especially in engineering, science, technology, and the social sciences. Criminologists are to study effective means of punishment and deterrence, not waste time reading Foucault's *Discipline and Punish*. Sociological students of inequality are to comb through Census Bureau statistics about the relationship between household income and housing in order to make informed policy recommendations, instead of rereading Karl Marx's book on poverty called *Capital*.

In addition, since American universities gradually lost funding beginning in the late 1970s, social scientists are expected to write grant proposals in order to help fund their universities, including portions of their own salary and the salaries of their graduate assistants. In quantitatively-oriented sociology departments, faculty are expected to get grants as a requirement for tenure and promotion. As such, grants have become "publication equivalents," in some respects – especially if they are large grants – replacing traditional scholarly publication as a valued professorial activity. I have worked in sociology departments that reward faculty who write grant proposals with courses off and even salary increases; these are rewards for simply writing the grant proposal, even before it has been awarded.

In this sense, sociological professionalism has segued into entrepreneurialism, with faculty evaluated in terms of their ability to "bring in" grant dollars in order to augment eroding university budgets. An entrepreneur is someone who starts a business. Not only are senior faculty expected to write grant proposals. Many even entry-level assistant professor jobs in sociology these days require evidence of the ability to get grants that produce "indirect" cost payments for their university, thus reversing the decline of their budgets. The requirement that professional sociologists seek grants limits the field of sociology to people who use quantitative methods, do surveys, and investigate problems of interest to government and business. Public intellectuals, renaissance men and women, and gadflies need not apply!

Value freedom

The final feature of much contemporary sociology is a commitment to objectivity, or what Max Weber called "value freedom." Weber (1946) in a famous essay entitled "Science as a Vocation" outlined this notion of objectivity in scholarship and teaching. He maintained that sociologists should check their political values at the door when they enter the classroom and the office, scrupulously removing their political and social biases from their teaching and research. This defense of objectivity is a standard component of graduate students' socialization as they learn not only how to manipulate statistical data but also write and think with the dispassion of a Max Weber, who self-consciously eschewed a politicized, and thus, he felt, unprofessional, sociology.

At the time Weber wrote his stirring essay setting up a firewall around the value-free classroom and research office, he was trying to establish a professional sociology as yet in its institutional infancy. Weber feared that a polemical, partisan sociology would imperil the legitimacy of the new-found discipline, subjecting it to ridicule by those who dismiss the findings of sociology as either obvious or trivial. Weber in particular wanted to put distance between himself and Marxists, who argued for the unity of theory and practice – the application of social-science knowledge and social theory to aid and abet the socialist revolution. Although Weber was quite critical of capitalism's tendency to become overly "rational," stifling creativity and diminishing the self's unique individuality, resulting in what Weber termed "the loss of meaning," Weber made his point success-fully and persuaded subsequent generations of sociologists that objectivity was to be prized above all else.

Two issues are in play here: Weber, in developing his doctrine of value freedom, was putting distance between himself and Marx, requiring later sociologists to appropriate a contradictorily value-free Marx as they integrated him into the sociological canon as a "conflict theorist"; in valuing objectivity, Weber initiated a debate, that has been intensified since post-modernism, about what it means to be objective. In this second respect, defenders of a strict positivist standard of objectivity differentiate them-selves from social scientists and social thinkers who, they contend, fail the test of objectivity and thus are marginalized or "othered" as non-scientists or even anti-scientists. This debate about objectivity raises the science question for theorists and epistemologists who debate what it means to do science, and about the appropriate means of doing it. For an enlightening discussion of the science question by a critical sociologist influenced by both the Frankfurt School and postmodernism, see Stanley Aronowitz's *Science as Power* (1988).

As I explore in my chapter on methodology, to follow, postmodernism is a frequent target of those who claim that it rejects objectivity in favor of relativism and even nihilism. But I have argued that there are postmodern versions of science that read science simply as one competing text among others that must fight for its right to be heard, and taken seriously. This version of science, of empiricism, denies that quantitative methodology is a royal road to truth. How you conduct and write up a study does not establish the study's truth value, its objectivity. Fiction can edify, as can art and film. This returns to an issue I discussed earlier about how method pretends not to be an argument – rhetoric, by another name – but in that respect it secretly argues. The most "objective" version of the world, the supposedly positivist version, is in fact as perspective ridden, as contextual, literary, and corrigible, as more self-consciously subjective versions, whether qualitative methods (participant observant, fieldwork, ethno-methodology), literature, or art.

This can be seen by examining science's busy, heavily figured text for what it is: A pastiche of gestures, reviews, additions, deletions, revisions, compromises, rearrangements, self-justifying letters to the journal editor *that could have been written differently*. Science denies this, pretending that it is a perfect mirror of nature, a representation that does not lie on the page as a poem might but is the outcome of rigorous scientific and statistical method. The problem here, as elsewhere in this book, is that positivist sociologists, in imitating the supposed objectivity of the natural sciences and especially of physics, are embracing a model of scientific objectivity that was abandoned as soon as Einstein wrote his first paper on relativity in 1905. Positivist sociology is nearly a century out of date in its replication of Newton's physics! Where Newton suggested that the scientist can stand outside time and place and analyze the world object-ively for what it is, without error, Einstein realized that the scientist is always in-the-world, captive of time and space that together distort what is seen, and measured.

Einstein revised the Enlightenment's standard of objectivity – mirror-like knowledge – because he recognized that the mirror distorts. There is no god's-eye-vantage from which we can know the world objectively. Heidegger, a follower of Nietzsche, phrased it this way: Existence, simply being alive and in the world, precedes essence, a timeless knowledge of certain objective truths. What is crucial for resolving the science question is whether Einstein's and Heidegger's acknowledgments of **grounded knowledge**, knowledge that is influenced by how the knower "knows" or sees it, for example whether she is female, African-American, or gay, require us to renounce science altogether. In other words, if we can't be totally objective, must we deny the existence of the world of objects (and other subjects) altogether, abandoning science for art?

Einstein clearly didn't think so, nor do I, nor must postmodernists or critical theorists who contend, as I do here, that positivism has become a powerful ideology, a way of restricting knowledge to sheer facts in the here and now. Trying to be objective about a world that defies total understanding is what we do already, as situated actors in our everyday lives as we struggle to pay our bills, make vacation plans, save enough for our kids' college, read and evaluate the newspaper, decide for whom to vote, even take sociology classes. Harold Garfinkel relied on the philosophical writings of Husserl, who was Heidegger's mentor, to argue that the everyday self is already a scientist in the way she negotiates an objective world, dealing constantly with imperfect knowledge, garbled conversations, conflict over meaning and values.

Everyday selves inescapably deal with objectivity, and with social objects. We don't doubt for a minute that we lack all the answers, but we nonetheless feel a certain efficacy in the way we learn to negotiate and even remake our worlds. Garfinkel, inspired by Husserl's later writings on science, argues brilliantly that it is best to view science and sociology as everyday activities and not as what Husserl called "transcendental" ones, literally transcending space, time, context, history, culture, gender, race, class in achieving perfect objectivity. Scientists, although frequently well-educated and credentialed, are selves, people who deal everyday with contingencies, such as imperfect knowledge, inadequate funding, jealous colleagues, broken computers, overheated offices, too little time and too much to do. The scientific self, much like the bricklaying self, the schoolteacher self, the construction-worker self, must make choices from the givens at hand, doing science much as we all do life, without knowing everything. This knowing self is, by definition, subjective, subject-like, having feelings, prejudices, hunches that color the scientific outcomes.

As I discussed in the preceding chapter, Garfinkel argues that what Husserl called the natural attitude is prior to the theoretical attitude, the attitude achieved by bracketing out preconceptions and prejudices. He says that we will learn more about how people "do" social organizations like workplaces, schools, and families by observing them do their magic (and sometimes their evil) from the ground up, instead of imposing on them the burden of being rational actors – people who are objective and knowledgeable and who operate according to how social laws say they will. Much of Garfinkel's work is implicitly a critique of the structural functionalism of Talcott Parsons, who governed American sociological theory from the 1930s through the 1950s. Garfinkel's ethnomethodology rejects Parsons' model of the self as a "unit actor," preferring to listen to people's own accounts of their behavior as they accomplish what a Parsonian might call "social structure." Garfinkel believes that people construct or sustain the enduring patterns of social life, termed "institutions" by Parsonians, through language and other sense-making practices conducted in the natural attitude, in everyday life, which of course is the way we approach everything, from the time we get out of bed to when we turn in at night.

Garfinkel, then, is saying that the self, the everyday person like you and me (even those among us who have several degrees on the wall and many academic publications), is quite competent to make sense of her world and then communicate (about) that world with others. Indeed, it is through everyday sense-making that people construct their worlds so that Parsons can, from the outside as it were, say that there are social institutions such as family, politics, religion, mass media. Garfinkel portrays a competent, communicating, if not totally objective, self who in effect is a sociologist. Sociology conducted in the natural attitude is a process of ordinary people like you and me doing our observing, interviewing, theorizing from the ground of our lifeworlds – the everyday scenes of household, family, kids, their homework, miles traversed to school and work, coming home in the evening, working out, watching television and, while at work, doing writing, teaching, gossiping, playing tennis, e-mailing, and Web surfing. The sociologist has an everyday life in which, among other things, she does sociology, which is a curious process of learning from selves how *they* do sociologies that equip them to pay the bills, help their kids with homework, go shopping, plan for a future, and make sense of important events such as September 11, and the disintegration of the space shuttle *Columbia*. As I write this paragraph, I remember that I had a conversation with a colleague at work about a chapter in a book I recently published in which I explored the theoretical meaning of the World Trade Center attack; I continue to read about the possible causes of the space shuttle *Columbia's* explosion, which I heard as it happened when I was playing tennis – a huge boom, preceded by a series of chugging sounds like a roller coaster. In these moments, I was doing sociology, no less than when I sit here, at the computer, composing a story for you to read. It is especially difficult for sociological selves to separate their lives into neat compartments: Our lives as citizens, parents, friends, tennis players, and our lives as sociologists. The fact that these spheres blur proves Garfinkel's point about how we do science in exactly the way we do the rest of our lives: Life is a practical accomplishment of people who compose themselves as they watch, read, learn, chat, write.

This book, then, can be read as an ethnomethodological account of virtual selves, selves who experience and construct the world using information technologies that allow us to achieve a globality and instantaneity only dimly imagined by modernist theories of history, which relied on slow and local media such as newspapers, letters, book publishing. My account of the virtual self is necessarily about my own life, and the lives of people I know and observe. Sociology is strengthened by autobiography and ethnography. You can begin to write sociology as you grapple with the forces that made you who you are. Keep a diary or journal in which you reflect on these matters. Great intellectuals have done this, to their advantage. Putting things down on paper helps you think them through; your writing sometimes surprises you as your unconscious surfaces and leads you in new directions. Sociology is about self-discovery. Not only has the everyday self changed with the Internet, having become at once more fragile, susceptible to the electronic tentacles of the culture industries, and more efficacious, capable of writing the world and joining community through the power of the pixel, which augments the power of the pen. The sociological self, as Garfinkel understood it, has also changed, capable of acquiring global, multicultural knowledge and of achieving global dissemination, as scholars link up in virtual communities with minimal resistance. Compare the transaction costs of sending an e-mail to a like-minded colleague in Europe or Asia, whose work one may have discovered using www.Google.com, with the costs in time and money of attending the American Sociological Association annual meetings in Chicago or Atlanta, let alone the International Sociological Association World Congress meetings in Durban, South Africa.

Virtuality makes possible instant community, instant communication, but also the potential for an institutional de-differentiation that invades the private sphere of everyday experience as institutions such as culture, media, education, and especially the economy collapse in on the self, who was formerly shielded to some extent from the outside world. The increasing permeability of the boundary between public and private achieved by the Internet (as well as television, cell phones, fax machines, pagers) represents a threshold between modernity and postmodernity. The postmodern is here understood as the potential for the self to imprint itself on the world, and to risk being imprinted by the world. The postmodern moment, when the boundary between the self and world becomes quite flimsy, can be viewed either positively, as the occasion for self-creation and social change, or negatively, as an occasion for more of what the critical theorists term domination – the colonization of people's everyday lives by culture and power, reinforcing their subordination. The postmodern boundary between self and world is the topic of my final three chapters. I worry that this boundary is dissolving as selves are saturated by the world. Selves are also enriched by having the world at their fingertips. But before we get there, we need to have a discussion about what my more scientific colleagues down the hall call **methodology**, the systematic ways in which empirical researchers learn about their worlds. I am in favor of methodology, as I will explain, but I contend that there are many legitimate methods. We shouldn't become overly optimistic about methodology's ability to do our thinking for us.

CHAPTER THREE

Does Postmodernism Make You Mad or Did You Flunk Statistics? A Chapter on Methodology

Quantitative sociologists hate postmodernism because they believe that it rejects science. Postmodernists hate science because they think that it pretends to see the world from the outside, which they believe is impossible. Methodologies can't solve intellectual problems but are simply ways of making arguments for what we already know or suspect to be true.

Many sociologists really hate postmodernism! I once worked in a sociology department in which colleagues circulated a cartoon lampooning the word-play of postmodernists. In another university, I found that same cartoon posted on a staff member's door; she was married to a guy in my department, who I knew didn't like postmodernism. I have had, and still have, colleagues who characterized me as a "postmodernist," even though I am not one, exactly, and even though they don't have the slightest idea what one is. A good book on postmodernism that clarifies some of these misunderstandings is Charles Lemert's (1997) *Postmodernism is Not What You Think*. Like me, Lemert is sympathetic to many postmodern ideas, but, also like me, he uses non-postmodern ideas in his empirical discussions and theorizing. Even to write or talk about postmodernism earns the wrath of mainstream people!

In this chapter, I want to discuss various methods (or methodologies, as my empirical colleagues often call them) for conducting social research. Every introductory textbook talks about the scientific method, including both quantitative and qualitative research. Here, I want to broaden this discussion by examining both empirical research and theory as sources of valid insight about the virtual self and postmodern capitalism. Indeed, I go beyond sociological methods proper to include literary, poetic, and artistic methods for gaining social understanding. A good place to begin this discussion is the raging debate over postmodernism, which, as I will explain, is really a debate about science.

Ten Reasons to Reject Postmodernism

I have known little that angers and agitates people as much as postmodernism. Even women's studies, African-American studies, Marxism, critical theory don't arouse as much animosity. Queer theory gets some people steamed, especially when they think it is secretly postmodern. Foucault was gay and postmodern. Postmodernism has blended with all of these perspectives; indeed, one of the things people dislike about postmodernism is its imperialist nature, the way it takes over all fields, or seems to. Postmodernism underlies many complaints people have about those of us who do it, or at least read it. What they really dislike is our postmodern point of view, but sometimes they don't say this because it would appear intolerant and parochial and so they say other things: He's not rigorous; he doesn't have data; he publishes in the wrong places. I once applied to be chair of the sociology department at a major southern university, persuaded by a famous friend of mine there to do so. I was turned down, I was told, because certain members of the department there didn't like the fact that I said in my application letter that I play tennis; they viewed this as sarcasm. What they were really saying is that they didn't want a postmodern or Marxist chairperson, but they couldn't bring themselves to say that and so they found something, anything, to complain about. I'm not special; we all suffer slights. My point is that mainstream people go to great lengths to disqualify postmodernism, even if they end up talking about tennis. (I could have this all wrong, perhaps because postmodernists are paranoid. Maybe mentioning I play tennis suggested I wasn't serious enough about my profession to be chair!)

Let me make a list of the things that I know people dislike about postmodernism, and then respond to each of these.

I   Postmodernism is difficult, wordy, abstruse, abstract, and invents words!

It is true that much of the work of Jacques Derrida, an Algerian who founded deconstruction, requires enormous philosophical erudition. His book *Of Grammatology* (1976) is a very difficult read, requiring much philosophical and literary background; I rarely inflict it on my students. He invents words and uses existing words in new ways. But Derrida is trying to make a point about language, stressing its inherent flexibility and its ambiguity. He is demonstrating that clear language does not necessarily resolve philosophical quandaries. Indeed, language breeds more language, as people try to clarify, and clarify again. This is an infinitely long process because even definitions need to be defined. Derrida would probably say that the criticism of postmodernism as unclear and wordy implies that people have access to clearer, cleaner languages that do not involve themselves in the endless, infinite process of interpretation. But a Derridean believes that there are no such languages, even mathematics: There are no languages that perfectly mirror nature and don't need to be explicated, explained, defined, worried through. Positivism is the illusion that such languages exist. And it is a powerful illusion, posturing science and math as royal roads to truth and suppressing philosophical investigation and interrogation as muddle-headed. Although I wish that Derrida would be more systematic at times, he is a literary theorist who views the boundary between philosophy and literature as quite permeable. Philosophical language can be creative and metaphorical, suggesting insights by the way it writes and talks.

2   Postmodernists are relativists, denying truth

This is one of the most prevalent criticisms of postmodernism, and the least valid, in my opinion. Postmodernism says that there is no supreme vantage point, outside of history and beyond time and place, from which we can see and then write about the world in a totally objective way. The perspective or vantage point of the knower, seer, writer, scientist matters hugely to his or her conclusions about the world. Some weeks after the *Columbia* exploded, there were two separate investigations into the causes of the explosion taking place. One was being run by NASA, which sent up the space shuttle. The other was run by an expert commission, headed by a former military officer, charged by the government to find the causes of the disaster. Why would there need to be two separate investigations, especially since NASA employs many space and aeronautical experts? The answer is to be found in Derrida, who recognized that what you know is relative to your vantage point; knowledge is perspectival, as I have already discussed in this book. The independent commission was set up to investigate the accident because the government wanted to avoid the appearance of a possible cover-up by experts at NASA, who not only want to protect the shuttle program but also their own jobs. This is not to say that NASA experts would flat-out lie but rather they might, consciously or unconsciously, minimize their own culpability for launching a craft that may have been unsafe, and that they may have suspected was unsafe. Derrida and Foucault do not deny the existence of an objective truth; they would recognize that the space shuttle *Columbia* exploded for a reason, and that investigators can uncover the reason and then communicate it to the world. They don't deny science and its pursuit of truth. They simply make the point that all knowing, writing, observing, counting, and teaching take place within contexts, including language itself, that necessarily taint their information. These don't introduce error so much as they introduce perspective, the way you see something, especially where your basic assumptions are concerned.

Let me take another, more sociological example. Criminologists have hotly debated the efficacy, utility, and morality of the death penalty for years, especially since the US Supreme Court under President Reagan once again opened the door to legal execution of convicted murderers, delegating the decision to execute murderers to individual states. My own state, Texas, executes felons at a much greater rate than any other state, with our local courts having little mercy for offenders, even where DNA testing now demonstrates that people convicted in the past may have been convicted wrongly. Anyway, academic criminologists have begun to examine the death penalty, and in particular the issue of whether capital punishment deters murder. Many criminologists decided that the issue of deterrence is best studied by examining homicide rates in contiguous states (states next to each other), one having the death penalty and the other without it. One could then test whether, within relatively homogenous socio-economic and cultural environments, the existence of the death penalty actually served to reduce the homicide rate. The data collected in this way suggest that it doesn't. But why doesn't it, criminologists wonder? Because most homicides, more than two-thirds of them nationally, occur between intimates and constitute the proverbial crimes of passion, committed in the heat of the moment. Lovers' quarrels, domestic abuse, and robberies might fall into this category. In these cases, there is little or no premeditation; that is, the person who acts murderously doesn't reflect carefully on what he is about to do, including estimating his chances for beating a murder rap and escaping the electric chair or death by lethal injection. But other criminologists, who are more disposed to favor the death penalty for either professional or personal reasons, argue that the question of deterrence is best answered by asking people whether knowing that their state has the death penalty would actually deter them from committing murder. Here, the vast majority of Americans answer that the death penalty would deter them. Who is correct? Is there a "truth" to be found about the death penalty? Derrida would notice that how you ask the question of the death penalty's possibly deterrent effect has much impact on your answer. If you take the contiguous-states route, the death penalty is not deterrent. If you poll citizens, the death penalty is deterrent. Just because the criminologist is working from perspective, a central Derridean idea also shared by phenomenology, does not mean that there is no truth. There is, but getting at it depends on what and who you ask. Thus, according to postmodernists, less important than establishing the relationship between truth and method is stipulating the ways in which your method already depends on certain theoretical assumptions and perspectives. No method is value free. Although there *is* a truth out there about whether capital punishment deters murder or not, there isn't a single correct method for discovering this truth.

3 Postmodernists sometimes seem to deny the existence of the real world altogether

This criticism of postmodernism is an extension of the criticism just discussed, about relativism. Foucault has done a great deal of work that could be called empirical social science. He has studied the history of punishment and the history of sexuality in multi-volume series of books, thus earning a place in the literatures of criminology, social control theory, sexuality, and **gender**. Lyotard (1984) has written on science. Baudrillard (1983) has addressed advertising and other aspects of consumer culture. All of these approaches are empirical, examining the real world, even if they are non-quantitative. The incorrect impression that postmodernism ignores reality probably stems from the fact that postmodernism denies that there is a single reality upon which everyone will agree, and which can be described using a single language, especially mathematics. Postmodernism's non-representational, non-positivist theory of knowledge is sometimes confused with an idealism that denies "reality" altogether. Actually, postmodern theorists pay attention to the ways in which culture and discourse construct the world's meaning, thus

requiring that culture and discourse receive critical attention. Culture
and discourse are "real," every bit as real as the World Trade Center
towers. But the world is not simply a text, even though all texts are worlds
– nucleic societies of readers and writers through which power is
transacted.

4   Postmodernists oppose progress and are too cynical

This all depends on what we mean by "progress." To be sure, postmodernism, like the Frankfurt School's critical theory, stems from Nietzsche's
unsparing critique of the Enlightenment, which sometimes gives the impression of nihilism (there are no values) or cynicism (all values are bad).
Also, postmodernists, especially Lyotard and Foucault (but probably not
Derrida), reject Marx's "grand narrative" or large story of progress because
they contend that no story, however large and all-encompassing, will
capture every nuance. Marx's theory was secretly authoritarian, these
postmodernists contend, because Marx, following Hegel, wrote a total
theory of world history in which, as Hegel termed it, history is the slaughter
bench of individuals, who are sacrificed to the cause of History as expedi-
ents. But postmodern theorists are generally sympathetic to progressive
social movements, such as environmentalism, post-colonialism, and gay
and lesbian rights precisely because such causes unite the "margins," those
who, as Other, have been left out of the white male heterosexual European
narrative of progress. Whether contemporary Marxists can accommodate
these sorts of difference and marginality is an open question. I would argue
that postmodernism in general has been more attuned to marginal people
and groups than has an orthodox Marxism that still invests its theoretical
and political energy in the white-male proletariat, even where there is scant
evidence that the traditional working class is likely to become a revolutionary actor in the near future.

5   Postmodernists take classical and contemporary works of culture and "deconstruct" them into meaninglessness; this thwarts the traditional civilizing function of the liberal arts

Although Derrida first suggested deconstruction as a legitimate intellectual activity, he never embraced deconstruction"ism," a methodology

to be applied to any and all texts. For a wide-ranging discussion of deconstruction, see Jonathan Culler's *On Deconstruction* (1982). Indeed, Derrida did not even intend deconstruction as something done "to" texts, from the outside as it were. Deconstruction is the tendency of all texts to unravel, to come apart at the seams as their glosses, inconsistencies, contradictions, deferrals of meaning eventually get the better of the seamless impression they try to create – including Derrida's own works, and certainly this work! He wants to make the point that writing is a mistaken-ridden, partial, and necessarily incomplete project that, in being read by strong-willed readers who supply their own meaning to what they read, is necessarily transformed. This is the sense in which Derrida implies that reading is writing, a strong version in its own right. It must be, given that texts suppress and defer a variety of their internal problems, begging questions that can only be answered in new texts (and so on). Thus, there is no single correct reading of Shakespeare but only versions of him, indeed as many versions as he has had readers. This no more renders the text irrelevant than postmodernism ignores social reality in favor of nihilism or solipsism (thinking that the world is a figment of one's imagination). Deconstructing literature draws attention to novels' tendencies to suppress tension and defer meaning. Novelists such as Mark Twain intend to tell the whole story, even if they write sequels. The greatest works are full of inconsistencies and blind spots that cry out for elucidation. That may be why we consider them "great." This does not weaken their authority but reveals the human artifice behind them; they were written by people, and can be rewritten. Indeed, they are being rewritten every time that they are read (think of the Bible or Shakespeare), as readers resolve their quandaries of meaning in their own imaginative ways.

Every text is **undecidable**; that is, according to Derrida, you cannot once and for all grasp its meaning, which can then be clearly communicated, in a book review or Cliffs Notes. Critics of deconstruction also indict deconstruction for supposedly reducing "great books" to the level of ordinariness, treating them critically on the same level as television, journalism, comic books, pornography. That is exactly what cultural studies does, unashamedly! Although there are many links between postmodernism and cultural studies, the critical analysis of culture industries does not necessarily require Derrida's deconstruction. Cultural studies makes the valid point that mass culture and media culture are worth studying by anyone interested in the politics of culture. Derrida would agree that every text, no matter how "high" or "low," is susceptible to being deconstructed, that is, to deconstructing itself, as readings probe its text or discourse for evasions, inconsistencies, deferrals. But Derrida did not introduce deconstruction in order to end civilization as we know it, or to "deconstruct" Great Books curricula of the kind found at Columbia University and the University of Chicago. There is a tendency for people who drink deeply of postmodernism to broaden the canon of so-called great books to include marginal voices, as well as media productions, just as there is a tendency for people who do postmodern theory to be interested in cultural studies. But Derrida's thesis of texts' deconstructibility is not culturally nihilist. In fact, most of Derrida's own published deconstructions address very important works of western philosophy, such as the writings of Hegel and Rousseau.

6   Postmodernism comes from Europe, especially France, and is un-American

Homegrown Midwestern empiricists of the kind who dominate many PhD-granting US sociology departments tend not to like theory of any kind, especially European theories, because they are somehow beside the point, which is getting at the facts, using mathematics and statistics. Americans often use the term "pragmatic" as a positive thing. "Useless" is its antonym, which many people think postmodernism is. As a former quantitative colleague said to me, about social theory generally, "So what?" The American rejection of postmodernism is frequently anti-intellectual as well as ethnocentric. I know that these are fighting words. But, after having worked in several primarily quantitative sociology departments, I am convinced that empirical sociologists, many of whom are men in plaid, dislike postmodernism because it is the most exotic of the already offensively exotic species of theory. It plays with words; it intellectualizes; it speculates beyond the data; it is unashamedly political, supporting weird causes such as the rights of queer people. I had a colleague, who was very quantitative but only mildly productive in publishing his work, tell our whole department that postmodernism is "speculative bullshit," exuding overdetermined anger (anger that has many sources and manifestations) at European theory as a whole. He also disliked me because he thought I was self-important, which goes with the theoretical territory, I suppose. To be sure, French postmodern theory makes an easy target for down-to-earth, number-crunching empiricists who would rather count than theorize.

7 Derrida and Foucault talk only about texts and not about "reality," making them inadequate inspirations for sociology and social science

It is true that Derrida in particular performs many textual readings, of Hegel, Rousseau, Marx, even Shakespeare. He tends to view the whole world as a text, even though he of course knows better. We didn't get to see the political and social-science side of Derrida until his *Specters of Marx*, in which he declares his Marxism and theorizes the Internet's impact on society and culture. Foucault has always talked about "reality," although he understands, as does Derrida, that reality is mediated through, and constituted by, texts, especially what Foucault calls discourses (systematic habits of speech and figuration implanted in everyday life). His point, in his voluminous studies of madness, crime and punishment, and sexuality, is that professional and punitive discourses such as psychiatry and criminology exercise power over people in achieving social control. Foucault realizes, in a way paralleling the Frankfurt School, that it is no longer adequate to understand power and domination as simply "done" to people; they are now to some extent self-imposed as external control and self-regulation are blended to the point of identity. But this doesn't mean that Foucault ignores "hard," empirical social structures such as prisons, economies, and families. He simply theorizes and studies the discursive practices that, to some extent, constitute these institutions. He contends that discourse constitutes selves, as much as it is constituted by them. In this respect, he blends the analyses of culture, power, and identity.

8 Postmodernism opposes science, and especially mathematics

Derrida, Foucault, and Baudrillard have written little about science. Lyotard has delved further than the others into the philosophy of science. It is possible to apply deconstructive insights in the realm of the sociology of science, reading science much as a postmodern critic might read literature, film, or advertising. As I have been saying, science is an authored project, not a photographic representation or mathematical machine. It is different from literature only in that it suppresses the author, covering over the literariness of its text, indeed denying that science is writing at all; it is secret writing, as I have suggested. "Literariness" means "having the qualities and appearance of literature." So the appropriately deconstructive project is to *authorize* science, bringing to view its literary artifice, its having-been-written-from-a-certain-vantage and disgorging its subtle argument, its political rhetoric, for one state of affairs over others. This is not anti-science at all, but only anti-positivist, which, more than other scientific epistemology, suppresses the author so deep in the densely figured mathematical journal page that the page seems to be sheer representation, when in fact it is science fiction – the author's way of being human through chemistry or demography.

A postmodern and critical-theory version of science is eminently possible, as I have shown in my work, and as Marcuse has shown in his writings on new, gay, or happy science, an image of non-positivist science that he develops in his blending of Freud and Marx. The reading of postmodernism as anti-science is an act of sheer projection – supposing that another person or theory will do something bad to you because, secretly, you want to do something bad to it. Blending Freud, Schiller, and Marx, Marcuse suggests that science is a vital play impulse, a self-creating and productive mode of cognition that freely plays with concepts and with data in order to envision the world. This is, as he tells it, a literary process, a practice of authorial artifice. He does not theorize this discursive component of free cognition, of science, because he was writing at a time, the 1950s, before French postmodern theorists had begun to develop their discursive perspectives on power and culture. The *Tel Quel* group, centered in Paris and including the founders of postmodernism such as Derrida and Foucault, did not form for another decade. There has remained a symptomatic silence between German and French theory, especially on the issues of science and culture, that has only recently begun to be bridged (see the work of Ryan, Kellner, Huyssen (1986), Luke, Aronowitz, myself).

9   Postmodernism, because it is amoral and relativist, leads to amoral and immoral activities, such as September 11

I would never have thought that anyone with intellectual credibility could possibly blame postmodernism for that distressing day in September, 2001. Although Dinesh D'Souza (1991) and Allan Bloom (1987) had already weighed in on the intellectual scandals of campus postmodernism in their twin diatribes composed during the Reagan years, these are not criticisms taken seriously by many in the academy, even though their books have sold briskly in the trade markets. But this past summer I came across a debate between a *New York Times* cultural correspondent and the noted theorist Stanley Fish (e.g., 1989), who has produced interesting work on the relevance of Derrida for literary criticism and legal studies. The cultural correspondent argued that the relativism of postmodernism has entered the culture, indeed the global culture, and that this relativism and amorality had led, at least indirectly, to the attack on western icons such as the World Trade towers and the Pentagon. If I hadn't read this argument with my own eyes I wouldn't have believed it; it was too silly. But there it was, in the pages of the *Times*, along with Fish's well-argued rebuttal in July's 2002 *Harper's*, in which he exonerates Derrida for having caused the airplanes to be hijacked and their passengers flown to their deaths, and the subsequent deaths of thousands more. It is one thing to call postmodernism relativist; that is wrong, but fairly innocent. It is quite another to blame postmodern epistemological relativism for a global climate and culture of amorality and immorality, licensing wanton attacks on hallowed western institutions and American citizens.

Although Derrida and his student Gayatri Spivak (1999) have written on post-colonialism, as has the noted Arab theorist Edward Said, these thinkers have not licensed or launched an intellectual jihad against the west but simply tried to understand the "othering" of marginal groups, non-western cultures, gay and lesbian people as an outcome of a certain Enlightenment view of Europe, of European science, and of what lies beyond, both culturally and intellectually. I have already suggested the causal chain that takes us all the way from the Enlightenment, through the Holocaust, to the creation of Israel, to Bin Laden and September 11 in the concluding chapter of my *Postponing the Postmodern* (2002). I argue that September 11 is bound up with hostility to Israel, which was created because European culture was deeply anti-Semitic, which springs from the Enlightenment. It is not the Nietzschean-inspired critique of the Enlightenment and positivism developed by Derrida that led to various immoral acts and organized catastrophes during the twentieth and early twenty-first centuries. It is positivism itself – a worldview that views nature and other people as things to be manipulated. Adorno and Horkheimer were the first to recognize that fascist authoritarianism redirects anger about authority figures against Jews, Slavs, Gypsies, queer people, who are "othered" and then exterminated as mere objects, not also selves. Their critique is consistent with Derrida and Foucault's later discussions of othering and otherness.

10   Postmodernism is not serious or rigorous, but merely wordplay,
mastered by any fool

The notion that any amateur can master postmodernism is false on the evidence. No amateur, unacquainted with western philosophy and literature, can begin to fathom Derrida's dense work. And yet Foucault (1972) praises the amateur and amateurism because he wants to disestablish official knowledges, which he regards as discourse/practices of power and control. In this regard, his healthy respect for amateurism, for grass-roots knowledge, is similar to Garfinkel's own conception of practical reasoning found in his ethnomethodology, about which more will be said later. The real amateur for Derrida and Foucault is the reader, who enters the text in a subordinate power position with respect to the writer, who may even be the recipient of royalty payments generated by the purchase of her book. But deconstruction quickly turns the tables as readers further enter the sense and sentience of texts that cry out for interpretation, and even correction, by readings that, as such, become writings. Pick any difficult and lengthy work of fiction: Tolstoy's *Anna Karenina*, Shakespeare's *Hamlet*, Thomas Pynchon's *V*. The literate but perhaps unpublished reader works her way into these texts, cracking the code and becoming immersed in the plot. Almost immediately the mind wanders, imagining the world of the main characters, the author's intention and sensibility, the relationship between the fictional characters and one's own life and times. This interpretive intervention, done by amateurs, is called forth by the sheer indeterminacy of all writings that do not easily give up the key to understanding themselves, even if they possess glossaries of terms at the end. Even glossaries are fictions, requiring further elaboration, and perhaps glossaries of glossaries, definitions of definitions, endlessly. I have a single glossary in this book, but I also intend the main text to be a kind of glossary, too, defining itself as well as terms I use in my official glossary. I say this because I want you, dear reader, to think theoretically about which is the "real" glossary, and why! So there is a sense in which postmodernism praises the amateur in the figure of the reader, she who ventures forth into the thickets of novels and science with a compass, compassion and common sense and thereby begins to *transform* what she is reading into her own version – a reading of *Hamlet* appropriate to America in the early twenty-first century, perhaps drawing analogies between Shakespeare's protagonist and certain contemporary political figures, who experience their own tragedies. A transforming reading might notice that Shakespeare probably composed this tragedy in the year 1600, the time when the Enlightenment commenced, and tease out of this fact certain insights into the continuity (or discontinuity) between Shakespeare's life and times and our own. In any case, there is nothing wrong with amateurism if the amateur becomes an author in her own right, perhaps one day even breaking into print. It is liberating to know that anyone can do deconstructive detective work, auguring a literate public.

Postmodernist Intolerance

I have just given you the much-misunderstood sides of postmodernism, which is viewed with contempt by cultural conservatives and quantitative methodologists alike. But this would be an incomplete portrait without discussing intolerance that flows the other way, from the Derridean humanities toward natural and social sciences that not only rigorously analyze the world but use numbers and statistics to do so. There are humanists galore who unreasonably despise not only positivism, the rather circumscribed enfant terrible opposed by critical theory and post-modernism, but all empiricism, which bases knowledge on direct observation, experiments, surveys, and large data sets. It is worth remembering about my account that the early Frankfurt School, in the 1920s, 1930s, and 1940s, conducted many empirical social research projects. The Frankfurters wanted to support and enrich critical theory with empirical studies of the family, of authority, of the working class, of mass media. They found a world of difference between empiricism and positivism; they believed that one could develop empirical research methodologies, per-haps even using mathematics and statistics, that did not adhere to narrow positivist strictures about value freedom, perfect representation, and the pursuit of social laws.

By the 1950s, the Frankfurt thinkers had largely given up empirical social research, convinced that even their non-positivist work risked being atheoretical. Instead, they began to write more systematic works of social theory, such as Marcuse's *Eros and Civilization* and Adorno's *Negative Dialectics*. Although these books addressed the empirical world, they did not discuss data in the usual sense of responses to surveys or economic indicators. By the 1970s, when American sociology was becoming much more quantitative and statistical, there was a widening gulf between critical social theory and quantitative social-science empiricism. For their part, the French postmodern theorists never pretended to be either social scientists or empiricists. Their work was composed largely as commentary and critique of works of philosophy and literature, as I have already discussed with respect to Derrida. By the end of the twentieth century, many theorists and humanists took for granted not only differentiation between theory and empiricism but opposition. As well, the distinction between empiricism and positivism had faded as theorists demonized empirical research, much as they were demonized by Midwestern empiricists as nihilist. Intolerance abounded on both sides.

All of this is quite contrary to the unified epistemologies of the original social theorists, Durkheim, Weber, and Marx. These thinkers discussed the empirical world; they had little time to engage in meta-theory, theory about other theories, although Marx began his career by explaining his dissatisfaction with Hegelian idealism. And yet their pages were not littered with the figures and gestures of mathematics; they were accessible to well-educated and even amateur readers interested in the division of labor, suicide, bureaucracy, religion, economic markets, the degradation of work and workers. This is not to suggest that Marx agreed with Durkheim and Weber on all issues; of course, he did not, differing with them about the weighty issue of what Hegel called the "end of history."

There are differences in the substance of the founders' theories of modernity, but great similarity in their intellectual methods: *They essay the world*, recognizing that empiricism is theoretically framed, indeed collapsing those categories altogether. I seriously doubt that any of the three great theorists of modernity would have compartmentalized the empirical and the theoretical; they would have regarded their writings as totalities, seamlessly unfolding the world as they knew it, and sometimes advocating a different, better one. Again, one should not oversimplify: Durkheim and Weber, although they essayed, believed that sociology should be a science and seek to describe social laws; in this, they were positivists. Marx believed that positivism, especially bourgeois economic science, was an ideology, promoting false consciousness among workers, who, upon reading about the inevitability of their social fate, reproduced it in their everyday lives, going to work dutifully and refusing to commit the revolutionary deed. They differed, but they were similar in how they put pen to paper, making up the world as they went along. In particular, none of them relied on methodology, a rigorous protocol for conducting empirical research. And they didn't rely heavily on quantitative techniques, even though they dotted their pages with numbers, especially as they discussed wealth, the suicide rate, and population growth.

Just as Marx, Durkheim, and Weber essayed, so they were systematic, addressing typical patterns of social structure and social behavior, patterns that endure, but can change. In Lyotard's famous term, they wrote "grand narratives," big stories not just about France or England but about "modernity," a global society emerging first in the factories and families of western Europe and Great Britain. Whether or not they overemphasized the west is a fair question, but not the most important one here. More important is the scope of their theories, which was global, general, even "total," again to borrow Hegel's word. The tried to explain "everything," not just particular things like their home countries, the world between 1850 and 1865, industrialized nations. They sacrificed nuance for scope, a methodological decision at its most crucial. Methodologists call this a problem of the **level of analysis**, typically, within sociology, distinguishing between individual-level and aggregate social phenomena – your household income versus the pattern of all household incomes, for example.

Postmodern theory tends to be intolerant of sweeping stories, including the classical nineteenth- and early twentieth-century theories of modernity. One of the characteristics of postmodernity, it is said, is that it resists global, total narratives but can only be captured in fragments, requiring local, individual-level, even intuitive methodologies. Some contend, with good reason, that the postmodern only discloses itself in architecture and art. Grand theories tend to become grandiose, beating the reader over the head with the author's perspective, which is necessarily selective. Postmodernists, thus, often counsel flying below the radar in order to capture nuance and local flavor.

This aversion to grand, global theory is curiously matched by the frequent postmodern aversion to mathematics, especially as deployed in the human sciences. Numbers are too abstracting, like grand theory, sacrificing the particular and personal to the general. The notion that we cannot summarize human experience in either concepts or numbers runs deep among many humanists, including postmodernists. This is what makes the project of a postmodern science so important, retaining the possibility of counting things and people, keeping track of the economy, analyzing DNA, calculating the infant mortality rate. Postmodernists are correct that counting and numbering are always already theoretical acts, rooted in certain assumptions about what-will-be-counted. But because math and science are theory-laden does not mean that they are to be sacrificed to expressive narratives rich in experience but lacking concepts, structures, numbers, generalities. I am arguing here that one can do natural and social science, counting, graphing, summarizing, testing, as well as develop general theories disclosed in grand narratives *as long as one recognizes that methodological decisions are always already theoretical ones*, involving the author's philosophical and sociological assumptions about the nature of the world. The text of math and science is never free of context; but that doesn't mean that we should abandon counting and analyzing as impure activities. All intellectual activities are impure in the sense that knowing helps constitute what is to be known; knowing constructs knowledge. Text and context blur, just as all versions are deeply grounded in the body of the author, her world, her time, her gender, her race, her class. The postmodern aversion to science and math because they are perspective-ridden is misguided, especially where deconstructive insights and techniques can bring these literary gestures to light, in effect theorizing them.

When I read science or math in sociology presentations, I attempt to authorize them, replacing figure and gesture with the concepts and theories that underlie them. I exhume their arguments, their rhetoric, their advocacy. One can decode science in this way, especially science clogged with methodology, technique, statistical operations. By the same token, one can translate theoretical constructs into empirical terms, not so much making them testable, whatever that might mean, but grounding them in examples. What are we otherwise to make of "negative dialectics," "total administration," "undecidability"? In this sense, both science and theory can be read from the outside, translating them into terms of each other. Methodology poses and solves intellectual problems, typically translating technical terminology into other languages that illuminate them, from the outside. In sociology, there are already well-established quantitative and qualitative methods, involving surveys, testing, measurement, interviews, direct observation, experiments, narratives. One of the main problems of our discipline is that forays in method have overtaken forays in theory and conceptualization, substituting figure and number for concepts. "How" we study problems, and analyze data, has gotten the better of "what" we learn. Again, this is in large part because sociology, beginning in the 1970s, became a science-like discipline in order to impress deans and foundations. We need to undo this trend, albeit without dogmatically rejecting all math and method, especially where we redefine methodology as a textual, theoretical practice, a process of opening up texts so that readers can see the machinery of argument and make their own arguments in turn.

My position is that there is nothing wrong with methodology if method is understood as a way of writing, of composing an argument, of intellectually engaging with the world, of translating one's own language into others and others into one's own. We all use "methods" in our intellectual work, some of them quantitative, qualitative, theoretical, intuitive, narrative, autobiographical, archival, experimental, fictional, representational, non-representational. They are all legitimate "versions," to use a Derridean word, in that they are all ways of expressing ourselves; they are literary postures that, at a profound level, reconfigure the experienced and observed world as *something other*, creating distance, which is frequently quite uncomfortable, between the reader or viewer and her comfortable conception of the order of things. Adorno valued distance, as well as dissonance, as a source of liberating insight. The problem for him and for his close colleague Max Horkheimer (1974) is that in late capitalism people tend to become so immersed in the world that it is very difficult for them to see the forest for the trees, to grasp the big picture, and to tell large stories that help explain the "totality." Critical theory could be described or defined as an intellectual methodology for gaining distance, for thinking about the world as something other, going beyond everyday appearances to understand its deepest structures and its most distant reaches. This is one way of talking about "globality," which is an interesting theoretical term used both approvingly and disapprovingly. The critical theorists were noticing that our experiences of the world are framed by cultural discourses that position us in the world as consumers, citizens, family members, educators and the educated. This notion of being positioned by culture has become an explicit topic of French postmodern theorists such as Foucault, who approach the issue of distance and closeness in ways very similar to the Frankfurt School. It is no accident in that Foucault studied Marcuse closely and learned from him.

Meaning, Not Method

As I have said, every writer has a method, whether the method involves computers and data-analytic software packages or simply a pen, for writing fiction and theory (a certain kind of fiction!). My conception of sociology, especially in a time when the self is struggling to assert her identity as a literary (reading and writing) subject, would deemphasize methodology, without making it totally irrelevant. It can't be totally irrelevant because one needs to learn an intellectual style, or, preferably, styles. But method is more about how one composes oneself on the page than about truth, which, I contend, is less about intellectual techniques than about meaning. For every truth, there are many possible methods. I will go further: Multiple methodologies enhance the search for truth, allowing us to view the world and ourselves from different angles, and with differing depths and dimensions. As I write these words, I am a composing self, banging away on our new home computer. It is early in 2003, and the US is about to go to war in Iraq, for quite dubious reasons I strongly feel. I and my kids made a lawn sign the other day that said "No War." It was stolen off our lawn within a few hours, in plain daylight. A neighbor who witnessed this political statement (a protest of a protest) said that high-school kids tossed the sign into the local creek, and it sank. Enough about me. What is the problem here: The writing self? The war in Iraq? Wayward adolescents? The subject of methodology? Maybe all of them! My writing could well be enriched by looking at the problem, or problems, from a different angle: Why is the US threatening war in Iraq? What geopolitical theory is President Bush using? What do he and his military and intelligence teams know that I don't?

Before I sat down to write this section of the chapter on methods, and after I helped my 11-year old daughter with her homework – preparing for a test on World War II – she asked me "What was the Holocaust?" We talked for a while, and I decided that I would download some stuff from the Internet next day at work. (We don't have it at home, for theoretical reasons regarding the colonization of everyday life and the acceleration of childhood. Recently, my daughter, prodded by lunch-table banter among boys in her grade, looked up www.dildo.com on my wife's work computer. That initiated an interesting discussion!) I also decided to give my daughter two of my favorite books, the harrowing but necessary *Eichmann in Jerusalem* by Hannah Arendt (1994) and Sartre's *Anti-Semite and Jew* (1948). I was going to lend the Eichmann book to an Israeli student who plays on our university tennis team, but he said that this transforming moment in Israeli history was so intensely troubling to him that he couldn't yet read the book; he is 26, and a pilot in the Israeli air force as well as an engineering student with nearly straight A's. I will not yet show my daughter photographs of the inhuman bodies that the Allies found at the liberated camps. She has nightmares.

This is, of course, a discussion about methods. How to teach and learn about the Holocaust. Whether or not to have the Internet at home. How to compose a chapter on methodology. I can only conclude that multiple methods enrich single methods, but that all the methods in the world, a real cacophony of voices, don't get us to the truth without the difficult process of *just thinking it through*. Method doesn't solve intellectual problems but can quickly become a problem where we expend all of our energy refining our measurements and improving our experiments. At the end of the day, all methods are distractions from the real business of thought and theory. You need a method – how to teach my daughter about the Holocaust – but these methods don't absolve us of thinking for ourselves. In the wrong hands, they become formulas for disaster.

Let me summarize my views of methodology:

1   There are lots of good methodologies – quantitative, qualitative, narrative, autobiographical, fictional, poetic, artistic, filmic. None is inherently superior to the others, and none avoids its own blind spots, its perspective-ridden nature. That is, every methodology tends to ignore certain problems by focusing on other ones. And some of the best methodologies are found outside of sociology, in the humanities and in art.

2   Methodologies, especially quantitative ones, that pretend to be totally free of bias and perspective are not only deceiving themselves and their audience. They pretend to be free of bias in order to assert their own intellectual superiority, especially by comparison to "soft" methods such as participant observation, ethnomethodology, sheer fiction.

3   Methodologies are really literary strategies; they are ways of making arguments. In this sense, methods *prove* what the scientist or sociologist knew all along. They are intellectual imprimaturs that make their work seem legitimate and authoritative. Typically, researchers write their methodology sections of their papers and books last, cleaning them up and presenting them as if they solved intellectual problems. This is not to deny that methods – systematic ways of knowing – are important. Indeed, every literary strategy is a method, by definition. But people have high expectations of methodologies that they cannot meet; they are merely ways of writing up one's argument. As such, they are rhetorical devices, not inherently superior to arguments that don't have methodology sections, such as a poem or a film. Methods make the reader believe that she is reading science and not fiction; but it is all fiction anyway.

4   Since the 1970s, the burden of sociological argument has been shifted from theory to quantitative methods in order to reverse the decline of disciplinary prestige in the United States. Papers are evaluated by reviewers in terms of their methodological sophistication, not the sophistication or reasonableness of their theoretical arguments. Quantitative sociologists might deny this. But my study, *Public Sociology*, for which I read hundreds of article reviews by specialists before the

articles were published or rejected for publication, demonstrates that our discipline has become *methods-driven*, as I term it. This is reflected in the reviews I read, in the articles themselves, especially those published in high prestige journals such as *American Sociological Review* and *Social Forces*, and in graduate-school sociology curricula, which are heavily weighted toward methods and statistics courses. US sociology is much more quantitative than 30 years ago, even though there are pockets of people who use qualitative and literary methods and who emphasize the importance of theory.

5   People who value quantitative methods tend to view non-quantitative methods as illegitimate – as non-science. They especially reject and resent interdisciplinary methods and theories, such as postmodernism, critical theory, cultural studies, feminist theory, queer studies. They place impermeable boundaries around the discipline of sociology, and also strong barriers, perhaps even a moat, between the empirical social sciences and the humanities.

6   By the same token, many theorists and qualitative methodologists reject counting, math, statistics out of hand, returning to an intellectual position formerly known as neo-Kantianism. This position sharply distinguishes both the methods and substance of natural sciences and social sciences. This position rules out of court the analysis of large data sets, including census data. This prevents learning about shifts in household income by gender and race, unemployment figures, crime patterns, data about migration and immigration. There is mistrust and defensiveness flowing both ways, across the methodological divide separating quantitative and non-quantitative scholars. Along with this mistrust one finds basic differences in what, and how, people publish: Quantitative people tend to publish articles, like physicists and chemists do, whereas theoretical people tend to publish books. This reflects and leads to struggles within universities and departments about what constitutes "real" research. Highly quantitative sociologists may view published books as worthless or nearly worthless when they make hiring and tenuring decisions, whereas theory and qualitative people may devalue co- and multi-authored journal articles delving into the fine details of a particular research problem, about which one can spend a whole career writing. When I was a university dean, I found few scholars genuinely "polyvocal" (capable of speaking, or learning, diverse methods).

I hope I have demystified methodology for you, at least a little! If you remember only one thing about this chapter, let it be this: Your methodology won't rescue you from intellectual quagmires. You must think your way out of them, using insights and ideas, not algorithms or technical terminology. In the next chapter, I return to my discussion of the virtual world and particularly of virtual capitalism. I ask whether our economic order, in which we see UPS trucks and "telework," is significantly different from the economic arrangements of Marx's time. If so, how do these differences have impact on selves and on sociology?

CHAPTER FOUR

Adventures in Capitalism

Postmodernity hasn't surpassed capitalism, but we are in a postmodern stage of capitalism in which information technologies like the Internet change the relationship between the self and society. Selves are increasingly invaded by culture industries that seek to keep them shopping and conforming. Is rebellion possible?

So far, I have talked about the virtual self, sociology's encyclopedia of concepts and theories, and methodologies viewed as literary strategies (and not divining rods). In this chapter, I want to explore the economic underpinnings of the virtual self, both beginning and departing from Marx in certain respects and in all respects updating his theories. This will flow into the next chapter, where I discuss the family and gender, and the ways in which women position themselves with respect to feminism. In this chapter, I discover that postmodernity has not succeeded capitalism, but that capitalism makes use of postmodern technologies of production and information in order to gird itself against a socialist revolution. In the next chapter, I discover that women who emphasize their femininity tend not to be feminists, leading me to think differently about the impact of the women's movement. In each chapter, I caution against celebrating courier services, white-collar work, cell phones, the Internet, and girl talk as deliverance from a more primitive and less enlightened stage of civilization. In significant respects, I find that we are sliding backwards, actually regressing. That topic will concern me in my final chapter as I take stock and speculate about whether virtual selves are better or worse off than selves before them, and what they can do about it.

Capitalism Colonizes the Self

More than ever, the self conjures itself out of the flotsam and jetsam available to it. This is not to say that selves were ever somehow prefabricated or authentic, arising from people's true essences. Self, in a society rooted in inequality that makes people's very existence inherently problematic, has always been an achievement, an uphill battle. To imply that subjectivity has been eclipsed is not to suggest that selves used to be healthy and whole, with industrialization creating unprecedented psychological catastrophes. However, I observe that the Internet makes it easier than ever for people to assemble themselves, authoring their own identities or at least appearing to do so. It is incredibly difficult for anyone not stranded on a desert island to resist forces of acculturation, socialization, and social control in face of what Foucault called a disciplinary or panoptical society, a society in which there is nearly total surveillance and self-regulation and thus ample opportunities for inauthentic existence, building selves out of parts that are, in effect, unhealthy. Make a list of healthy things you do, and unhealthy things. What would you like to change? Are you working on any of them? Sometimes, just knowing that we are defeating ourselves is a good beginning, even if we don't have enough energy or resources to change it right away.

Think of the overeater or the alcoholic. Temptations abound in a society with a fast-food restaurant or bar on every corner, and advertisements beckoning people to overeat and drink too much. One of the signatures of postmodernity is "supersizing," leading me to speculate that we are returning (regressing) to an era of Roman indulgence. At least a third of my daughter's classmates are overweight, some seriously so. What are their parents thinking? Perhaps they are so harried that they can't cook healthy meals, with rice, beans, broccoli, lean (or no) meat. Capitalism requires advertising in order to stimulate consumption, without which production would spew out unsold products and thus stagnate. Production must lead to shopping in order for profit to be realized. In contemporary capitalism, which satisfies the basic needs of more than three-quarters of its citizens, those who live above the poverty line, people must be motivated to consume more than they need. As Marcuse argued, we need to identify "false" needs, needs that are, in effect, imposed on people or, more accurately, self-imposed. They are self-imposed in the sense that we don't think about driving down to Krispy Kreme doughnuts on Sunday morning; we just get in the car and go, especially if our kids are whining for it. We consume more than we really need, largely on credit, because capitalism would stagnate if we didn't. This is not to ignore the fact that the vast majority of the world's billions live below poverty, for whom the issue is not false needs but basic needs. And a good Marxist will explain that the wealth of capitalist countries is achieved at the expense of third-world countries that provide both raw materials and cheap labor for the manufacture of running shoes, DVD players, children's toys, even canned and frozen food.

The issue, then, is not simply that people consume what is bad for them and for the ecosystem – plastic-wrapped hamburgers, gas-guzzling SUVs, margaritas in huge schooners. There are two even more important issues: People are manipulated to consume useless and dangerous junk in the interest of profit, far beyond the threshold of basic needs; and people, robbed of identity grounded in a nurturing community, assemble themselves in the image of what they find in cyberspace and over the airwaves. The **cyberself** is the term I use to describe this self-assembled, manipulated experience of the world. This is no different from the selfhood always required of subordinate people throughout history in the sense that people today, like selves during the middle ages or the industrial revolution, are "subjects," vassals, servants, workers, the powerless. They are "subject to" the will and whim of rulers, who exploit them and manipulate them for their private purposes. However, in post-World War II capitalism, the person is granted the illusion of freedom, of selfhood, in order to function more productively as citizen, corporate employee, and consumer. Indeed, in a cyber-capitalism, the "self" refers to the ways in which we invent ourselves in the electronic supermarkets and amusement parks to be found along the American interstate highways as well as on the information superhighway, which rolls not only through the wheat fields of Kansas and the suburbs of San Francisco but through the bedrooms, studies, and home offices of what used to be considered the private sphere.

Capitalism invented the self in order to manipulate it into frenetic, ceaseless citizenship, corporate obedience, and shopping. In a fast capitalism, psychology and social psychology are speeded up to an unprecedented rate as subjects – now selves – position themselves as cyber-citizens able to "access" the world simply by going online as well as to the mall. Selves are encouraged to create themselves by a postmodern culture industry that recognizes that identity – selfhood – is plastic, especially as children are brought up in households without strong parental guidance and role models. The education and socialization of children by parents have given way to effectively parent-less families in which children "learn" about the world and their places in it from television, the Internet, playground peers. Parenting has gone the way of writing letters, slow boats, radio. Parenting is no longer done primarily by caring adults in the home but is carried out through information technologies that at once entertain and educate. My daughter's classmates spend hours after school chatting with each other using AOL instant messaging. Although children can learn certain intellectual skills by using computers, "distance education" and chat rooms distance children from parents and teachers, who do more than impart information and skills. They nurture, guide, lecture, inculcate. Just as distance education in colleges and universities thwarts academic community, which can only be enjoyed in a face-to-face classroom and campus setting, children cannot be abandoned to television, telephones, and the Internet without losing contact with caring adults. Love and caring attention are better conveyed face-to-face, in real time, than transmitted by disembodied subjects, asynchronously. I am so exercised by all this that my next book, on speeding up fast capitalism, will address the acceleration and administration of virtual childhood by the culture industries and the accompanying decline of the self.

Capitalism was not always like this. Indeed, the very concept of "the self" did not exist at the beginning of capitalism, which dates from the eighteenth century. Before that, for the 2,000 years of prior civilization, the concept of the self or person was nowhere to be found in religious or philosophical thinking. More important than the individual person was the cosmos or universe, within which people were mere specks. No one thought that the person had needs, as we now call them, apart from the obvious needs for food and shelter. The consumer was not yet sovereign because people were not conceptualized as bundles of wants that could be satisfied by going to the mall, or even the corner store. You grew what you needed, or hunted it, or traded for it, for almost all of human history. Money began to change this, which is one reason Marx spent time in *Capital* reading money as a text, a postmodern exercise before the fact. Money's story, he found, was that people who are no longer self-reliant but go to work in factories and then shop for their needs are distanced from each other by the paper money sitting quietly in their wallets and purses. Money also leads to the wrong priorities, such as wanting it not for what it will buy but for what it signifies about the successful self. Later sociologists call this a status symbol.

Industrial societies emerged very slowly and gradually from the middle ages, which were nearly 1,000 years of ignorance and inertia. What made capitalism possible was the fact that a few Europeans saved enough to start businesses. They could save a little because technologies of agriculture and artisanship, leading eventually to industrial production, were becoming more efficient, allowing for inventories of crops and goods that did not have to be immediately consumed. As people gradually gave up farming in order to go into commerce, they began to move to bigger villages and towns, eventually, over hundreds of years, causing these towns of a few thousand inhabitants to swell into cities like London and Paris with millions of dwellers, consumers, producers. At the dawn of capitalism, very few people were well-off, let alone wealthy. Most were just getting by, much like their rural predecessors. As a result, social theory did not yet have a notion of the self and her needs. As well, political democracies, which rest on the parallel concept of the citizen, did not begin to emerge on the world map until late in the eighteenth century, with the American and French revolutions. Read a Charles Dickens novel, for example *A Tale of Two Cities* or *A Christmas Carol*, and compare life then to life as we know it. Dickens' characters couldn't take for granted central heating or electric lighting. They were cold in the winter, and often hungry. He paints a bleak portrait of urban life near the beginning of capitalism.

Two hundred years after Adam Smith published his bible of capitalist economic theory, with the end of World War II and the subsequent shift from Ford's urban factory to FedEx's suburban distribution centers, capitalism entered a new stage in which people had to be convinced to view themselves as insatiable beings who can only enjoy the good life by consuming goods. The self as a theoretical construct emerged much later in capitalism than Smith, Thomas Jefferson, Charles Dickens, Karl Marx. The critical theorists, writing originally in the 1920s, noticed this as they tried to figure out where Marx went wrong in predicting a socialist revolution. They concluded that capitalism's new battleground is the self, a bundle of needs, which it must produce in order to bleed off dissent and to promote shopping. This self is positioned by television news, which distorts political and social reality, by credit card advertising, which solicits buying beyond one's means, by the Internet ideologies of psychological plasticity and mobility, low transaction costs and globality.

In an earlier book of mine, I argued that in a "fast," postmodern stage of capitalism the boundary between the text and world fades as books ooze out of their covers and into the world. By this I meant that our lives are cluttered and commanded by all sorts of discourses, which I define as ways of talking about, and representing, the world. One might characterize discourse in general as the attempt to *figure* the world, whether using words, symbols, numbers, images, even music. The human capacity for "figuration," our ability to use symbols in order to express ourselves and mold our worlds (by building communities, nations, languages, religions, cultures) is perhaps the most basic human capacity, although Karl Marx argued that an equally basic capacity is working. Without minimizing the importance of sheer physical survival in the struggle with nature for resources and food, one could notice that life-sustaining work, such as farming and industrial production, falls under the rubric of figuration inasmuch as working on nature involves people in "figuring" activities, imprinting themselves (their "selves") on the landscape and their industrial commodities. Marx in his graduate-school manuscripts that form the basis of his humanistic philosophy of work, and of communism, argued that working is a type of **praxis**, a Greek word for self-creative activity. In this, he recognized that work, required for survival, not only figures the world, transforming it; it also figures us, transforming the worker and, under ideal circumstances, expressing his or her true nature. Make a list of your ideal jobs. What attracts you to them? Creativity? Complexity, so that you wouldn't be bored? The absence of a boss? Monetary compensation? Helping others? Do any or all of these jobs express yourself in the way that Marx imagined?

According to Marx, ideal circumstances for expressing ourselves through work involve both controlling the working process and owning the means of production, including the end result of work – what Marx called commodities. In a society without economic exploitation of working people, every human being would realize himself or herself in their work, "externalizing" themselves through their chosen projects. These projects – carpentry, music, metal craft, poetry, teaching – combine the material reproduction of the species and creativity. Marx criticized capitalism for *alienating* people's creative impulses, disciplining them by subordinating, regimenting, impoverishing people's innate creativity.

Writing in the mid-nineteenth century, Marx expected that capitalism would fall because workers would rise up to overthrow it, having been provided with a theory explaining the sources of their alienation and a workable vision of an alternative society, communism. Marx and Engels, his friend and co-author, wrote their brief tract *The Communist Manifesto* to convince the working class to escape the yoke of capitalist oppression. They argued in a related book that workers are oppressed not only by economic structures but by ideologies such as religion and capitalist economic theory that portray the everyday world as unchangeable, an outcome of certain social laws. These are the laws announced by Comte's social physics, and, after him, by Durkheim, Weber, and Parsons as the iron-clad laws of modernity.

According to Marx and Engels, ideologies produce **false consciousness**, a worldview that disqualifies radical social change as impossible and convinces workers to accept their present circumstance. They are in effect persuaded to exchange the prospects of socialism and communism in return for short-term benefits, such as a job – after all, a vital necessity! – and perhaps a modest rising standard of living along with weekends and short vacations. Religion promises that people will go to heaven for enduring earthly suffering. According to Marx, all pre-modern and modern societies require that the powerless have "false consciousness" so that they accept the status quo and decide not to revolt against their masters.

Marx thought that the socialist revolution would occur under two conditions. First, economic crises, which he felt were unavoidable in capitalism, had to sharpen to the point that workers are thrown out of work. Second, workers would have to believe that they can make a new world and organize a different economic and political system. They must have "true consciousness," their false consciousness and fatalism having been dispelled by theoretical writings that announce the possibility of an end to capitalist alienation and poverty. An example of this type of theoretical writing is *The Communist Manifesto*. Marx did not question for a moment that workers could have their consciousness uplifted by theoretical and political educators, who write stirring works of social theory and social criticism that not only indict the old but make way for the new – a world beyond capitalism. Marx did not doubt his or Engels' abilities to write their way out of economic misery and oppression. He did not need or develop a theory of writing, of texts, of books – of culture and the culture industries – because he felt it was obvious that one could pierce ideology in plain writings, accessible to the masses.

Marx's mid-nineteenth-century optimism about the overthrow of capitalism, although probably justified in the year 1867, when the first volume of *Capital* was published, was dashed by the 1930s, when Franklin Roosevelt helped steer American and world capitalism off the shoals of the Great Depression. Roosevelt realized that Adam Smith's pure market economy was inherently unstable. Over time, the market, without significant government intervention, has a tendency to produce highly unequal outcomes, with a few big corporations becoming very wealthy at the expense of smaller businesses and mere individuals. This is exactly what Marx had predicted in the 1860s. However, Marx failed to foresee the ability of the state or government to intervene in the marketplace, initiating various fiscal policies and heavy investment in make-work projects such as the WPA and later the military and NASA, and establishing progressive taxation which redistributes some wealth from rich to poor. Marx, in other words, underestimated the resilience of capitalism, especially where capital recruits the government or state to interfere in Adam Smith's pure market on its behalf. Marx himself recognized that the government is not a bipartisan actor but is, as he termed it, "an executive committee of the bourgeoisie." Is this true for all political parties? It is interesting to note that the United States is the only capitalist democracy without a large socialist party. You might research socialist and communist parties in Canada, England, and western Europe and consider why all of these countries have organized opposition to capitalism.

During the 1950s and 1960s, capitalism developed even more resilience. By the 1960s, the welfare state was firmly entrenched in most capitalist countries, both stimulating economic growth and redistributing wealth modestly through taxation, thus keeping the poor employed and shopping. The aftermath of World War II saw unprecedented affluence in the US, western Europe and Scandinavia, and in Japan and various Pacific Rim nations. Capitalism needed not only for the state to forestall economic crisis, it now needed the "culture industries" of radio, television, journalism, films, and especially advertising to intervene in, and redress, people's psychic crises.

People in post-1950s capitalism began to have more leisure time, more consumer durables, more savings – and thus greater temptation to remove their noses from the grindstones first imposed by the Protestant ethic. Capitalism now needed to divert people from the promise of liberation from both scarcity and work, at once keeping them busy in the workplace and providing them recreation, entertainment, meaning in the private spheres of household, leisure, and vacations. Selves needed to be "surplus repressed," as Marcuse termed it, in order not to seize the revolutionary opportunity first announced by Marx nearly a hundred years earlier. In particular, they must be led to engage in ceaseless shopping, **productive consumption**, so that the economy would continue to hum and so that they would be distracted from asking the big question: "Is the good life actually the 'goods' life?" You could do your first sociological survey: Ask people you know what they have on their agenda for their next purchases. See if people have clear ideas about what they want, and how they will save for them. Do their responses differ by gender? Are they intending to increase their work hours in order to pay for them?

Post-World War II capitalism accelerated in such a way that it was increasingly difficult for people to stand outside of their everyday lives and gain a critical perspective on what was happening to them. In this condition of domination or what Herbert Marcuse termed "one-dimensionality" people's imaginations are gripped by a deeper false consciousness than were Marx's nineteenth-century workers. In post-World War II affluent capitalism, according to Marcuse, people develop **false needs**, for endless shopping, trivial entertainments, the acquisition of status symbols (that acquire what Baudrillard, writing from the vantage of French postmodern theory, calls "sign value," the value attached to the brand Nike or Honda). Both Marcuse and Baudrillard recognize that people no longer really need an SUV, $100 running shoes, a DVD player, a plasma television, a cell phone that shows pictures and displays one's e-mail, a vacation to Disney-World. So they are led to want not the actual product but the brand name, the acquisition of which is stimulating and gratifying. When buying Nike Shox, for example, we don't want the actual shoes as much as we want the life depicted in the advertising campaign. We don't want the Lexus, we want the experience of driving the Lexus portrayed, both in images and words, in the advertising campaign. The brand becomes identity.

Marcuse judgmentally calls needs "false" that are imposed (superimposed) on the self by the culture industries and not freely arrived at through rational self-reflection. Selves lose the intellectual resources, the time, the space for rational reflection. Their lives are so "administered" that their needs flow almost immediately out of television screens, magazines, and now the Internet into their minds and bodies, which are "totally mobilized" for the project of endless shopping. A Marxist would notice that endless shopping is not only diverting, leading people away from political projects and social movements. Shopping for false needs also reproduces economic value – collected as profit – for a capitalist economy, that, at least in the United States, is capable of satisfying basic material needs for much of the population. We have moved from an ethic of saving to one of spending, aided and abetted by credit cards, a plastic invention unimagined by Marx. Workers in the nineteenth century, and certainly for the 2,000 years of civilization before that, had a great deal of difficulty even meeting meager needs for food, clothing, and shelter. Saving a little extra beyond that didn't begin to happen until well into the Industrial Revolution, which didn't have significant impact on most people's material well-being until the early twentieth century, when Henry Ford brought about the era of mass production, which accelerated capitalist productivity and increased overall wealth.

If people save too much, this imperils the economy, which requires ceaseless production to be matched by brisk consumption lest companies stagnate and go out of business. When this happens, workers are laid off and they cannot buy, creating a downward spiral of stagnation and unemployment. This is exactly what Marx predicted would happen to bring about the downfall of capitalism. Therefore, the economic system requires that we shift from the Protestant ethic of saving for a rainy day to an ethic of spending, even spending beyond what one has in the bank. Not only does this stimulate the economy; it keeps people busy and preoccupied, spending their "free" time shopping, being entertained, and traveling, and then working extra hard in order to defray their looming credit-card debt. This is a vicious circle. Any critical sociology of work will notice that leisure time, time spent away from work, is not genuinely free because people do not escape the pull of the culture industries, and of industry. They are influenced to shop, spend, engage in self-improvement, travel – anything that primes the economy and diverts them from reflecting on their lives.

Selves' psyches are engaged by the culture industries, which induce people to spend hours watching television and Web surfing, consuming advertising images that form identity. The self is also a body, which is a happy hunting ground for fast-food marketing and the contradictorily telling marketing of diet aids, health clubs, and fitness equipment. The body is not off limits to fast capitalism, but becomes yet another productive project for selves who are led to overeat and then diet. There is an additional factor at play here: Christopher Lasch's 1979 book on *The Culture of Narcissism* discusses the way in which selves in post-World War II capitalism are led to turn inward, becoming self-oriented and self-referencing. By **narcissism** he refers to the paradox of selves whose psyches and bodies are colonized but who then embrace private experience as an adequate source of meaning and shun politics and public issues. The self becomes both a battleground and a refuge, a haven in a heartless world that destroys the barrier between private and public life.

As I explore in the following chapter, it is predictable in this context that women would become preoccupied with makeup and hair, with clothing, with the whiteness of their teeth, with dieting. Post-feminism, especially in what is sometimes called its third wave, has become narcissism as women in their 20s and 30s refer to themselves as "girls" or "chicks," embrace femininity and its conception of the body as an object of the male gaze, and distance themselves from the strident politics of their 1960s sisters. Feminism has become a combination of the demand for equal pay for equal work, a basic principle of a market economy that is blind to the gender of workers, and self-absorbed attention to makeup, hair, and clothing. Sixties radical feminists proclaimed that "the personal is political," anticipating and echoing the Frankfurt School's contention that the self has become a site of contest and control in a late-twentieth-century capitalism. But third-wave feminists with blonded hair, painted nails, and capri pants embrace the gendered self, rejecting organized political and social movements as irrelevant, especially now that pay equity and reproductive rights have been legally defended.

Are Hamburgers a False Need?

Marxist critical theory possesses an inherent optimism: People, when free, will make good choices about their lives. Their selfhood will be healthy, non-dominating, neither abused nor abusive. They will not engage in binge drinking or eating. They will eschew cigarettes and cocaine. They will neither lie nor steal. They will be generous and courteous. There will be no road rage as drivers allow others to change lanes and edge into traffic without conflict. Resentment, Scheler's (1961) *ressentiment*, will be a thing of the past as people embrace their lives and do not heroize the rich and famous. Celebrity will be devalued; people will participate instead of spectate. Democracy will be direct and not only representative as people control their communities and workplaces, building consensus out of difference without papering over disagreement. Capitalism will be leveled as technology is harnessed to satisfy basic needs, in Afghanistan as well as Atlanta. The environment will be treated with respect, as a dialogue partner or loved one whose fragile ecology is a social issue. Animals will enjoy rights as slaughterhouses go the way of coal locomotion. (On the mass production of meat, see Upton Sinclair's original expose of meat packing, *The Jungle* (1951), and Eric Schlosser's (2001) update, *Fast Food Nation*.) Race and sex hatred will fade as police no longer apprehend drivers simply for being black and women run large organizations without male resentment.

At the center of this image of good lives chosen freely is a notion of personality that is strong and self-determining. Far from being caused or positioned by impinging social forces, including discourse itself, the self is the sum of its projects, as Sartre explained in his existentialist treatise *Being and Nothingness*. Faced with freedom, people no longer have excuses for their apathy. It is "bad faith," in Sartre's terms, to blame others for one's circumstances. Instead, people will choose projects that define them, externalizing themselves in nature and society, through work and language. These projects ward off mortal aloneness, giving life meaning where, existentialists insist, it has none. At the center of Marxism is the conviction that life can be given meaning by free agents who define themselves by their activities. The later Sartre of *Critique of Dialectical Reason* adds a social dimension to this earlier existentialism where he argues that people define themselves intersubjectively, with relation to others, with whom they form communities. This opening of existentialism to community and history necessarily introduces issues of power and domination, which are central to Marxists. By 1960, when Sartre wrote the *Critique*, he had become a Marxist, concerned to analyze social relations and thus the prospect of emancipation. He linked this analysis to the everyday worlds in which people pursue their projects and deal with other people, imaginatively linking his existentialism to Marxism in a way remarkably similar to critical theory. For their part, the Frankfurt theorists cited Sartre's book *Anti-Semite and Jew* approvingly as they developed their own "studies in prejudice."

Sartre would acknowledge that the self is invented in the sense that people are their projects, their work, love, family, education, travel. People author themselves – Derrida would say through their reading, which is a kind of writing, implying sense and inferring meaning where the author is muddled or mysterious. But a crucial difference between Sartre's existentialism and a postmodern perspective on the self is that Sartre portrayed the person, the self or subject, as actively choosing her destiny whereas postmodern selfhood is in a sense chosen for the person by the large, impersonal, frequently electronic media that position the subject, which is otherwise empty of content. Although life is a useless passion for the Sartre of *Being and Nothingness*, in the sense that people inevitably die, a perspective adapted from Heidegger, the self is a strong agent, an author, a decision maker who defines herself by her work and intimate life. She authors, whereas for postmodernism she is authored, largely by the discourses of the culture industry, such as the Internet.

Postmodernism arose in disagreement with Sartre and Merleau-Ponty, his French left-existentialist comrade, about the self. Theorists such as Foucault and Derrida abandoned subject-centered philosophies because they were keenly attentive to the ways in which culture and power form the subject, both through discourse and practice. As well, they opposed the Enlightenment arrogance positioning the self at the center of the universe, which was conceived as a happy hunting ground for the human will to control. Francis Bacon announced that knowledge is power – power over the "other," he, or it, who is less-than-human. This was a Promethean conception of humans that gave license to the defoliation of forests, human genocide, wars of attrition. The critical theorists and postmodernists humble the self by positioning it theoretically not at the center of the universe but at the margins, from which knowledge is gained only through inference and indirection, not by grand systemizing that spins sticky conceptual webs trapping the knower in elaborate structures – theories! – from which there is no escape.

Critical theorists and postmodernists disagree on certain issues relating to the self. The Frankfurt theorists are closer to Sartre in that they want people, beginning from the ground of everyday life, to change the world, even though Adorno, profoundly affected by the Holocaust's impact on philosophies of liberation, announced in *Negative Dialectics* that the opportunity to change the world has passed irrevocably, after Stalinism and the Holocaust. Adorno and Horkheimer ended the 1960s in profound despair about organized leftist politics, including official Marxism and the New Left. However, the logic of their critical theory suggested a critical, rebellious, imaginative subject who, like Sartre's self, defines herself by her political and social projects, from work to family.

Even though many in western capitalist countries are more affluent than their counterparts in the nineteenth century, the self in post-World War II capitalism is more dominated than in Marx's time. This is because, as Marcuse argues in *Eros and Civilization*, technological progress has to be matched by an increase in "surplus repression" lest the prospect of overcoming scarcity deter people from shopping and citizenship, ending capitalism as we know it. Although critical theorists viewed the self as subject to manipulation by ideology and advertising, they would not have agreed with postmodern theorists that the subject is so plastic as to be positioned by cultural media such as television and the Internet. The self's identity, for leftists, is firmly grounded in society and history, notably in class, race, and gender, which recruit identity for political ends. The self is conceptualized as a contested terrain, a battleground, on which the struggle for hearts and minds is carried out. For postmodernists, by contrast, identity is not grounded in history and politics but is a pastiche, a mosaic, made up of ephemeral fragments that fill the person with content, meaning, values. For theorists such as Derrida, Foucault, and Baudrillard, this is always true because they regard the concept of the subject or self as a philosophical artifact of the Enlightenment, which was corrupted by the equation of knowledge and power. For the postmodernists, subject-centered philosophies are, in Derrida's terms, philosophies of presence, pretending that concepts can mirror nature by putting us in its presence. In fact, he maintains, concepts are undecidable, forever begging questions, deferring meaning, engaging in circular reasoning. As I said in the preceding methodology chapter, this is not an irrationalist rejection of rational philosophy, science, and mathematics, but rather an argument that philosophy, science, and mathematics are merely versions that must compete with other versions – art, theory, ethics – for credibility and credulity.

I agree with the French theorists that the Enlightenment was flawed by hubris, installing an imperialist methodology of science that neglected to notice that science does not best myth but is the more mythic the more it pretends to break from speculative philosophy, constructs, values. Value freedom is the most impregnable value position of all, as we have learned over the history of positivism. However, that is not an occasion to reject all subject-centered philosophies, such as dialectics and humanism. To do so invites an apolitical relativism that does not hold the self responsible, as Marx, Sartre, and the Frankfurt theorists did, for initiating social change. To say that the self is agent and author does not necessarily repeat the mistakes of the Enlightenment, which positioned the self to conquer nature and eliminate all otherness. Agents and authors can be humble before the task of rewriting history as well as the texts that shape history and are in turn shaped by it. They must be humble if liberation is not to be postponed until a distant future time, after the Party (any party) has eliminated all opposition. Of course, liberation delayed is liberation denied, as the history of the organized left, especially of the Soviet variety, has demonstrated.

Postponing the Postmodern

If the term "postmodernity" has any credibility, it describes a historical moment, such as the present, when the subject or self becomes object to itself, an assemblage of gestures, styles, commodities, roles, accommodations that, taken together, constitute personality or selfhood. What is distinctive about the postmodern moment is that it is the first moment in history when the self becomes an object, a topic. Postmodernity could be defined as the stage of social history when people become "selves," objects for self-manufacture and marketing. Although the psyche or personality obviously existed before the postmodern moment, for example during modernity, before postmodernity selfhood was off-limits to social theory because the person was viewed as beyond the scope of social forces, of what sociologists term socialization. Only as modernity segues into the postmodern do we make the self a critical and theoretical topic, recognizing, as we must, that the self is manufactured and marketed as it becomes "object," where before the subject and object, or self and world, were at least somewhat distinct. For excellent accounts of the postmodern moment, from perspectives sympathetic to Marxism, see David Harvey's *The Condition of Postmodernity* (1989) and Fredric Jameson's *Postmodernism, or, the Cultural Logic of Late Capitalism* (1991).

Although the critical theorists did not use the term postmodernity to characterize late capitalism, preferring formulations such as "totally administered" and "one-dimensional" society, they drew attention to the objectivity of subjectivity, or eclipse of reason, as a hallmark of post-World War II societies. Self becomes object where the object is "preponderant," holding sway over thought and consciousness. This is a thoroughly historical process for the critical theorists, and not something written into our social nature, as it was for Freud, who understood the subject or self to be an outcome of the conflict between superego (conscience) and id (primal life instincts, such as sexuality). The relation between subject and object changes with the times, especially as in later capitalism consciousness, the body and needs must be mobilized in order to reproduce the existing society, notably through conformity, consumerism, and self-absorption. The self becomes a discernible entity when, in effect, capitalism requires shopping, especially for self-improvement products, in order to soak up all the commodities that labor and technology churn out. Instead of working on the body politic, virtual selves work on their own bodies, but contradictorily, clogging themselves with supersized junk food and then burning it off at the gym.

Many American people live in middle-class suburbs and neighborhoods. They have relatively secure livelihoods, and the majority have working spouses. Economic desperation is a vague prospect for most. Most of these middle-class and working-class Americans still must work hard to make ends meet; they are leveraged to the limit, given their consumer styles, penchant for vacations, immediate gratification, and, contradictorily, saving for the children's college years. These Americans neither own nor control the means of production, as Marx called them. They are not poor, but neither are they rich. They are relatively powerless, although they have seeming "freedom" to shop and travel, even if they remain indebted through most of their adult lives. They seem to live on Easy

Street, unlike their parents and especially their parents' parents, who endured the Depression. But around the corner lurks unemployment, as our unplanned economy lurches from boom to bust. Given the possibility of credit buying and the economy's need for ceaseless consumption, these Americans I am describing invent themselves – their selves, literally – in order to reproduce the existing social and economic order. The production of selves makes way for economic reproduction.

Kellner (1995) calls our popular culture a media culture, as opposed to a literary culture. Although the Internet is highly textual, the writing and reading we do is different from the way people used to read novels, biographies, and the newspaper. We rarely read straight through, from beginning to end. If you are like me, you have a number of reading projects going; our house is littered with open magazines, newspapers, books, and my own manuscripts. Books used to stand at one remove from the world, requiring studied contemplation and consideration. With the decline of textual forms of ideology – systematic claims made on behalf of the world's alleged rationality and justice – what used to be called "reading" has quickened, as people are required to make nearly instantaneous sense of the busy, multisensory worlds in which they live, making snap judgments about their conduct in order to survive as successfully situated beings. We drive to work on crowded streets, weaving our ways amidst other drivers chatting on cell phones; we meet and greet co-workers and then answer our voice mail and e-mail, which have accumulated since we left work the day before. We plan for our children's afternoons and evenings, as well as summer camps. We track our investments and retirement portfolios. We worry about our bosses' satisfaction. We do our work, which increasingly involves not physical production but cognitive and interpersonal manipulations.

In postmodernity, we "interface," instead of converse. We do not read memoranda but rather "review" them. We jump from task to task quickly, using computer software that allows us to open and close computer "windows" rapidly, becoming "multi-tasked." When we return home, we do not read texts in the traditional sense. We may glance at the newspaper and periodical magazines. We may write and answer some more e-mail, perhaps using a personal account. I recently spoke with the administrative assistant of an Internet billionaire in the Dallas area. I was trying to track him down using e-mail in order to propose a joint project to him. He is famous for answering his e-mail directly, even though he is very busy. She told me that after returning home from a recent trip, he had 2,230 e-mails awaiting him! Although he certainly must be a wordsmith, reading and responding furiously, he is not a wordsmith in the pre-Internet sense of someone who reads carefully and composes slowly, bothering to polish and refine. We read quickly through mail and perhaps pay bills. We do not sit down to write long letters that we send using the US mail service. We rarely write in a diary. We do not read challenging works of fiction or non-fiction, at most consuming fast trade books, such as spy novels or gossipy biographies, in order to fall asleep. You might make a list of the things you have read in the last week or month, and the things you are reading now. Are you reading anything except school books? Are you reading the newspaper? Novels? Books of social criticism? When is the last time you read a book from cover to cover?

Contradictorily, reading and writing occupy our days, as I have acknowledged, and yet it is a different kind of reading and writing than we used to do. We read road signs, peruse menus, glance at advertising, manipulate Web pages. We use textual means to chat, "messaging" colleagues and anonymous strangers in chat rooms. Literacy in the strict sense has not disappeared, only the reading and writing of distanced texts that require strenuous interpretation and imagination. Using fast epistemologies, we deal with the many discourses and demands of the moment, becoming nearly indistinct from the figural world that requires our attention lest we run off the road, miss an important e-mail from the boss, pass up a travel bargain on the Web, or forget to pick up all of the kids in our neighborhood car pool. The pace of daily life has accelerated since World War II, diminishing the quiet time spent reflecting, reading, essaying, writing letters. This quiet time is the time spent mediating, as well as meditating, carefully examining truth claims and the meaning of life. In my 1989a book, I linked all of this to the frenetic demands of a high-octane capitalism that requires restless, ceaseless shopping as well as a jumble of activities so intensive and distracting that we forget to worry, remember, hope, criticize. Capitalism has always understood that idle hands are the devil's workshop, tempting people to be laconic and even worse – revolutionaries. Since the arrival of the Internet, Web, cell phones, pagers, voice mail, and faxes, fast capitalism has quickened, requiring heroic efforts to slow it down, to carve out time in order to make sense of it all.

An electronic media culture makes images of selfhood readily available. It is as close at hand as television, cell phones, and the Internet. People shop for selves in the same way they shop for other consumer durables at a time when transaction costs have been dramatically reduced. One of the characteristics of postmodernity – although I contend that this is a stage of capitalism and not its transcendence – is the distinct sense that **identity** is in play, permitting selves many daily opportunities to remake themselves in the images they acquire through their electronic involvements. The self is at once an object, to be considered from the vantage of its reflection in the various mirrors of everyday life, and a commodity, to be purchased or at least rented. One could argue that the psychological ground of modernity is the self itself – systematic self-consciousness and the experience of being in the world. If so, then the ground of postmodernity is the alienation of self-consciousness into the world, its becoming an object (and commodity) for consideration, appropriation, and manipulation. We can see our own reflection in the computer screen. I recently watched an ad on television for, as I recall, J. C. Penney's. It showed a young woman in her twenties daydreaming while sitting next to her boyfriend, who was talking her ear off. Visions of the latest fashions were dancing through her head, and catchy music was playing. Suddenly, she came to attention and told him she was going shopping. The voiceover urged young women to go shopping at Penney's for the "fashions [they] crave." It is clear that Penney's wants this young woman to crave a new self.

Although the modern self was not without self-consciousness, this self-consciousness was shielded from invading social forces. Modernity valued freedom and self-sufficiency, whereas postmodernity views the self as positioned and self-positioning with respect to dominant discourses of culture and society. These discourses, in their nature, are fragmentary; one cannot speak of truth within their vocabularies. In postmodernity, it is recognized that the self is a pastiche, an assemblage, of partial discourses and not a window on the whole world. The postmodern self is not a truth teller but only a participant.

The postmodern abandonment of truth signals a repositioning of the concept of the self. This postmodern self is perfectly at home in a culture that is fast, decentered, ever-changing, electric. The modern self is grounded; it rests on what postmodernists disparagingly call "foundation." The modern self *is* a foundation – values, personality, identity. The postmodern self abandons this founding selfhood – a stable subject – in favor of the concept of a positioned and self-positioning self, a self that is manufactured and marketed. The postmodern self, in its powerlessness to change its own circumstance, let alone the world, reflects powerlessness at large, abandoning the notion that the self is a foundation impervious to social conditioning and control.

Capitalism has always closed the door of fundamental social change, through ideological texts and discourses, while cracking open the door of personal betterment (upward mobility, as sociologists term it). This individualistic notion of self-improvement has always been a tenet of liberalism, "possessive individualism," as Macpherson (1962) called it. Liberalism viewed the self as sovereign and autonomous, a truth teller and steward of the good. As well, liberalism charged the self with a significant degree of responsibility for its own fate, requiring it to be thrifty, hard-working, abstinent, and a participating citizen. However, as modernity slides towards the postmodern, the self is increasingly viewed not as an active subject in charge of its own fate, if not of society's overall fate, but as a byproduct of enveloping social and cultural forces that, in Freud's term, are overdetermining, shrinking the degree of personal autonomy nearly to nothing.

Just as there is continuity and discontinuity between modernity and postmodernity – they are two different stages of capitalism – so there is continuity and discontinuity between modern and postmodern concepts of the self. Although the postmodern self is less an active agent than the previous modern self, it is more accurate to say that the postmodern self is allowed to be active in fewer domains than the modern self. Previously, under liberalism, the political theory of democratic-capitalist modernity, the self was active in the democratic body politic. As well, the self, as I have noted, determined personal values from the foundation of stable identity, insulated to some extent from the impinging influences of what postmodernists later term "the social." In postmodernity, politics and the public sphere are declared meaningless, requiring selves to withdraw from public life. As well, the very foundation of selfhood, rational goal setting and value judgments, has been denounced as a mythological residue of the Enlightenment. Subjectivity is abandoned as ideology, the myth of the autonomous self capable of personal and public reason who, as the Enlightenment exhorts, achieves power through knowledge, notably science.

Like Derrida and his French colleagues, the critical theorists reject the image of the all-powerful subject who views the world as his oyster, to be plundered, devoured, digested. They reject the Enlightenment's imperious disdain for otherness – nature, mystery, the ineffable – and its myth of science as the undoing of myth. However, unlike the French postmodern theorists, the German critical theorists believe in **enlightenment**, even as they notice the seventeenth-century Enlightenment's betrayal of enlightenment in favor of the dogma of a value-free science. The Frankfurt theorists, with Marx, believed in reason's potential to order and reorder the world, notably societies. They differ with capitalist reason as an incomplete version of possible reason, which would free people from bondage to live in productive harmony with nature. Their belief in the emancipating powers of reason allowed them to theorize the subject, the self, and to lament its decline.

Critical theorists felt that talk of the subject or self must be historical and empirical. They wanted to assess, with open eyes, the extent to which the person could order and master her world. Under domination, which stretches back before capitalism to antiquity and which threatens to outlast capitalism especially as it borrows tools from fascism, selves are nearly thoroughly manipulated by economic, political, and cultural forces. Adorno would read *Self* magazine as a symptom of mass delusion, not of people's innate ability to master their worlds and lives. In the early twenty-first century, precious few selves can initiate a regime of reason, given the preponderant social forces arrayed against freedom, forces that appear to be objects or object-like in their intractability.

Imagine Adorno considering the proposition that people can "go online" and shop for a self, or indeed shop at all! I suspect that Adorno would have agreed with much of Foucault's analysis of the disciplinary society. Like Foucault, Adorno drew attention to the way in which the self has been neutralized. In this analysis, a number of themes are combined by the French and German theorists: In a totally administered disciplinary society people are subjected to electronic surveillance, which tracks consumer taste and enforces social control; they shop in nearly frictionless ways; they entertain themselves at home and in their offices; they work on themselves. At the same time, they resist electronic grids by forming cellular and Internet communities that afford meaning and connection.

Here, I am especially interested in the way that the self is transacted in the malls, over the airwaves, and through the electronic cables of the information superhighway and Web. People increasingly derive their identities from what they own, beyond the basic necessities required for physical survival. Vance Packard (1959) wrote a book about "status seekers," and Thorstein Veblen (1979) talked about the "leisure class" and what sets them apart from those who simply toil. These popular treatments derive from Marx and Weber, who understood the importance of status in a capitalism gradually growing more affluent. Although Marx expected the demise of capitalism in the mid-nineteenth century, given its economic contradictions, by the 1930s it was well understood that Marx's apocalyptic optimism about the end of capitalism needed to be revised, partly through a reading of Weber who uncoupled class and status, in light of relative abundance, consumerism, the culture industry, false needs. By the 1960s, it had become obvious that capitalism had staved

off its demise, at least temporarily, by linking identity and shopping in a
way unforeseen by Marx, who wrote when the basic issue for "identity"
was simply getting enough to eat (Ewen 1976).

In studies such as *Economy and Society*, Weber said that Marx painted an
overly simplistic portrait of capitalism. In suggesting that there are non-
economic factors in social explanation, Weber was not telling Marx something he didn't already know. Marx stressed the role of economic misery in
social development precisely because misery, for most of human history,
has been an ineradicable fact of social life. And although capitalism had
the potential to end poverty and blunt scarcity, Marx saw dramatic irony
in the fact that misery for workers increased under capitalism, given
capital's seemingly nature-like tendency to fall into a few private pockets.
Marx theorized that poverty and misery would intensify under capitalism,
leading to a socialist revolution and then the building of communism – the
classless utopia of his dreams.

Marx realized that consciousness, culture, ideology all play important
roles in social life, the more so the more workers need to be diverted by
belief systems that portray capitalism as the legitimate end of history. In
The German Ideology, Marx and Engels (1947) outlined the role of ideas –
ideology – in prolonging capitalism. They could not foresee the extent to
which consciousness – what I am here calling identity – would become
plastic, susceptible to what the French call "positioning." As I have said,
Marx did not foresee the culture industry's impact on consciousness,
sensibility, and thus society. He did not expect capitalism to outlive the
serious economic crises pitting capital against labor in what appeared to
be a final death struggle. Although Marx, especially in the later phases of
his intellectual career, emphasized the economic, he did not ignore identity and ideology, especially where he needed to explain why impoverished
workers did not revolt.

For Marx, capitalism defends itself by promoting a belief that the world
is inert and cannot be qualitatively transformed in the direction of a more
humane society. But consciousness can be elevated, educated, edified,
notably by grasping the "historicity" – fluidity and openness – of the
social, which makes social change possible. For Marx, there are no stable,
singular, timeless "subjects" or selves but only selves that endure history,
variously made and remade through the influence of impinging social
forces. Selves can become free, together, once they seize the moment and
claim authorship of history. At that precise moment, they attain full
awareness of their history-making role, their fundamental complicity in
their own fate, which they cannot pass off on others by saying "history

has no subject," as Althusser (1970) in his structuralism claimed. The self is fully free only when she masters her work, lives in harmony with nature, and shares freedom with other humans. And yet all selves possess the potential for freedom, which they must recognize in order to begin the process of liberation, which is at once a personal and collective effort.

Marx, albeit without naming it explicitly, developed the sociological concept of social structure, suggesting that the person is organically, materially, and historically situated and makes choices in the context of those conditions. That understanding is common to materialist social theories that stress the constraints on human behavior; indeed, positivists who seek social laws begin from much the same intellectual foundation as Marx in this respect. Intriguingly – and this is the core concept of a dialectical social theory – Marx argued that people could change the material and historical constraints on behavior, and even transform their relationships to their own bodies, desire, and surrounding nature, through the exercise of intellectual and political agency. A socialist revolution, in particular, would transform the conditions under which we labor, love, and do science, art, and philosophy. These transformations, leading to what Marx termed communism, would maximize our freedom to make choices and exercise control over our bodies, nature, communities, families, and workplaces. This would not be total idealist freedom, with science fiction-like scenarios of unconstrained wish fulfillment, as Freud termed it. It would rather be the situated freedom of people who come to grips with their imbeddedness in nature, body, desire, history – existence, to use Heidegger's and Sartre's term, a key concept from existentialism. Existence is the experience of the self in the world, not abstract philosophical ideas.

Existing in a world with others and nature constrains freedom but does not thwart it, if by freedom we understand the potential for self-realization, self-creation, self-discovery. All of these "self" prefixes suggest a direction for a critical theory sited in cyber-capitalism. More than ever, we need to attend to self-assemblage, the ways in which people electronically create themselves in the figural, flickering, spectral world of the Internet. This self-assemblage has always taken place in a society in which people are at risk of destitution, deprivation, lack of control and the loss of meaning. Today, in the affluent capitalist west, if not everywhere on the planet, the lack of control and loss of meaning are more immediate problems for many than is deprivation. I would argue that time and meaning are the scarce resources of a post-Fordist capitalism. This is not to say that capitalism has evolved beyond class struggle, the basic contradiction, as Marx understood it, between capital and labor. This structuring struggle is still at the epicenter of capitalism, even as its manifestations change in response to capitalism's changing global and cultural environments.

Marx did not dwell on the scarcity of time and meaning. He was pressed to theorize the scarcity of food, clothing, housing. The unequal distribution of wealth, in an otherwise forward-moving capitalism, would nudge people toward revolutionary agency. People would seize the moment, becoming agents (and, I would add, authors), only when theorists convinced them that they have only their chains, their poverty, to lose. In itself, what Marx called "immiseration" wouldn't trigger the socialist revolution; after all, most of human history had seen unrelieved misery and poverty, without progressive political action in response.

Money – wealth – remains scarce today, especially for the billions of people who live outside the capitalist west. Poverty and misery are omnipresent because the global distribution of wealth is severely skewed in favor of capitalist and what used to be called state-socialist countries such as Russia. Capitalism is the root cause of this uneven development, with some nations possessing disproportionate productive wealth. As Marx theorized, the fact that some nations and people possess inordinate wealth – capital – means that others will remain impoverished, necessarily, given the fact that when some "win" others, indeed many others, must "lose." Dialectically, Marx supposed, this would come back to haunt owners of capital, who, by impoverishing the many, would lack customers for their products, leading to the slowdown, stagnation, and eventual collapse of capitalism.

The self is very much at issue in a stage of capitalism that requires, in effect, excess. Once basic needs are met, the marginal utility, as economists call it, of indefinite, infinite consumption drops. (A good example of marginal utility: You crave donuts. You eat the first, but aren't satiated. You eat another, and another. By the time the fourth donut is staring you in the face, you are beginning to feel sick with sugar. The "marginal utility" of eating this fourth donut is lower than it was for the first one, which you really wanted.) This has the potential to de-rail an economic system that, as Marx recognized, is crisis-prone. The fundamental crisis of capitalism is the lack of spending, of shopping, where consumption meets or matches production. It is imperative that people buy what their labor produces for capitalists to realize profit. The alternative is stagnation and even business failure. Economic recessions and certainly depression would destabilize capitalism dangerously, throwing many out of work, both compounding the downturn in shopping and threatening the revolt of the masses.

Capitalism bleeds off potentially revolutionary dissent by keeping people employed, for which their shopping is a vital requisite. Staying employed allows people to meet their material needs and also to indulge in a pleasurable excess, extra, or surplus consumption, allowing them, as Marcuse recognized, to emulate the lifestyles of their bosses, a tantalizing psychological and socio-cultural projection in post-World War II capitalism.

Selves come into play politically where they are vital transmission belts between production and consumption. Capitalism must learn from social psychology in bridging self and society, implanting socially useful needs without appearing to violate the self's liberty and autonomy. This is a ruse in that people are hardly free to turn off the many stimuli that bombard them from their screens, periodicals, and billboards. People must be taught to consume beyond what they need for survival, or even for satisfaction. The culture industries gear them up to be endless consumers, promising "euphoria in unhappiness," as Marcuse termed it. But they don't do this crudely, through sheer manipulation. Advertising is not propaganda, but rather representation, freezing images of plentiful and stimulating everyday lives lived by selves who seem remarkably similar to ourselves. Advertising succeeds precisely because it presents an argument to the self, suggesting that happiness lies in self-improvement – attention to the self as object or topic. This is fundamentally new in capitalism; for most of human history, people weren't encouraged to view themselves as needful objects, people with sensibilities who cannot live without pleasure, entertainment, stimulation, acquisition.

Adam Smith already noticed this shift from penury to luxury, from subsistence to credit buying, in the eighteenth century. But only with suburbia, two-income families, and credit buying beginning in the 1950s did we have the material conditions necessary for what one might call the objectification of the subject – the subject becoming object to itself, through the category of needs. Freud initiated all of this, and with him the emerging discipline of psychology, as he theorized about need, a fundamentally new category as yet unexplored by philosophy and social theory. Freud opened the door to this type of thinking about the self where he said that each person is compelled by Eros – the life instinct. As such, people seek a primal gratification in socially acceptable ways, notably in their work and love lives. This invention of the self – before which there was simply human nature – roughly corresponds to the distinction between needs and wants, the first being basic, such as food and clothing, and the latter being discretionary – a second car, private schooling, brand-name clothing, a remodeled kitchen.

With cable television, niche channels appeal to the sophisticated consumer self. Indeed, you can shop for a new self, purchasing exercise equipment and aphrodisiacs. There are whole channels devoted to food, cooking, and home improvement. The home-improvement channels are very popular, especially a show, a knock-off of a British series, called *Trading Spaces*, in which people redecorate part of their neighbor's house, with only a thousand-dollar budget. I have watched this show with my wife, and the "new" room never seems much better than the "old" one. Indeed, sometimes it is worse. On the one hand, this is evidence of people's restlessness, their unhappiness with themselves. On the other, you could read *Trading Spaces* as empowering for people who want to be self-reliant and not waste their money on expensive redecorating jobs. I read the show as answering to a desire for self-reliance as well as for change. Of course, this is not political change, just a makeover. This notion that you can change your life if you change your environment is postmodern.

Speaking of decor in suburbia, think of the Cleaver household portrayed on *Leave it to Beaver*, a popular sit-com during the early to mid-1960s, when I watched the Beaver and Wally learn moral lessons from their disciplined dad Ward and receive nurturance, and after-school cookies, from their doting mother June. These are the people, newly middle-class, whose parents probably worked with their hands and endured the Depression. The Cleavers hadn't yet entered postmodernity, with cell phones, CNN, and the Internet, and yet they were materially comfortable and could afford discretionary items such as cars and vacations. There was a subtle struggle between mom and dad in this situation comedy over how indulgent they should be as parents, and as consumers. Ward represented an earlier Puritanism, insisting that his boys hold down after-school and summer jobs, whereas June, largely for implied reasons of her gender, indulged the boys, wanting them to avoid the penury of her and Ward's upbringing. This is the struggle between saving and spending that defines the history of capitalism, and which has been largely resolved in favor of spending, especially the mortgaged kind. In real life, as well as in the screen version, class and gender blend to the point of identity: It is never entirely clear that Ward does what he does because he is a breadwinner thrust into a certain class position or because he is a Neanderthal male, or that June mitigates Ward's puritan gruffness because she is a woman or a domestic laborer.

Leave it to Beaver portrays the acquisition of selfhood in 1950s and 1960s America. The show, like others of its genre and generation, is transitional between stages and sensibilities in capitalism, located somewhere between 1750s Puritanism and the excesses of post-1950s capitalism. The Cleavers were probably only a generation away from their working-class roots, in an earlier Puritan capitalism. Wally and the Beaver, if the show was still in production, would today be yuppies, spending beyond their means and raising their own Gen-Y children amidst the perils of AIDS, the date-rape drug, and too much homework. In the following chapter, I explore the Cleaver family further as I discuss the impact on women of watching June Cleaver, the feminist rebellion against the housewife role, and now our entry into an era called "post-feminist." Adventures in capitalism, the *Wall Street Journal*'s advertising slogan, involve gender, sexuality, and families. Feminists have long noticed that the economy and family are intimately related; they call this the work–family relationship. Postmodernists help us understand that the boundary between these two institutions is blurring as institutions undergo "de-differentiation," with the functions and structures of one institution blending with those of another. With the Internet, people "office" at home. For an intriguing study of "telework," consult Penny Gurstein's *Wired to the World, Chained to the Home: Telework in Daily Life* (2002). Her study links the concerns of this chapter on capitalism with the concerns of the following chapter, on family, feminism, and femininity. The Cleavers now both work, they use after-school care, their household is wired for the Internet, and parents and kids all have cell phones!

CHAPTER FIVE

Girl Talk

The impact of feminism on America has been exaggerated. Post-feminism returns to 1950s notions of femininity and its sharp differentiation from masculinity. Although many women now have jobs, they reproduce their own cultural inferiority through girl talk. But do women talk like girls because they don't like what it means to be "women" in today's society?

My mom didn't have a paying job. She stayed home and took care of me and my sister, even though she attended Bennington College, an exclusive college for women. Today, Bennington women work and have careers, and many have families. When I was 8, in 1960, women were called "girls." Ten years later, college women were calling each other "women." By 1980, the word *girls* referred to little kids, but not grown women. The women's movement, fueled by feminist theories, empowered women not only to go to college and embark on careers but to re-name themselves as a way of gaining control of their identities, their bodies, their families, their culture. A significant piece of post-World War II American feminism has involved the politics of discourse, as well as a politics of sex, bodies, and families. Today, confusingly, grown women are "girls" again. In this chapter, I want to explore girl talk, and figure out what it all means for virtual selves and their virtual children.

What Girls Do

Today is the rare snow day in the Dallas area. It sleeted last night, and the roads are frozen. There is no road salt, unlike in our former hometown of

Buffalo, NY and so schools are closed. My kids are staying home and having a great time. We went sledding down a nearby hill, which was a rarity for them. And then we came home and huddled around the television for a little vegging out. One of my wife and daughter's favorite channels featuring home-improvement and "lifestyles" shows, on which we all watch *Trading Spaces*, had just begun to air a half-hour show depicting an attractive 28-year-old Hispanic woman from Chicago who felt that her hips and thighs bulged too much and her breasts were too small. We were taken through her decision to have plastic surgery on both defects and then the surgery itself, followed by her joyous aftermath. My daughter watched in amazement at the fat-sucking liposuction and the boob job, which were performed during the same two-and-a-half-hour surgery. Most amazing to my daughter was the young woman's discourse about how her self-esteem was low because her breasts were too small and thighs too big, demonstrating self-absorption and vanity typical of the post-feminist generation. And after the operation, the woman professed to be happier than ever now that she had "a cute figure."

I talked to my daughter about this, as did my wife, a feminist sociologist and women's studies director at our local university. I am teaching a summer course in which we read books on fast food and diet, part-time work, and women's conceptions of their bodies. The course is called "Fast Work, Fast Food and Fast Bodies in Fast Capitalism." One of the books we read is Hesse-Biber's *Am I Thin Enough Yet?* (1996), a study of young college women and men who talk about what's wrong and right with their bodies. The author finds that many young college-age women are susceptible to anorexia nervosa and bulimia, two serious eating disorders of women who can never be thin "enough." Hesse-Biber, as I do, interprets this as evidence that young women haven't necessarily taken to heart the messages of their feminist mothers and older sisters; their self-worth is tied up with how they look, not just to men but to themselves in the mirror. Although 1950s women participated in girl talk and tried to beautify themselves for men, eating disorders were less common than they are today, when young women feel the additional pressure of watching svelte beauties on television and in the movies.

I can't remember June Cleaver obsessing about her looks or shopping; that she applied makeup and shopped was implied. Her sexuality was concealed. She spent most of her time on-screen resolving her sons' quandaries, with just the right mix of solicitude and humor. But it was never in doubt, as we revisit the show – and its decade – that June and Ward were preparing their boys to deal with issues of workplace authority, family roles, and the organization of leisure time. Nor was June ever shown working on herself, engaged in the various pursuits of self-improvement that consume yuppie selves today. And June probably didn't go to the gym or take painting classes, the way yuppies today do. It is hard to imagine June meditating, or doing yoga. But she may have attended PTA meetings and probably belonged to various women's social groups. She was a good wife who crafted her wifely and motherly sensibility according to the suburban norms of her day. June's sacrifice of labor, time, and emotional support for her boys was a component of her selfhood and not an act of sheer self-denial. It was how she as a suburban mom fulfilled and defined herself, much as suburban soccer moms do today, spending countless hours driving their kids to and from practices and games in their SUVs, planning their complex and overscheduled lives armed with cellular phones.

I am noticing here that the Internet makes possible a virtual self, an electronically-mediated and -facilitated selfhood, that represents work on the self fundamentally new in capitalism, even as people like Ward and June Cleaver worked on themselves, and on their children's selves, at the end of the late 1950s and early 1960s. Capitalism, as I have been saying, made selfhood an issue because people must be encouraged to consume far beyond their daily bread; they must also be distracted from the big picture. People only developed needs, or more accurately, wants, once capitalist industrialization had proceeded far enough that sheer survival was no longer at issue. The instant that survival was not an issue for many, capitalism had to invent the self, which would extend non-discretionary needs, necessary for survival, into discretionary wants. This did not happen overnight but emerged gradually as the human sciences, philosophy, and public culture invented selfhood, much as the English Victorians invented domesticity, romantic love, and the very notion of the precious child. These inventions, of the self and the beloved child, were historically and socially linked, reflecting the ways in which the newfound self was sited in public institutions such as the marketplace and mall and in private spheres such as family and gender. You can do research on the Victorian era, when a sharp distinction between femininity and masculinity was established in order to persuade women to leave factory jobs and spend time in the household, tending to their husband's and children's needs.

We learn gender, among other things, from television. This is what cultural studies demonstrates to us. The project of cultural studies came about during and after the sixties, as scholars began to realize that the many hours people were spending in front of televisions had impact on them and on their children. We learn gender by watching actors whom we idealize and imitate. June was a feminine woman, a model for other women and girls. Of course, there are other cultural models of femininity since then. "Norma Rae" in the movie with the same name was strong and feminist. Today, we are returning to the heavily gendered sitcoms of the sixties that depict women and men as being from different planets, except today many women, who are otherwise depicted as feminine and subordinate to their husbands at home, also work. Culture is complex and sends confusing and sometimes contradictory messages about gender and other aspects of the self. This makes it all the more difficult for kids to grow up sane. Let me take an example from my daughter's sixth-grade cohort of friends and classmates. Unlike in June's era, and even in my era, girls are encouraged to play sports. My daughter's friends have joined soccer, softball, and volleyball teams. Some do gymnastics. And some do cheerleading, which is the second "state" sport of Texas, after football! My daughter's friends are taught to be athletic *and* to be feminine. To accomplish this, they wear makeup and painted fingernails to athletic events in which they participate. They combine what they learn from gendered sitcoms and movies with what they learn by watching Mia Hamm play Olympic soccer.

Make a list of your favorite shows, movies, and bands. My daughter likes Avril Lavigne, an unaffected teenager from Canada who isn't glamorous or particularly feminine. Discuss how women and men act on screen and on stage. Are they playing traditional feminine and masculine roles? Do the women have jobs? Do they do all the housework? Are their husbands sensitive to their needs? Think about what you like about the women depicted in these cultural vehicles. Are these women different from June Cleaver? Are they different from your mom? Your mom is probably younger than June. Talk to her about her views of gender, and particularly about how women should act.

Today, with boys grown and grandchildren, June Cleaver would spend her day working out, taking cooking classes, volunteering for the League of Women Voters and Meals on Wheels, and helping Ward run his retirement home office. June would be adept at planning vacations using the Internet. She would still focus on her boys, but she would be less self-denying. Indeed, her newfound focus on herself – her body, needs, spirituality, friendship networks – could be redefined to encompass her boys, flesh of her flesh. Many American women use the Internet in order to get out of the house, or better, out of themselves, planning their busy lives and fulfilling their social needs, albeit virtually. Working women do much of this in the office. I don't think I know any working women in the academic world, from secretaries to faculty, who fail to use the Internet daily in order to fill themselves with the surrounding world, interacting with it adeptly and thus positioning themselves in it. Indeed, if Gilligan (1982) is correct that women and men conceptualize and deal with the world differently, given basic differences that she identifies in their cognitive and emotional sensibilities, it is not surprising that women are adept at using the Internet, with its inherent multidimensionality and visual depth and complexity, whereas they may be less adept at linear "male" tasks. Of course, men, too, surf, and for many of the same reasons as women: sociality and community, entertainment, news groups, shopping, sports, sex. I am simply noting here that as June Cleaver moves from the Fordist America of her original situation comedy to the networked global world of the present, she acquires computer skills that allow her to enrich and improve herself.

Cyberselves could be said to objectify themselves in their surfing, leaving tracks that reflect themselves and, in so doing, altering their identity. Television, radio, and movies also fill the self with content: The critical theorists were convinced that cultural commodities needed to be analyzed in terms of their circuits of production, distribution, and consumption. It is not enough only to criticize the ideology of situation comedies; these shows must be situated in the Hollywood entertainment industry, which itself must be situated within corporate-capitalist advertising. The critical theorists' point is that culture has become a commodity, like any other, that can be analyzed both in terms of profit and the corresponding exploitation of labor power, and in terms of its ideological contribution to public discourse and people's formation of selves. Of paramount interest is the connection between the public and private, in particular the economy and selfhood, which they insisted must be kept in mind by a critical theory that seeks to explain how capitalism has outlived Marx's expectation of its demise. It has done so in large measure because people have made the wrong political and personal choices, opting to reproduce the marketplace of capitalism, gender roles that favor men, racial domination of non-white by white, and the domination of nature instead of refusing to work so hard, to mistreat women and people of color, and to despoil the environment.

At issue, in so many words, is lifestyle, Weber's wonderful term for the lives we lead, and the selves we are. People's lives, which seem freely chosen at a stage in history where the most advanced nations have solid infrastructures of civil liberties, are in fact imposed by culture, which convinces people to drink too much, eat animal fat, vote Republican, teach their children sharply distinguished gender roles, overspend on frivolities, and stress themselves out by working too hard. The self, for those above the poverty line, lives what Adorno called a damaged life, a life conducted according to the wrong priorities – indulgence, excess, amnesia, conformity. This life hurts oneself and harms others, who share the same neighborhood, region, nation, planet. The damaged person is overly self-regarding, "self" having become an obsession for people steeped in post-Freudian psychology who have been taught to look out for number one, to make "self" thematic, to be in touch with themselves, even to take the road less traveled.

Self-care and finding Mr (or Ms) Right are two preoccupations of people, primarily women, in the Internet age. The Internet did not create, but it certainly accelerated, work on the self. The self becomes a cyberself when it is assembled – self-assembled – via the Internet and with other electronic means such as cell phones and chat lines. Identity is acquired through these electronic prostheses, which allow, indeed require, one to fabricate, alter, experiment with one's self-presentation to others. In addition, one engages in "self work" as one scans the Internet for content with which to fill oneself. This can involve chatting and newsgroups, although it can also involve simply surfing various Web pages, reading them as one would read a pulp publication. I notice that a great deal of this self work, toward the end of self-assemblage, involves what one might loosely call self-improvement – gathering information about weight loss and body maintenance, sports, hobbies, lifelong learning. Other self work involves looking for romantic partners, which often leads to chatting and e-mails.

Doing Gender Online

Women go online to build a life, and thus a self. Inasmuch as women have shouldered responsibility for domesticity – the reproduction of selves, in both biological and cultural terms, through the social institution of the family – it is no surprise that they continue to bear this responsibility. That more than 75 percent of US women under the age of 55 work outside the home for wages has not relieved them of housework and emotional labor. Research on housework (e.g., Hochschild 1989; Shelton 1992) shows that in an era when the majority of American women do "two shifts," as Hochschild terms it, both in paid labor and domestic labor, the only discernible change in the gendered division of labor since June Cleaver's era is that women do less housework and childcare than they did when they didn't work outside the home, but that men don't do more. The book *American Couples*, by Blumstein and Schwartz (1983) documents this nicely, just as it explores the ways in which American couples, both straight and gay, negotiate these tense political realities within the privacy of their own bedrooms and kitchens. As this book demonstrates, there is nothing really "private" about such matters inasmuch as questions of who does the dishes and changes the diapers are intimately bound up with larger economic and political issues of earnings, schedules, and what some feminists call the political legacy of male supremacy.

If French feminists such as Irigaray (1985) and Kristeva (1980), following the psychoanalyst Jacques Lacan (1977), are correct that women and men reason differently – an argument also made by Carol Gilligan in her work on feminist psychology – it is no surprise that women have taken to the Internet. The Internet is flexible, polyvocal, visually-oriented, talkative, at once synchronous and asynchronous, available from home and office (and even via cell phones), inexpensive. These features make it perfect for women who do three shifts – housework, emotional work, paid work – and who are perhaps not as "linear" as men, who are less likely to use the Internet playfully. I do not agree with French feminists and other radical feminists who essentialize women's cognitive and emotional differences from men. What differences there are can better be explained by different socialization given boys and girls and by structural inequalities in power and wealth. Women learn their difference from men as a mark of their subordination, which ought not to be viewed as eternal, either by male patriarchs or by feminist theorists. But leaving that issue aside, it is notable that women who surf compose nothing less than themselves, while men who surf conduct their business, including work-related electronic activities, entertainment, and pornography. The Slovenian theorist, Slavoj Zizek, has also built on Lacan in his rich studies of selfhood and culture, for example in his 1989 book *The Sublime Object of Ideology*.

Self-care ranges from Web pages on childrearing, children's learning disabilities, home and auto repairs, medical advice and self-treatment, and networking. Chatting and e-mail are forms of self-care, too, in that women are more likely than men to experience isolation, especially if they office at home. The care of the self – a title of one of Foucault's books – is facilitated by the Internet, which creates an electronic symbiosis between self and world, recreating what Freud called the oceanic feeling, referring to the way in which infants, before "individuation," feel that they engulf the world, from which they are indistinct. The oceanic feeling washes over the adult self who surfs, bringing the world closer and indeed inserting the person directly in the world. After all, the Internet spans oceans, continents, hemispheres, making it truly oceanic, a veritable state of mind into which the self slips as soon as her fingers begin caressing the computer keyboard.

Of particular interest here is women's search for relationships. Although Internet behavior is clearly gendered, with women and men adopting different tones in e-mails, surfing in different places, and doing self-care somewhat differently, both men and women use the Internet for romantic reasons. They search for partners, for stimulation, for variety, for chat, for a taste of dating and mating culture to which they may be unaccustomed. Romantic and erotic use of the Internet is rapidly growing, with a proliferation of pages devoted to love and sex – "lifestyle," as they are often tellingly named. Dating and relationships pages, such as www.Match.com, do brisk business, for a monthly fee. They offer straight, gay, and "alternative" matching services, catering to every taste. Even this is gendered, though, with men disproportionately consuming pornography and women mainly looking for dates and electronic connections. Students of pornography well understand that pornography is a male-dominated industry catering mainly to men, and so it is not surprising that men would use the Internet for this purpose, especially since they are afforded both privacy and access. It is also unsurprising, given the gendered division of labor established by Victorianism, that women would use the Internet less for erotic stimulation and more for making emotional connections, which has become the preserve of women, who are assigned responsibility for maintaining the family – a haven in a heartless world.

For women, thus, the Internet is an affair of the heart, whereas men deploy the Internet to satisfy their libidos. That begs the question of whether the Internet successfully delivers the goods, to either women or men. This issue is at the center of any discussion of selfhood today for we are, in effect, asking whether the two-dimensional cyber-world, spanning oceans quickly and accessible to those who own or have access to micro-computers, is as fundamental, and as fundamentally satisfying, as the three-dimensional world of face-to-face interaction, body-to-body encounters, travel, sports events held in real stadia (especially the funky retro ones, with irregular shapes and real grass). Are electronic "connections" as fully human as the real thing, achieved in three-dimensional space and in real time? To phrase the issue that way is analogous to the distinctions, here, between falling in love over the Internet or falling in love face-to-face, and between having an orgasm while masturbating while viewing an erotic Web page or having an orgasm entwined with another person.

The Internet is a prism through which we can assess the impact of cyberculture on politics, particularly feminist politics. A feminist take on the Internet is appropriate, as I have been saying, because the Internet is an attractive vehicle for women's self-care and their pursuit of emotional connection, which could include feminist consciousness-raising and or-ganizing. But are self-care and making connections a valid and viable feminist agenda? Information technologies such as the Internet and Web tend to be depoliticizing, individualizing politics beyond anything that even "self"-oriented leftists and certain feminists from Friedan (1963) to Brownmiller (1975) could accept. To be sure, the left and progressive social movements need to attend to the self, both because the self has become a political battleground (feminists' credo that the personal is political) and because ignoring the self almost automatically invites au-thoritarianism and determinism. But Internet-based interaction so person-alizes and privatizes politics that we risk losing a purchase in the public sphere, which liberals such as John Stuart Mill (1978) and neo-Marxists such as Habermas view as the foundation of transforming political projects.

This begs the question of whether the Internet can be a new ground of the political, creating an electronic public sphere, an issue to which I return in my next chapter. My provisional answer is that Internet-based politics, both consciousness-raising and networking, can begin a valid political process, which is conducted within the more traditional coordin-ates of the public sphere, but that e-politics cannot substitute for more public and permanent political projects, which, if successful, emerge in full-blown social movements and institution building. These social move-ments must never sacrifice selves to larger goals, whether in the name of a nation, a personality cult, or abstractions such as Democracy, Freedom, or the State, requiring attention to the politics of the personal, the family, body, sexuality, marginal groups, children, animals and nature.

Is Post-Feminism Progress?

Since Betty Friedan published *The Feminist Mystique* in 1963 feminism has been a political agenda. It has sought to shift power from men to women, sharing it equally. Male power has been characterized as **patriarchy** – rule by men. Feminists astutely understood that the feminist political agenda required a rethinking of power, which has been anchored in a long male-dominated tradition of political theory beginning with Plato. In this tradition, power and politics have been conceptualized as occurring in the public sphere, within public institutions such as parliament, Congress, the economic marketplace, corporate boardrooms, military campaigns. Feminists accept that politics and power are sited in public institutions such as the polity and economy, and now the military and the media. But, beginning with Friedan, they notice that male political theorists have missed an important dimension of politics and power by ignoring the politics of sexuality, intimacy, family, household, housework, childcare, emotions. Writing at the time that the Cleavers were living a fantasy life across Americans' television screens, Friedan notes that many middle-class American women, such as June Cleaver, were desperately unhappy, bored, and miserable with their lot as homemakers denied a role in male-dominated public institutions.

Thus, feminists reconceived power and politics to involve a politics of the personal, opening up dialogue about what I am calling the politics of subjectivity. Much like various western Marxists from Germany, Hungary, and France, feminists insisted that critical theories must not ignore what happens behind closed bedroom and kitchen doors or on the screens of power, but pay ample attention to the interior lives of citizens. They also insisted that this attention to selves would prevent radical movements from congealing into the edifice of Soviet-style authoritarianism, becoming a dictatorship over the proletariat. The Soviet experience has been instructive for the left, which has struggled with the legacy of Soviet "statist" socialism. Post-Kruschev revelations of the enormous extent of Stalinist terror disabused democratic and humanist leftists of a 1930s optimism that the Soviet Union, with its Politburo, KGB, and collective farms, represented the apex of civilization. Instead, the debunking of Soviet Marxism has been an essential catharsis for the western left, including feminists, who in their own context of liberal, albeit capitalist, democracies wanted to blend democracy with socialism in ways unanticipated by Marx. Feminists insisted that democracy begin at home, as men share housework and childcare so that women could pursue careers and so that children are exposed to mommies and daddies who, in their own choices and activities, live outside the Victorian-era sexual division of labor, which assigns women to domesticity and femininity, and men to public life and masculinity.

In 1975, Russell Jacoby published his path-breaking book *Social Amnesia: A Critique of Conformist Psychology from Adler to Laing.* Jacoby was a student of Marcuse's at Brandeis, and he works within the framework of critical theory. In a chapter in *Social Amnesia* entitled "The Politics of Subjectivity," Jacoby criticizes the growing obsession with the self in left-wing theory. Feminism is one of his targets. Jacoby contends that the pendulum has swung too far from Marxist economic determinism, which ignored selves in favor of structural analysis. Now, according to Jacoby, there is a cult of the self that replaces social analysis and criticism with a self-oriented focus on everyday life. This is no politics at all, Jacoby argues, leading to what I am calling self-care and self-improvement. Following Adorno, Jacoby suggests that we view the person as dominated by impera-tives to conform and consume that require us to look deeply at the self in its evident plasticity as a political entity. This has been the point of departure for Frankfurt scholars such as Marcuse, who used a Marxist reading of Freud's psychoanalysis in order to explore the whole topic of human needs.

This notion of the relevance of the self for politics and society leads to new insights into domination. But the notion that selves are enlisted to shop for things they don't need and thus refrain from political activity also suggests, as Marcuse recognized, that the self has become a battleground. This is similar to feminists' insight that the personal is political, given the invasion of sexism into the household, family, body, desire. And so the question for theory becomes one of priorities: How much do we concen-trate on traditional political and economic issues and how much do we concentrate on issues of the politics of self? This is essentially a question of balance. A related issue is whether we see the politics of the personal leading to large-scale social change or whether changing selves is suffi-cient as an end in itself.

Jacoby argues that the 1960s and 1970s politics of subjectivity was, in effect, liberalism – the political theory of John Stuart Mill. Liberals believe that people can change the world using rational arguments and represen-tative democracy. They believe that it is more effective to change people's minds through debate than to attempt to seize power through mass political and social movements. They prefer the New Hampshire primary to the Bolshevik Revolution. Liberals and Marxists fundamentally agree on the importance of political liberty, but they disagree on the means to achieve it. Liberals in general oppose revolutions, with the twin exceptions of the American and French Revolutions.

Indeed, there is a species of feminist theory, appropriately called liberal feminism, that would earn Jacoby's disapproval. Liberal feminists believe that political progress proceeds in small steps, and is achieved through rational persuasion and legal changes that ensure women's civil liberties and prohibit overt discrimination. Liberal feminists also want to change the culture in which boys and girl learn rigid definitions of masculinity and femininity, a key concern of all feminists. Clearly, all feminists support rational argument, legal change, cultural change but they place different emphases on where, and how, change should start. Socialist feminists agree with Marxists that women, like men, are oppressed by large-scale social structures such as capitalism and patriarchy. Indeed, some of the most creative theoretical and empirical work has been done within the framework of socialist feminism, elucidating the complex historical and institutional interlocks between patriarchy and capitalism, which are seen to be mutually reinforcing, if non-identical.

The problem leftist feminists have with liberal feminism is that it under-estimates the obstacles to rational argument and legal change, failing to grasp the immense power of the patriarchy, especially within capitalism. Rule by men – and by capital – is not likely to be relinquished without a fight, making husband-by-husband conversion, although desirable, a very unlikely path to overall social-structural change of the kind desired by all feminists. Yet in making a case against liberalism, which is essen-tially the case I am making against Sherry Turkle's (1997) and Kenneth Gergen's (2000) optimism about the self-changing capacities of the Inter-net, one must avoid rejecting the politics of subjectivity, which are more than ever necessary at a time when the self has been deployed politically. Everyday life matters now more than ever inasmuch as it is a gathering point for institutions, such as work, family, education, entertainment, which have become so intermingled that they are no longer identifiably distinct.

So we must tread lightly in appraising the feminist cyber-politics of subjectivity, which involves self-care and the search for intimacy instead of feminist consciousness-raising and political organizing. This is not a disjunctive alternative: Women can use the Web to prepare their income taxes and obtain medical help just as they participate in chat rooms devoted to ending violence against women. But the emphasis within American feminism has shifted over the last two decades, from a struc-tural materialism that coalesced under the banner "women's movement," to "girl power," which is Generation-X's take on the empowering of young women, particularly in the realms of body image and adornment, romance and popular culture. Inasmuch as the Internet is styled for women, acknowledging that women surf in search of identity and escape, it is easy to recognize this shift of feminist sensibility simply by browsing Web pages and advertising. There is virtually no reference to a political feminism, which is framed as old-fashioned, and many references to women as "girls" who assemble themselves (makeup, fashion, hair, body) and position themselves with reference to men.

Some call this post-feminism, reflecting the sentiment that the angry political feminism of the 1960s and 1970s has been surpassed by a more conciliatory and self-oriented feminism that bleeds into femininity, from which it is scarcely distinct. Feminist "girls" position themselves socially within the same old Victorian categories, which are now stylishly post-modernized, of attractiveness to men. The only difference between Victorian femininity and this blended feminism/femininity is that Victorian women stayed home. At one level, this is a very significant difference in that working affords power, both in relationships and in the larger socio-political environment. This is the argument of liberal feminists (or, perhaps, post-feminists) such as Naomi Wolff, who summarizes the feminist agenda, as she wants it to read, as "more for women." But leftists of a more structural bent contend that participating in capitalist wage labor or even the professions is not sufficient in itself to spell liberation, especially if one works for male bosses and in occupations that are gendered such as waitressing and secretarial work, reproducing the sexual division of labor in the family.

Post-feminism is liberal feminism dressed in designer clothes and shoes. It is feminism blurring with femininity – blonde highlights, red lipstick, tanning-salon tones. It is the feminism of *Ally McBeal*, not *Norma Rae*. It is relentlessly suburban and heterosexual, addressing soccer moms and not inner-city black women. Friedan anchored her feminism in the suburbs, where she identified boredom as a symptom of women's Victorian-era malaise – women who don't have careers. Now, suburban women, whether or not they have jobs and careers, whether or not they homeschool their children (an interesting blurring of family and education, premised on the antique notion that children are best lessoned by mom), use information technologies to organize and occasionally elevate their families and themselves. These electronic prostheses include cell phones, pagers, fax machines, microcomputers, answering machines, telephone land lines replete with caller ID and call-blocker, Palm Pilots. Post-feminists use these devices not to raise consciousness among the sisterhood – who has heard that term in a decade or more? – but to care for themselves and their loved ones, filling gaps of information, meaning, and romantic connection.

Post-feminism is defined both by its distance from the political, which characterized an earlier, angrier feminism, and by its appeasing attitude toward men, who are now viewed as valued partners. Post-feminists don't want to appear "bitchy" or "butch" but rather feminine. When I moved to Texas in the mid-1990s, I walked into a cleaners with a bundle of clothes. A woman probably in her thirties was talking to the proprietor, also a woman. She was complaining about having to bring in her boyfriend's shirts for laundering. After a few moments, she realized that I was standing there and probably listening. She said, apologetically, "I hope you don't think I'm bitchy." This isn't simply a generational phenomenon, with Gen-X'ers, born after 1967, monopolizing this perspective on gender relations. Many baby boomers are post-feminist, too, viewing themselves as post-political because they balance marriage, children, and career in a way that makes them mainstream, not marginal. In avoiding politics, post-feminists also avoid gay and lesbian constructions of sexuality, which are viewed as too extreme. Much as liberal feminism was for the most part heterosexual, so too is post-feminism, which makes thematic women's relationships with men, rejecting Rita Mae Brown's definition of a feminist as a "woman-identified" woman.

Although not particularly grounded in theoretical doctrine, post-feminism is decidedly apolitical. Post-feminists shun politics as old-school, replaced by the self and one's immediate community of children, husband, girlfriends, colleagues. Although, as I have been saying, the left, since feminism and critical theory, bridges personal/political and local/global – perhaps the most important legacy of the New Left and sixties – to be "left" requires politics to start at home and on the screen, both literally and figuratively, but not to end there. Although the personal is political in an advanced stage of capitalism now that selves are mobilized to consume and conform, politics, to be political, must be public, transforming communities, corporations, countries. Self-care, achieved through electronic connections and the instantaneity of the World Wide Web, does not count as political unless it inserts itself in a larger political discourse and the public sphere. That this discourse and public sphere are notably missing from today's landscape is a result of what Jacoby in the 1970s disparaged as a politics of subjectivity that starts and end with the self. Virtual selves must surpass virtual politics.

The discourse of post-feminism is interesting. "Women," the sixties through nineties term for people who used to be called girls or ladies, are now "girls" again, and sometimes "chicks," which is the derogatory and sexually-objectifying name given to women by non-feminist men. The feminist self has dissolved, replaced by a supposedly post-feminist self who takes for granted having a job but who "returns" to the pre-1960s femininity launched originally by the Victorians as a signifier of women's inferiority. It is now "okay," even "cool," to have a blonde flip (like women in the 1950s and early 1960s), colored nails, even plastic surgery. Women wear hip-hugging jeans that reveal their navels in the studied sexuality of adolescent girls. This is constructed by girlie discourse as an extension of feminism, instead of regression behind it. Men, who still run the patriarchy, are loving it; women are self-objectifying, girlifying themselves in their makeup, clothing, hair, and even their discourse – girl talk. Listen to the patois of women in their twenties and thirties and compare it to the rhetoric of the 1960s and 1970s sisterhood, who understood that the body, family, and discourse are battlegrounds. Post-feminist, post-1960s women re-compartmentalize the self, body, and household as off limits to feminist expectations and their political intrusions. "It's okay to be feminine" has replaced "the personal is political" as the rallying cry of this younger generation of women.

Two other aspects of women's discourse should be noted. Do women today change their last names when they get married? Do they identify themselves as feminists? Most of my college students say that they want to get married, which, for most of them, will involve taking their husband's last name. And most of them reject the label *feminist*, which they regard as political. They may hold feminist values, such as equal pay for equal work, but they shun the label. You will have to decide these issues for yourselves: Should you keep your last name if you get married, and do you view yourself as a feminist? How women position themselves using language has a lot to do with their eventual power positions in relationships.

I have talked about the feminist self, her discourse and her relationship to her body and family. Girl talk does not happen in a post-ideological vacuum; post-feminism as ideology follows from basic economic issues, involving women's pay and especially their labor-force participation. Women's salaries still lag behind men's. This income gap, although gradually narrowing, reflects overt and subtle sex discrimination in the workplace. For the several decades since the second wave of feminism was launched in the early 1960s, most notable was women's rapid entry into the workforce. That the majority of American women worked was more significant for feminist sociologists than that a minority of American women stayed home, or worked only part-time. Today, we need to pay more attention to the missing quarter of US women who are either too poor to afford childcare and thus can't work, or so wealthy that they don't have to work, or so post-feminist that they don't want to work. Their identities are affected by not working, and they are more susceptible to post-feminist rhetoric that belittles them as girls or chicks. Most of the women on my wife's tennis team either don't work at all or work only a few hours a week. They are generally college-educated, and they are either middle or upper-middle class. They construct their gender identities as liberated; they play tennis when they want, they take vacations, they spend freely, they seem to have influence over how their children are raised. And, with the exception of my wife, they are economically dependent on husbands in exactly the way that most of their mothers were, during and before the 1950s. Their girl talk is more sophisticated and cosmopolitan than their moms', but they have the same economic status as housewives. This is not to deny that all of them are primarily responsible for housework and childcare, a fact that doesn't distinguish post-feminists, from feminists, from pre-feminists. But inasmuch as their husbands work full-time, they are even more responsible for taking kids to school and lessons, for meal preparation and for household maintenance than are women who work and have husbands who work.

Post-feminism indicates that the feminist revolution is over. Indeed, it may never have happened in the sense that it had lasting impact on the way women view themselves, talk about gender, and relate to their bodies, households, husbands. To be sure, women now go to college and many, if not all, embark on careers. But these are for the most part secondary careers, subordinate to their husbands', and their income is viewed as supplementing the salaries of the primary breadwinners, who, as in the Victorian age, bring home all or some of the family wage. If feminism is at least partly about identity and culture – how women portray themselves to themselves – I contend that women have experienced regression, especially under the influence of visual, media, and Internet cultures. There is a seductive tendency to impose a linear logic on the women's movement, just as the Enlightenment philosophers and social theorists told a story about history emphasizing the inevitability of progress. Feminist historians of feminism, no less than progressive male social theorists, transform the period between the early 1960s and the present as one of progress, albeit with occasional "backlash" (Faludi 1991). This is a comfort to those who endured the Reagan and Thatcher years and now endure the era of the junior Bush. Although the country, probably beginning with Carter's presidency during the mid-1970s, has shifted to the right (so much so that Clinton and Gore supported the death penalty and then Gephardt, a Democratic congressman running for President in 2004, supported initiating the war in Iraq), many feminists still tell a seamless narrative about feminist progress.

I question this narrative in light of developments within women's culture and identity, especially post-feminism. Many younger women – my students – now embrace a sharper differentiation between the genders than did their sixties sisters and mothers, inserting themselves in a self-objectifying, self-trivializing culture of femininity. Feminism is defeated by femininity if the latter means women's subordinate status to men, including their objectification as love and lust objects. A media, advertising, and Internet culture both reflects and promotes this as women view themselves through the lenses of cultural representation – tight jeans, makeup, high-maintenance hair, dating scenes, images of traditional work and family, self-indulgent recreation and leisure. These frames are colonizing; they invade our minds and position our bodies. And, because of information technologies that convert reading into authorial opportunities, colonization occurs in two directions, as incoming and outgoing messages and representations. Marx understood that oppressed people tend to reproduce their own oppression by giving in, giving up, going along. They do this because they can imagine no different, better lives for themselves. This is true for women today, especially younger ones, who do not remember the feminist struggles of their mothers and sisters for a non-sexist culture.

Enter feminist cultural studies (see Walters 1992, 1994; Agger 1991, 1993). Influenced by European theories of interpretation and criticism such as postmodernism and critical theory, feminist scholars during and after the 1970s began to articulate a feminist cultural criticism that addresses women's unfortunate participation in their own oppression and men's production of oppressive images of women through discourses such as pornography. Feminist cultural studies was a branch of the larger project of cultural studies, an interdisciplinary theory and research program that focused attention on the politics of culture, television, film, fiction, advertising. Feminist theorists talked about "the male gaze," the lens through which male producers frame women as they produce movies, television, and advertising. These cultural representations of women lead to, and reinforce, their political and economic disempowering inasmuch as they influence both men and women to take women less seriously than men in the culture, polity, and economy. Images, like texts, are encoded with power dynamics. In reflecting lives full of girl talk and feminized bodies, culture reproduces those lives; they are ontologies, theories of being, of what is possible. The media-ted ontology of women is so powerful precisely because it is non-textual; the images of feminine women flirting with men, beautifying themselves, and engaging in girl talk wash over us. They are not phrased in theoretical terms, subject to rebuttal. The images of what is possible are exhausted by the depiction of the present – people like you and me living their lives oblivious to the possibility of something other, precisely the image provided by theory.

The cultural portrayal of women, their work and family roles, their clothing, hair, makeup, discourse, sexuality, and sexual orientation, is decidedly a political factor: This portrayal models appropriate womanhood for contemporary women, and for their children and future generations. June Cleaver has gone out to work, but Ward, her husband, still calls the shots and is generally absent in the lives of his boys, Beaver and Wally. June still has her blonde hair in a flip; she wears capri pants; she sounds girlish when she talks. Although she now brings income into the family, her production of gender is much the same as it was when the sit-com was originally broadcast.

Feminism flourished during the late twentieth century, but only for a short while. It has been replaced by what was always there, a sharp bifurcation, which has political overtones, of masculine and feminine. What appears to be simply biological differentiation slides into social categories of gender identity, a cultural estimation of what it takes to be a real man and woman. These social categories of gender are now transformed further into political categories, with the "stronger" **sex**, both biologically and socially, having more power and wealth. Post-feminists would argue that feminism did its job, getting women into the labor market and freeing their sexuality. These are substantial gains by comparison to women's lot a hundred years ago, after Victorianism but before suffrage. But male identity is still constructed, by women as well as men, as more powerful and worthy. Post-feminists, in their images of twenty-first-century liberation, borrow from men's roles, notably going to work and having sex. Although women want what men have in the way of income and sex, they don't want everything male, or I should say masculine. Women want to be feminine, to be "women," precisely because gender identities have remained intact, even though women now work alongside men and have sex with them. Gender is the strongest hold men have over women; differentiation between the sexes, captured in the concept of gender identity (masculine and feminine), conceals stratification, with one sex/gender elevated over the other.

Let me give only one example of this. I am convinced that in many organizations feminist women are treated differently than feminine women. Women are hired and promoted only if they are "real women," made up, coy, cooing – girls, not women. Stronger, less overtly feminine women are dismissed as butch or bitches. The hiring of feminine women is constructed by men as "affirmative action," when in fact it is anything but. The issue is not sex, but gender – how appropriate women view themselves and dress, act, and talk accordingly. Women are promoted into the boardroom, or as academic deans, only if their femininity positions them as subordinate in their personal and family lives; when they go home at night, they are girly girls whose femininity transcends their occupational roles alongside men.

How are un-feminine women viewed and treated? They are often labeled "lesbians" or "dykes" because they don't accept the traditional definition of femininity. This is because we tie gender to sexual orientation: Women who act "like men" (assertive, strong-willed, competitive) are viewed as lesbians, and men who act "like women" (gentle, empathetic) are viewed as gay. Of course, crueler terms are often used. A colleague, when she began her teaching career, didn't shave her legs. Regularly, she would receive teaching evaluations that questioned her sexual orientation (she is straight). At least 10 percent of Americans are gay or lesbian. Current research demonstrates that sexual orientation is for the most part not a choice, but rooted in our makeups when we are born. How do you feel about homosexuals? Do your friends tell homophobic jokes? Are you gay, but in the closet? Is it necessarily true that women who don't "act feminine" are lesbians? If not, why don't they act feminine? Does this have something to do with power? Ultimately, who decided what it means to be a real woman or real man – girly or rugged?

Femininity trumps feminism as the twentieth century ends and a new century begins. On a recent episode of a "reality" television show, in which young, attractive women compete for the hand of a hunk who supposedly has $50,000,000 (but really doesn't, revealing them to be gold diggers), a woman physician says that she isn't necessarily playing the game for the money, but then adds "Of course we wouldn't mind having that much money; we're women." Women, to construct and maintain their gender, try to live up to dim-witted, acquiescent, money-hungry, sexual standards imposed on them by men, who control the culture. Women who don't wear makeup or shave their legs, who spike their hair and otherwise shun the accouterments of femininity, are rejected by other women as dykes, women who, by definition, are failures. Femininity and masculinity, as a bipolar structure of expectations, are deeply homophobic, positioning people in a mainstream heterosexuality. In my daughter's sixth-grade class, the worst thing a kid can be is a "faggot." And the word "gay" refers to anything bad: "That test was really gay."

If feminism had been successful, women wouldn't only work; they would have transcended gender, both theirs and men's. And we wouldn't link gender and sexual orientation. Women wouldn't have to avoid appearing bitchy, nor would men have to be stoic and sullen. Nancy Chodorow's *The Reproduction of Mothering* (1978) brilliantly sites men's hatred of women in family relations. Little boys, neglected by their fathers, are raised by their mothers, against whom they rebel in order to achieve what Freud called individuation, growing a self. She argues that gender, pitting the masculine against the feminine, could be overthrown if fathers would get more involved in parenting, and women in working. Although more women work than 30 years ago, parenting is still largely the woman's preserve, suggesting that Chodorow is correct. All of this raises the question, first insultingly posed by Freud, about just what it is that women want, or should want. Feminine feminists, post-feminists by another name, want the right to work, but they also want their gender. They want the trappings of femininity and for men to call the shots in the bedroom if not boardroom. They want to be girls, and to engage in girl talk. More radical feminists want not only political and economic equality; they want to undo their imprisoning by gender. They want new selves, new families, new men, new children, new curricula, new culture, all of which would allow women to be men and men to be women. But no one would be a girl.

This has been a rather unsparing portrait of post-feminism, which looks more like anti-feminism than an extension of sixties ideas about gender equality. What woman in her right mind would want to regress from womanhood to childhood? Wanting to be a girl is ambivalent: On the one hand, post-feminist women embrace men's fantasies about having sex with young girls, and even their daughters. How else can we explain women in their twenties and thirties dressing and talking like Drew Barrymore and Reese Witherspoon, appearing at once clueless and sexual? On the other hand, perhaps wanting to be a girl suggests funda-mental dissatisfaction with being women today, that is people who occupy subordinate statuses by comparison to men. Post-sixties women some-times chant "girl power" in the way that we used to shout "power to the people!" Maybe being a girl is protest against innocence lost. Perhaps it is purposeful regression to a primal past unsullied by workplace discrimin-ation, sexual harassment, unfair wages, doing too much housework, and having too little time. Seen this way, the notion that "chicks rock" might be heard to be secretly subversive.

A crucial component of girl talk and girl culture is the appropriation of sexuality by women who are unashamed to want sex. Of course, in our heterosexual culture, to get sex requires women to sexualize and girlify themselves. In the next chapter, I will discuss why our society seems to be sex-crazed, at least judging by how people use the Internet, and even acknowledging that women surf in order to connect whereas men surf in order to get off. I will discuss these notions of connection and gratification from the perspective of critical theory, especially Marcuse's work. Both women and men are saying something important when they appear preoccupied with sex, their bodies, makeup, connecting, getting off. They are saying that they aren't being sufficiently satisfied in the realms of work and love, especially where private life, far from a haven in a heartless world, is being invaded by the culture industry via the vectors of virtualization. People are using the Internet to get their needs met, even if they don't sufficiently understand that finding dates or orgasms isn't going to cure what ails them – a fast capitalism in which people are deprived of meaning.

In my concluding chapter, I will step back and ask, again, whether we are in a stage of history that can legitimately be called postmodern in the sense that it breaks from modernity. I will return to the question of selves, exploring Garfinkel's views of sociology done in the natural attitude, in the midst of everyday life. I will sketch a new sociology relevant to today, situated in everyday life, and a new conception of selves who are, above all, sociological writers. The Internet makes possible unprecedented opportunities for learning, for reading, for writing, for culture creation. The social technology that invades the private interior of selves, commanding them to consume and conform, also potentially liberates people to engage in what Garfinkel called practical reason, taking control of knowledge and culture and ultimately of themselves by opening a global literary horizon heretofore off limits to everyone except the few who sign corporate publishing contracts and write Hollywood television and movie scripts. In this sense, a sociology of virtual selves necessarily takes us into the intellectual and political territory of a new interdisciplinary movement called cultural studies.

CHAPTER SIX

Virtually, a Sociology!

Selves can use the Internet to liberate themselves from the culture industries, doing creative sociology and other types of writing that create a democratic public sphere. This suggests a view of sociology as a literary strategy, a writing style, call it science fiction. Sociology retains its concern with social structure, but grounds social structure in discourse. A virtual sociology studies virtuality, while conducting its analyses and writing online, as well as in traditional pulp formats.

We leave the Cleavers behind, even if they still live among us, even if we are them! Although myths of a golden age risk romanticizing the past, there was a certain tranquility to the "original" Cleaver household. It was generally quiet and orderly. All family members were depicted as readers, if not deep thinkers. There was little mention of television, which hadn't yet attained the ironic distance from itself that we find when we watch an episode of *The Simpsons* on the Fox Network and notice that the characters lampoon Fox as a network full of trashy offerings. This is balanced against the fact that June didn't have a job, and thus a thin thread of autonomy. She was even more under Ward's thumb than are women today, who enjoy a minimum of economic independence. We can conclude that the past – the 1950s and early 1960s – was both better and worse than the present, better in that family was insulated against virtuality and the other extensions of the culture industry, worse in that women were economic appendages of men. In any case, we can't turn back the clock, except to watch the Cleavers in reruns.

From Pulp to Pixel

So far, I have examined both the self and sociology, especially how sociologists conceive of the self, which, by most accounts, should be the centerpiece of the discipline. Of special interest to me is how sociology and its conception of the self changes when we enter into a stage of modernity in which information technologies mediate our communication, entertainment, imagination. The virtual self composes himself in daily e-mail, Web surfing, chatting, cell phoning, faxing. It is a postmodern self less stable and centered than the self of previous modernities, when there was a clear boundary or barrier between oneself and the world.

Yet, at the same time, the Internet opens up a new world of self-creation, storytelling, global communities, interactive instantaneity, and possibly even political organizing quite unknown in a slower-paced stage of modernity. The Internet also requires a new sociology, a virtual one, that uses electronic media and composes itself differently, more publicly. A pulp capitalism has given way to a postmodern capitalism in which connection and self-creation are as close to hand as the home computer, laptop, or cell phone. At issue in this final chapter is whether the human benefits of information technologies outweigh the ample costs of institutional de-differentiation and the possible demise of the self. I will argue that we are now at a stage of society and culture – call it postmodernity, but without embracing all of what that slogan often implies in the way of a transcendence of politics, class, conflict, the local – in which the self can flourish only if it becomes a sociological self, using the efficiencies and social opportunities afforded by the Internet to theorize, to think conceptually about the world and then to write essays, stories, and even fiction that mobilize others to rethink their lives.

As I indicated earlier, Marx felt that he could right wrongs by writing, piercing ideologies of religion and bourgeois economics that keep workers in their place. He didn't worry about the tendency of texts in fast capitalism to lose their distance from the world, as weighty tomes that must be read slowly and considered carefully. Think of the Bible, a Charles Dickens' novel, a Shakespeare play. These, and others, are the great works of our civilization, imparting important lessons and affording sharp insights about the human condition. But they are not easy reads in the sense of *People* magazine or a Tom Clancy novel. Their movie treatments took centuries to appear, and they do not substitute for the real thing. Marx's own writings insert themselves into this tradition of public books, books written for "everyone," that do not require a college degree to read, but which are not light and frothy and exact a considerable toll from the reader. Marx inhabited a world in which public books were being written, and in which there were careful readers who wanted to understand society, culture, and humanity better. Although there was less literacy and fewer college degree holders, there were more curious readers of learned books, people who couldn't turn on television or fire up their computers in order to check e-mail and chat.

A pulp capitalism, in which these books abounded even as late as the 1930s, 1940s and 1950s – think of the writings of Lewis Mumford, Mary McCarthy, Susan Sontag and the sociologist C. Wright Mills – did not end overnight, with bookstores suddenly shutting down. With radio, television, popular magazines, tabloid newspapers, and now cell phones and the Internet, people gradually came to read less, and to buy or borrow fewer difficult books of analysis and theory. Their time is filled with other activities, even as their leisure expands: shopping, carpooling, commuting, working out, self-beautification, travel, surfing. Although one can read in the carpool line, on the Stairmaster, and in the beauty salon, this is a different kind of reading than Marx and Dickens had in mind. (They were contemporaries; Dickens published *A Christmas Carol* in the year that Marx wrote his important early manuscripts on freedom and alienation.) When one is sitting in line or working out, the literary fare is likelier to be a gossip or sports magazine than a hardback book, especially one without pictures or a plot line.

The Frankfurt School began to theorize the tendencies of discourse to decline in the 1940s, during their American exodus from fascism. Horkheimer, Adorno and Marcuse conducted media studies of radio, television, journalism, and movies that helped them understand what they termed "the dialectic of enlightenment." They were referring to the ironic narrowing of reason, which was installed as an antidote to religious dogma and myth. In one of their sentences from *Dialectic of Enlightenment*, Horkheimer and Adorno say that "[E]nlightenment behaves toward things as a dictator toward men." Once we assume that scientific methodology can solve all intellectual problems, science becomes mythology, aware of everything but itself and its own blind spots and biases. This results in authoritarianism, especially where science is harnessed to industrial-age technology and nature is conceptualized as a sheer utility for the human species. The way we treat nature, and animals, is often the way we treat other people.

After watching the Nazi Adolf Eichmann's trial in Jerusalem for organizing and implementing the mass killing of Jews, Hannah Arendt argued that evil has become banal, ordinary. Organization men, as Whyte (1956) called them sociologically, merely carry out orders, losing sight of right and wrong. The Nuremberg defense, mounted by the Nazi war criminals in response to the charge they committed crimes against humanity, is pathetic in its prosaic, everyday quality: I was only following orders. The Nazi high command was saying that it failed to possess a moral compass and the will to resist required to judge the morality or immorality of the death camps. It is one thing to kill an intimate in the heat of the moment; one temporarily loses one's mind. It is quite another thing to plan and carry out the extermination of a whole race of people – millions and millions of people, who must be rounded up and transported to a cost-effective death by poison and then either burned or buried in mass graves.

Although Americans understandably cringe when they remember September 11 – a date so shattering and vivid in memory that it needs no year attached – and the 3,000 or more lives lost on that day, and even including tens of thousands of additional lives lost in Afghanistan and Iraq as a result of the bombing of the World Trade Center towers, none of this compares to the Holocaust, when millions of lives were expended by the Nazis. The Nazis did not use terror, exactly, if that means the unpredictable irruption of death and destruction in order to destabilize civic order. The Nazi death count was predictable, given their rational science and technology of administrative killing; the camps were in effect factories that "produced" bodies, toward the extermination of a whole race of people – the aptly named final solution. The means and technology of killing were preserved and streamlined by the victorious allied nations after World War II, as capitalism was further rationalized. Thus, the critical theorists contended, a liberal capitalism which defeated fascism integrated aspects of fascism, producing a total system from which there is no escape.

Foucault has addressed many of the same phenomena in his studies of crime, punishment, sexuality. He argued in *Discipline and Punish* that former barbaric forms of punishment such as beheading gradually gave way, after the Enlightenment, to more "humane" means of correction such as prisons. But these seemingly more humane reforms are actually more totalitarian than are public beheadings and torture in that they involve inmates internalizing control and self-control as if they are being watched by an anonymous, distant but retributive authority, such as George Orwell's Big Brother. The disciplining of people is now more total in that we are continually bombarded by cultural and political stimuli flowing not only into our homes but into our heads, inducing us to buy things we don't need, to hate enemies, and to avoid committing the revolutionary deed, especially inasmuch as that requires talking to other people.

There has been massive depoliticization, the destruction of a public sphere of discourse and debate. Marx could assume that his and Engels' polemics would be read by thousands and vigorously discussed. Formerly, texts started arguments and enriched political life. Today, books have been eclipsed by a subliminal cultural discourse of everyday life, surrounding us and leaving us no room, or time, to consider carefully the claims made by advertising, music, television, movies, newspapers. And, in spite of their appearance, this enveloping cultural discourse *argues*; it is, like positivist science and social science, secret writing, concealing its authorship so that it appears to be a natural feature of our everyday environment and not an ideological text that defends and seeks to reproduce the status quo. We are not challenged by disturbing, difficult, distancing writing, texts that make strong points, and challenge conventional wisdom, precisely in order to shake our complacency. This is the argument made by Marcuse as he discusses the collapsing of critical thought into a "one-dimensional thought" which rests on the surface of things, not digging underneath them for either hidden causes or possible evolutions.

A crucial aspect of one-dimensional thought, a positivist fact-fetishism that learns to love the status quo, however meaningless or exploitative, is the suppression of selves' literary abilities and inclinations. People no longer read the difficult, distanced treatises of earlier modernist social theory; nor do they write such books, especially if they aren't tenured professors who can afford to compose works read by a few hundred, not a few hundred thousand. No academic book issued by Cornell University Press, let alone Simon & Schuster, will change the world, given the decline of discourse, which is a crucial discursive dimension of one-dimensional thought. French postmodern theorists such as Derrida and Foucault, both of whom have influenced British and American cultural studies and media studies, have paid more attention to textual and discursive issues than have German critical theorists, although this is somewhat surprising given the critical theorists' own discussion of the culture industry as an important new phase of a late capitalism. The shift from pulp to pixels has reflected and reproduced the decline of discourse, of writers willing to write big books on important public topics and readers capable of reading them, especially where such readings require a certain level of sustained attention and bracketing of conventional common sense.

I conclude this book, then, with reflections on the import for selves and sociologists of post-World War II, post-Ford, post-pulp technologies of information, education, entertainment. Cyber-capitalism, as I have been arguing, is not a qualitative break with an earlier industrial modernity, with factories and printing presses, but a continuation, yet in a direction which opens up new and unforeseen media of connection and self-creation – social change, by another name. At the same time, the Internet is a dialectical phenomenon in that it has both negative and positive features, a reality and an actuality, in Hegel's terms, which appear to be at odds with each other. As Marx discussed many times, technologies of production and information are inseparable from their social and economic contexts. Their potential for freedom or domination depends on the political and economic uses to which they are put. The Internet is typically used for conducting e-commerce, shopping and selling through what Tim Luke calls the vectors of virtualization. A few of us use the Web for scholarly research and the Internet for contacting colleagues in Bulgaria and the People's Republic of China.

Russell Jacoby in *The Last Intellectuals: American Culture in the Age of Academe* (1987) suggested that American authors have lost the ability, the outlets, and the audience to write the "big" book, the treatise or tome on important social topics that don't require readers with advanced degrees. These are not academic books, but they are scholarly, perhaps even sporting footnotes and a bibliography. According to Jacoby, the independent intellectual and freelancer have disappeared because urban bohemia has declined, independent bookstores have nearly disappeared, and publishing has become corporate and oriented to best-selling trade books, not niche works of social criticism. I have addressed this phenomenon of the decline of discourse as a distinctive feature of a postmodern capitalism in which images replace (or indeed become) the text and thus old-fashioned arguments, posed in the public books that Jacoby discusses, are buried in the bookless world of mainstream television, film, the Internet. As I said in *Fast Capitalism*, there is a lot of writing going on, but few real books being written.

This diagnosis rests on Habermas' (1989) analysis of the structural transformation of the public sphere, a central feature of his critical theory. He argues that the public sphere has been depoliticized as political and economic processes have been taken over by professional managers. At the same time, Habermas notes that the everyday lives of selves have been colonized by systemic imperatives to conform and consume, politicizing the seemingly apolitical realm of self, family, gender, culture. Jacoby, Habermas, and I lament the decline of the public sphere because we recognize that democracy requires active public debate, commentary, critique. Without the attempt to forge public consensus about important issues such as the war in Iraq, how to deal with a declining public educational system, overcrowded prisons that only reproduce a criminal class, politics will be left to professionals. But in today's postmodern capitalism, would we be better off deprofessionalizing politics and public life and turning them over to the people? Is the public elevated enough to make decisions for itself? Could people break away from "reality" television shows long enough to think the issues through? (I am shaking my head as I write this because I just viewed a few minutes of the latest reality television show, designed to find the "hottest" person in America!)

This issue sparked debate within the Frankfurt School. Walter Benjamin (1969), an early member of the Institute for Social Research, argued that the printing press and electronic media of transmission help democratize culture and art in an era of what he termed "mechanical reproduction." Adorno was less sanguine than Benjamin, and later Marcuse, about popular culture, which, from his mandarin vantage, he viewed as moronic and stupefied. Indeed, that was precisely the tenor of Horkheimer and Adorno's analysis of the culture industry in *Dialectic of Enlightenment.*

The critical theorists' dilemma is similar to Marx's own dilemma years before: How are people who suffer from "false consciousness," making their peace with their own alienation and shunning radical politics, to cross the threshold into the public sphere and seize political and economic power? Are they educated enough? Are they distant enough from the fray to make good judgments? Are they ready to risk everything? The Frankfurt School is often accused of pessimism born of their cultural elitism; they disdained ordinary people and their kitsch popular culture. Marx resolved this dilemma in his discussion of "educating the educator." Marx called for political enlightening, for study groups, for consciousness raising, for self-criticism, risking a dogmatic orthodoxy in order to develop sufficient political consciousness in workers that they could forge the revolution from the shop floor. Cultural pessimists like Adorno despaired because they feared that political education – theory itself – was too easily co-opted, integrated, by the dominant order; again, Marcuse's term for this was one-dimensional thinking whereby even radical ideas are rendered banal as they are taken over by marketers and other ideologists. Marcuse (1978) and Adorno (1984) put stock in art's capacity for critical insight and utopian imagining, but Adorno had even less patience than Marcuse for popular forms of art and music because they are so easily integrated or simply ignored by the culture industry and their critical insights blunted. Marcuse suggests the image of Beethoven piped into

elevators as muzak, his moving images of reconciliation and transcendence betrayed as they are converted into "easy listening." Today, whole
radio stations, tuned in by office managers in dental practices, promote
easy listening because they don't want their clients to work hard to grasp
the meaning of the music, which is soothing background noise.

Norman Mailer (2003) in his recent autobiographical book about
writing and literary careers, *The Spooky Art*, discusses the "lit biz," that
segment of the culture industry devoted to mass-market fiction and non-
fiction trade books. Mailer recounts a conversation he had with Gore Vidal
about the decline of the "serious" novel, the big, sprawling book like
Mailer's early bestseller about war, *The Naked and the Dead*. Using the
esteemed German novelist Thomas Mann as his model, Mailer defends
serious fiction, but notices that publishing houses and their senior editors
are less willing to sign such books, which demand diligence from the
reader. Big books also take up valuable shelf space in bookstores; two
thin hardback volumes might cost $21.95 each, whereas the big book,
which takes up the same shelf space as both thin books, might retail for
$29.95, driving publishers to want easy reads. This is partly about the
difficulty of the prose, and partly about length and profit. (Mailer notices
that best-selling fiction proliferates adjectives, such as "the steaming hot
pizza," so that the text can do readers' work for them, short-circuiting
their imaginations.)

Jacoby and Mailer both acknowledge the difficulties of living an independent literary life. Instead, writers bail out and go commercial, writing
romance novels, television scripts, or academic journal articles that secure
their tenure. In all cases, their critical insights are blunted. This is what
I mean by decline of discourse. Yet this decline is not mainly about the loss
of literary nerve but a structural, institutional outcome of corporate
publishing, media, and entertainment, the professionalization of academic
discourse as well as trade editing, and the eclipse of the bookstore. Perhaps
most important, it is a result of what the Frankfurters termed *domination*,
the tendency of critical ideas to be swallowed whole by the culture
industry and turned into popular sausages, to be bought and sold and to
afford diversion. I blend critical theory and postmodern theory where I
notice that "domination" in a fast, twenty-first-century capitalism now
takes the form of textlessness, a blurring of the boundary between what
Derrida and his ilk call "the text" and the world – culture and society. The
boundary is blurred in such a way that bookstores now contain everything but books in Jacoby's and Mailer's old-fashioned sense of large
literary works that matter, Mailer's serious novel which requires the

reader's diligence and commands her sustained attention. Indeed, Barnes & Noble is stocked with pot boilers, star biographies, diet manuals, calendars, stuffed bears, magazines, espresso bars, greeting cards.

As serious novels and social criticism disappear from bookstores, writers capable of writing such books vanish. They no longer have role models, nor an audience. Mailer details the odds, which are growing longer, against young authors finding risk-taking editors willing to sponsor their first books. Craft is being replaced by professional networking, necessary in order to get one's foot in the publishing door. Even to have one's first book published isn't enough, especially where the publishing house might not invest enough in marketing to give the book an honest chance. As a result, young writers do their writing elsewhere, in other venues, unlike the John Updikes and Mary McCarthys who used to dominate the literary scene.

What of the literary self today? The Internet, like network television and corporate publishing, frustrates the serious writer who resists the fads and pace of highly-accelerated communication. Mailer describes how he rented a bare room in Brooklyn, without telephone or television, in which he could do his writing, undisturbed. Like Graham Greene, he had regular writing habits, recognizing that to be good, one needed to put in long and regular hours at the desk, allowing one's literary unconscious free play. The Internet, like television, is a diversion, and an insidious one, because it invades one's private space and private moments, whether at home or in the office. It might have enticed Mailer away from his craft by distracting him with news, sports, pornography, good deals. It would also have offered him literary opportunities such as chatting and e-mail. It is easy to imagine a garrulous sort like Mailer succumbing to chat rooms as a way to waste time better spent on his next novel!

On the other hand, the Internet is made for literary selves in that it eases their burden when they need to do research, it connects them to other authors and to readers, it enables them to correspond with publishers and editors, and, perhaps most important, it allows them to post their work in progress to various Web sites. I am not alone among critical theorists (Douglas Kellner leads the way here) in putting up work in progress and even book prospectuses for the whole world to read, and, we hope, to comment. The everyday self – the self who doesn't fashion herself a writer or author – bleeds into the literary self and perhaps the sociological self (depending on one's topics) when the Internet becomes a vehicle for busy literary work. Although images and figures abound in cyberspace, and Web pages can be short, pages often have many links (the **hypertext**) and, unlike pulp media, the Internet allows readers to become writers. You can send e-mail to a posted/published author; you can enter a chat room about a literary or political topic; you can post your own Web page, which, like Kellner's, can contain chat, correspondence and even music (see www.gseis.ucla.edu/faculty/kellner/kellner.html).

Jacques Derrida demonstrates that reading is a secret version of writing, disqualifying Locke's image of the mind as a blank slate (or of the pen as a transparent tool). The reader is neither a blank slate nor a vessel, to be imprinted or filled with the self-evident meaning of writing. Instead, the reader must intervene in texts, working them through, taking liberty with them, exercising poetic license. This is demonstrated irrefutably by the Internet, which allows readings to become writings of their own – glosses, commentaries, critiques, new versions. It is easy to find dozens of Web sites put up by independent amateurs, having no corporate or publishing ties, who explore and extend the work of a major intellectual figure. There are sites on Foucault and on Marx. These sites contain the reader/author's commentaries, sources for further exploration, the author's own e-mail address for readers of the "reader" to respond in writing. This is a serpentine, "meta"textuality, writings beyond, and about, the text that become part of it, available to be viewed as a literary totality when one launches a search engine such as Google to research a famous author. Thus, Google's Marx is Marx's texts and writings about those texts, which began as readings.

A word sometimes used in postmodern theory to describe this chorus of voices within, and beyond, each text is **intertextuality**. The Internet makes intertextuality possible, fundamentally erasing or at least easing the boundaries between text and other texts and between readers and writers. As I noted earlier, one of the features of postmodernity – although recognizing that the postmodern exists within modernity as one of its recent tendencies, but doesn't extend beyond it – is institutional de-differentiation. The work/family boundary fades, as does the boundary between entertainment and education. Politics and the economy intermingle, Eisenhower's "military-industrial complex." This happens largely because, as Habermas put it, the social system bends everyday life to its purposes. It does this by mobilizing minds, bodies, and discourse, removing them, as best it can, from the realm of private choice. Foucault calls this disciplining, whereas Adorno and Horkheimer called it administration. Marcuse in his marriage of Freud and Marx explains how capitalism turns the self into a prosthesis, an extension, of society, politics, economy, and culture. The self becomes fair game for ideologists, advertisers, pornographers, survey researchers as the self is beaten down and its inviolable individuality gradually removed. In this light, then, institutional de-differentiation – collapsing boundaries, especially that of self and world – is not to be celebrated but resisted.

Are boundaries good? Do they take us toward the promised land, or to Orwell's dystopia? Orwell foresaw a society without boundaries; the demarcation between self and government is erased precisely because people think that their thoughts are being monitored, even if they aren't, which is exactly the issue touched on in Foucault's discussion of Jeremy Bentham's perfect prison which merges regulation and self-regulation. Orwell wants to restore the boundary between thought and state, and he does so through his allegory of Big Brother. He wants his readers to realize that they are *not* having their thoughts read, their every move monitored, and thus to set themselves free, avoiding 1984. The Frankfurt School wanted to preserve and restore boundaries between self and society, family and state, because they felt that strong selves capable of thinking for themselves would only grow to healthy maturity in families that aren't invaded by Big Brother, cable television, advertising, theme parks. In this respect, the critical theorists earned the wrath of later feminists who argue that the Frankfurt defense of the family risks being conservative, only reproducing paternal, patriarchal power. Christopher Lasch, a social historian inspired by the Frankfurt School, whose work I cited earlier in my discussion of narcissism, takes inspiration from the Frankfurt analysis of family's eroding boundaries in his book *Haven in a Heartless World: The Family Besieged*, a book which reads almost like a conservative defense of family values.

The issue of family boundaries demonstrates how tricky it is either to praise or bury boundaries in a postmodern era. Here Freud is of some assistance where he argues that the infant must begin to differentiate itself from the outside world, a process that continues through adolescence and indeed the whole life course. This individuation, involving a basic boundary-setting between self and others, is necessary for the development of mature selves, or what Freud called egos. But too much differentiation of oneself from others cuts one off from micro institutions such as family and macro institutions such as culture and politics. From within sociology Durkheim called this "anomie," being isolated from others and as a result lacking values and purpose. Marcuse in *Eros and Civilization* used Freud in support of Marxism to help explain the extent to which selves must be held in lock step to social-system imperatives of conformity and consumerism. Selves become too much in the thrall of others (the superego) and they lack the solid core of identity required to make informed decisions about eating meat, driving gas-guzzling cars, shopping on credit, neglecting one's children. The inner core of selfhood, which, as Freud argued, requires strong boundaries between oneself and the world, especially political ideology, popular opinion, and advertising, was called "reason" in earlier philosophical traditions from Plato to Hegel.

The concept of reason is suspected by certain postmodernists like Jean-François Lyotard of being secretly authoritarian. In the name of absolute values rationalists conquer other nations, put people to death for political treason, despoil the environment beyond repair, deny democracy. The problem with these values, according to Lyotard, is that they impose one standard of reason on other possible standards, resulting in a cultural imperialism and political tyranny. Like other postmodernists, such as Foucault, he argues that we should be cautious about embracing absolutes, which, upon closer examination, turn out to have blind spots and biases reducing them to the level of mere perspectives. Earlier I talked about how **perspective** is a devilish problem for sociologists who want to be scientists. Positivism denies perspective, but, according to Horkheimer and Adorno, is the more "perspectival" for all that, concealing its own biases in an apparently value-free text.

I identify myself as a postmodern Marxist and not a left-wing postmodernist because I agree with Marcuse's Freudian version of Marxism, heavily influenced by the early Marx, that it is important to hold onto a boundary-setting concept of the self who, at the end of the day, can be trusted to make good choices about life and politics. These choices are made by reason, or, better, reasoning, the capacity with which Harold Garfinkel endowed selves as they live their lives pragmatically, without knowing the social laws. The self needs boundaries around it; it needs to avoid total penetration, administration, integration. The self needs boundaries because, as Freud understood, all infants and children, in order to make their ways in the world, require a solid source of identity – "who I am." The self also needs boundaries for reasons that are historical and political, insulating itself against domination.

The issue of boundaries, fortunately, is dialectical: The intrusion of the world into personal life via information and entertainment technologies provokes resistance, people fighting back to take control of their own lives. As with any phenomenon viewed dialectically, the Internet can be used to entrap or to emancipate people. It can be a vector into people's brains, blocking thought and critique. Or it can facilitate people's ingress into the culture, allowing them to read and inform themselves and then to launch into writing, creating culture from the ground up. A good model of this is public television and radio broadcasting, where private citizens take over the airwaves in order to screen good shows and enhance community dialogue. There is not a single Internet but many, precisely because it is so difficult to commodify and control what is essentially a free good, available to anyone with computer access. To be sure, the poor, both in the US and abroad, lack the technology and sometimes even the literacy to engage in "Internetworking" and literary liberation. But the broad base of citizens in western and Asian capitalist countries has access to the Internet, in its nature more democratic than television, which is costlier to produce and transmit. Anyone can launch a Web page, send e-mail, create a listserv.

Virtual Selves, Virtual Sociologies

Garfinkel's ethnomethodology helps us understand that these everyday activities of reading, writing, posting, educating, chatting, organizing not only build communities but establish new social institutions. One of the problems I have with Habermas' image of the "system's" domination of everyday life is that *system* risks being an overly vague, anthropomorphic term; it also risks disempowering people so much that we are led to believe that they have no agency, and the system has all the agency. Habermas' predecessors, Horkheimer, Adorno, and Marcuse, risk the same oversimplification where they talk of an all-encompassing domination that completely removes people's free will. Although the critical theorists were certainly correct to recognize that domination happens to the self "itself" in these new, post-World War II stages of capitalism, their images of total domination fail to capture the ground-level, everyday ways in which people impose external power on themselves and sometimes work to undermine and undo that power. This is Foucault's argument against Marxism, although, politically, he clearly has much in common with the Frankfurt School's analysis of a late, fast, postmodern capitalism.

Garfinkel founded ethnomethodology as a distinctive theoretical and research perspective nearly 30 years before the Internet, which itself began as a US military initiative to maintain vital communications in case of a nuclear war. I am convinced that his discourse-oriented approach to social structure would have easily accommodated the Internet, even if he may not have come to all of my conclusions about literary and sociological selves. Garfinkel's main points were that people create social structure (typical and enduring patterns of behavior) and that people, in their negotiations of a complex social reality, are in effect already sociologists. In a sense, they are closer to the social pulse than are both quantitative methodologists and theorists, who examine everyday life from afar, and with a high degree of distorting abstraction. We can learn much sociologically from the way that people, who are practical sociologists, talk about social structure. Indeed, you can remove the preposition *about* from the preceding sentence. People talk social structure directly; it has no other reality than people's everyday language and behavior. For Garfinkel, people are sociological agents of change and stability. Indeed, in seventeenth-century French, a word for reason (as in people's capacity to reason) was *discours*, not only the equally plausible word *raison*.

The Internet, then, helps people do better sociology as they learn to sell their wares on eBay, organize their neighborhoods, build national and international communities of people dealing with a particular illness, and write about the world around them for millions and perhaps even billions of others, especially now that many search engines translate international texts. One of the strangest and yet most telling experiences I have had with the academic community-building potential of the Internet occurred when I found a Czech translation of an article that I had published in English over a decade ago. I clicked on a little icon allowing me to translate the Czech back into English, half suspecting that I would see my original article. But what I found was a very clumsy translation of a translation, demonstrating the ways in which the Internet bends and transforms writings simply by being read and written about. This is not exactly a matter of distortion; for all I know, the Czech translation was faithful to my original. This reveals how all readings write, how they transform texts just as they interpret them, begging new texts that distort in different ways.

The Internet is understandably celebrated as a vehicle of commerce, and of virtual capitalism. There is little doubt that global information technologies accelerate the rate at which Fordism, with its downtown factories and neighboring warehouses, is sliding into **post-Fordism**, with decentralized, suburban, exurban, and international production and distribution. This is especially important where markets for goods are "segmented," an economic term for what happens when consumers, especially affluent yuppies, demand many different sorts of products. E-commerce allows for demand-driven production, with orders preceding production so that consumers get exactly what they think they want, instead of selecting from a preexisting inventory determined by long-range planning and not short-term demand.

A Marxist would notice that e-commerce allows capitalism to thrive, with its uneven development, glaring social and economic inequalities, and destruction of the natural environment.

But there is a sociological side to the Internet that Garfinkel, but perhaps not *The Wall Street Journal*, would notice. It helps people to be better citizens, better social scientists, better readers and writers by breaking free of the culture industries and of centralized political authority. Now, sociological selves can "network," organize, agitate, polemicize, and build communities without the sanction of the networks, established political parties, advertisers, big corporations. They can create alternative communities, literary circles, political movements. You can see this already on the Web, where all sorts of non-traditional political organizing and radical scholarship are taking place. Even where net surfers may not yet understand themselves as sociologists and political actors, they are already doing sociology and acting politically where they break away from sedating and disempowering television and other mass-market cultural pursuits and spend time learning, educating, reading, and writing in a cyberspace that sprawls far beyond the reach of established authority and official culture. Although capitalism wants to charge for Internet use (think of the controversies surrounding Napster, which allows users to trade music, depriving rich bands and artists of a slice of royalties), it is not clear that putting a price on music downloading will succeed, given the Internet's inherently amateur quality, its resistance to being regulated.

Arthur Kroker (Kroker and Weinstein 1994) replaces Max Weber's image of the iron cage of bureaucracy with the electronic cage of the culture industries, drawing both from Heidegger and critical theory. Foucault would have had a field day with the Internet, which is certainly a grid of power. But there is a disorganized and amateur quality to the Internet that a critical social theory seizes on, especially a theory informed by Garfinkel's basic insight that people "do" their lives by talking, reading, writing. They are always already agents, actors, writers, critics, especially where they have access to cyberspace, in which they can display their wares and work products without passing through the gate-keeping of cultural capitalism. You don't need a publishing contract to post your novel or non-fiction work on the Web. You don't need a record contract to air your latest songs. Your page can connect to other pages, hypertextually, as you move beyond the constraints of the pulp publication, which may have footnotes and a bibliography but no instantaneous access to the sources you cite.

The Internet, then, matters not only for the way it facilitates new kinds of scholarship, authorship, culture. All of that matters greatly, especially as a learned, critical amateurism survives and thrives outside of the culture industries, which thwart independent production and distribution. But the Internet also matters for the self, even if the self doesn't write novels or political theory. The point is that the self, who is increasingly controlled from the outside by all of the economic and cultural forces bombarding us from morning to night (and about which we dream, unable to escape their thrall), can, by using the Internet, reconfigure herself, gaining knowledge and forging community with others who share their experiences of the postmodern moment. The Internet can mitigate loneliness, as well as aloneness, at a time when you can't take good friends for granted, your family lives far away and in different places, and people who share your interests can't be found around every corner. The Internet affords connection and creativity. It helps build community as well as identity, enriching people's everyday lives by taking them outside of themselves and into other worlds. The question is whether it takes them so far out of themselves that they are lost in space and don't return. The Internet helps make people dextrous in dealing with the world, enhancing their practical abilities extolled by Garfinkel as he tries to explain enduring social structures without recourse to the myth of a sociological invisible hand.

The Internet creates virtual selves, through whom the world streams. I am convinced that we haven't leapt from modernity to postmodernity, a society without the economic structures of capitalism, the male-dominated family, the nation, religion, culture. But postmodern theory helps us better understand the most recent stage of modernity, which is sometimes called post-Fordism or late capitalism. This is a stage characterized by de-differentiation of social institutions and by the de-compartmentalization of the self, who is now thoroughly opened up to the outside world. This brings greater manipulation than Marx and even Marcuse envisaged. But it also affords opportunities for *authoring oneself*, and thus changing the culture, unavailable to earlier generations. Although I wouldn't go quite as far as to say, like Mark Poster, that we have entered an age or mode of information, displacing Ford-era production, I share with Poster, Kellner, and Luke the insight that postmodern theory helps us understand consciousness and communication – discourse, by another name – in ways closed off to earlier modernist theories, even those of Habermas.

Not a postmodern-ist, I am using postmodern theoretical and technological tools, including the Internet, to understand the present. The Internet at once dominates and liberates selves who assemble themselves through the literary activities of reading, surfing, viewing, chatting, posting, messaging. The world can bear down on people who don't recognize that they are not empty vessels, who stare blankly at the screens of power (Luke 1989). The screen must always be mediated, read, reflected, theorized. People must process electronic information and stimulation; in Garfinkel's sense, they must engage in practical reasoning, making sense of what they see on the screen, and sometimes modifying it. Anyone who spends even an hour on the Web knows that there is lots of garbage out there, cranky pages composed by crackpots, commercial pages, especially pornography, designed to make a quick sale, a postmodern voyeurism for which one must supply a credit card.

Eric Schlosser, the author of *Fast Food Nation*, has just published a book, *Reefer Madness* (2003), on sex, drugs, and labor in the black market. People who surf spend many dollars and hours on sex pages, and in sexual chat. This needs to be theorized. Are we simply sex-crazed? Some of these same people frequent sexually-oriented businesses like strip clubs, where they drink a lot. My hometown paper, *The Dallas Morning News*, recently ran a story about how the biggest volume of alcohol consumed in commercial establishments across the state of Texas occurs in strip clubs. Much of this patronage is charged to corporate accounts. As one businessman said: "When a client gets off the plane, he wants to eat a steak, and then see a tall woman with big breasts." All of this bespeaks what Weber called the loss of meaning, and Durkheim anomie, a normlessness that leads people to seek cheap thrills, which are now to be found on the screen, no longer forcing them to visit strip clubs or licentious book stores. As any Marxist and feminist would note, sex has become a business, providing new revenue streams for culture industries that can no longer assume that people, in postmodern capitalism, will continue to buy books or have the patience to read them. The Internet is one of the primary features of a fast capitalism in which the boundary between the self and society becomes permeable, and in which there is tremendous acceleration of the cultural transaction of meaning. In a 24/7 world, all time and space are subject to what the Frankfurt thinkers called "administration." It is difficult to gain enough distance from the maelstrom in order to take stock and think the world differently.

I just asked why people are so preoccupied with sex these days. This returns to issues raised in the last chapter and to issues I am discussing now, such as why so many people use the Internet for sex. I consult Marcuse for an answer: People crave sex, and talk and images about sex, because they lack connection and gratification. Marcuse helps us see that capitalism as we have organized it causes people to be alone, lacking community and connection, and to be unfulfilled, especially in their work lives. People who aren't critical social theorists get confused about all this and seek sex, even anonymous sex, and make themselves sexualized ("girlification" as I called it in the preceding chapter) in order to fill a void in their lives. Sex is natural and basic, as Freud saw, and thus, as Marcuse argues, shouldn't be taboo. But there is a difference between using the Internet to have an orgasm with someone you have never met and finding yourself in a deeply gratifying relationship that is not contradicted by having a boring job. We all have a primal urge for gratification, which, according to Marx, Marcuse, and Freud, is played out in the realms of work and love. The issue is whether Internet sex or sexualization generally answers to our deeper need for connection and gratification, both of which are thwarted in our type of society that alienates work for most people and turns sex into a commodity.

In this context of prurient diversions and electronic stimulation, the Internet can either facilitate business growth along with cultural sedation, or it can become a "counter" net, a subversive force for self-exploration and self-expression, which together become politically significant. Virtual selves can theorize their worlds, understanding their conditioning by the cultural forces which stream through them. They can engage their own lives sociologically, gathering information and launching literary projects that both empower them and enlighten others. What I have been calling "theory," the activity of conceptualizing everyday experience and events in a way that gives them shape but also learns from them, changing theory, can be an everyday, ordinary activity not reserved for PhDs who have mastered Hegel, Heidegger, Marx, and Marcuse. Marx was quite right to insist that the revolution would only occur when workers comprehended the source of their economic misery – capital – and actively sought to overthrow it.

The Internet either saturates people with pre-formed meaning or it liberates our better literary natures as we critically engage other texts and ideas and, in response, compose our own versions. This is not so much a virtual politics, because politics and power cannot be reduced to Internet transactions, but a preparation for politics, combining critique, consciousness raising, teaching, the sharing of information – community, by another name. Virtual selves use virtuality to burst through the screens of power and create a three-dimensional public sphere in which a democracy of discourse prevails. Specialized knowledge, especially science, is demys-

tified as a literary version like every other. Selves, well-equipped sociologically to know and master their worlds, read in search of the authors,
and their arguments, who underlie every text. Viewed this way, good
sociology reveals method as perspective, a way of seeing or vantage, from
which certain problems are solved, but others created. My argument in
this book has been that "perspective" is a literary strategy – how we tell
our stories, and stories they all are. This shouldn't cause us despair but
motivate us to craft better arguments, deploying both facts and fiction.
Ultimately, sociology is science fiction, which must compete with poetry
and polemic for our attention.

The Internet moves us away from a conception of sociology as a fact-
gathering science heavily reliant on mathematics and toward a view of
sociology that stresses the practical reasoning underlying our everyday
lives, readers' ability to become writers. The intellectual and literary dex-
terity that the Internet affords selves helps move sociology away from a
view of society as overbearing social structure. Instead, a twenty-first-
century sociology emphasizes the discursive fluidity of the world, revealed
by studying the impact of the Internet. Studying the Internet reveals that
discourse, writing, images, texts matter, and, through the screens of power,
become matter – social contexts in their own right. In taking stock of
the power of discourse in this new century, sociology installs the concept
of discourse at its theoretical center. This does not weaken the concept of
social structure, which was sociology's centerpiece during its first hundred
years, but reframes social structure, much as Garfinkel did, in linguistic and
literary practices – writing, chatting, and posting.

The virtual self creates enduring social structures by chatting and
writing, demonstrating the power of the pixel. This power can be used to
liberate or dominate, as I have been arguing. We need a virtual sociology in
order to understand virtual selves who deal with the world in a much more
global, versatile, cosmopolitan way than did earlier selves in modernity.
One can surf the world with little friction, which represents a huge change
from the dawn of modernity, when courageous adventurers sailed from
Europe to find new worlds. It represents change even from the world of my
father, which relied on slow trains and slow mail for the transportation of
people and ideas. Even when I was a kid, we watched only a few black-and-
white channels, even though I was lucky enough to travel to Europe. The
other morning, my daughter accessed a Web page that had a translation of
the Japanese national anthem, for a social-studies project of hers. She wants
to visit Japan, and in the meantime to find Japanese pen pals with whom to
chat. Again, though, the Internet is dialectical, offering opportunities for

both progress and regress: My wife logged onto her computer recently and in the presence of a graduate student found unsolicited images from Asian porn sites of a woman having sex with a dog. She surmised that she received this promotional pornography because she sometimes does Internet searches for social-science data on income by sex of earner, thus earning, for all time, bulk electronic mail destined for voyeurs!

This is the world into which we have entered, virtually. To understand it, we need a virtual sociology, but one which borrows concepts and methods from theorists and practitioners who addressed an earlier modernity. This will enrich sociology's encyclopedia, and it will de-professionalize sociology, taking it beyond the academy and into the streets and homes. A public sociology will not require years of training in statistics and methods, but will be available to people who are inquisitive and read a lot. Such a sociology will address the pressing issues of power and personal life and not substitute advances in methodology for real intellectual gain. This sociology will be modeled on people's Web surfing and their critical investigation of their own conditioning by the culture industries that stream through them. By understanding cyber-culture's impact, we can remake the culture, as readers resist their disempowering and become writers. This virtual sociology, practiced by virtual selves, will investigate the Internet's impact on selfhood, society and culture, and the Internet's impact on the *concepts* of self, society, and culture.

A virtual sociology studies virtuality, while conducting its analyses, writings, and community building online, as well as in traditional pulp formats. This does not preclude quantitative methodologies but broadens the discipline to non-quantitative methodologies and to insights from other disciplines. A virtual sociology expands disciplinary boundaries, much as the Internet has broadened the self's boundaries, opening it to unfamiliar worlds. Although this risks decentering the discipline, which fights to preserve its boundaries within a cost-cutting university system, I contend that this will enrich sociology over the long run as it brings the discipline more clearly into public focus. Imagine Web surfers inquisitive about social issues doing Google searches that identify sociological pages on race, crime, family, drug problems. This has already begun to happen as sociologists post their work. In their heart of hearts they know that such publicly accessible Web work must be comprehensible, written not for other PhDs but for well-educated, curious amateurs. The Web is enforcing the norm of straightforward writing as virtual writers anticipate having their pages consulted by thousands and even millions of people, not just by professional sociologists who speak a restricted language.

For professionals, sociologists who have and seek jobs, this will beg the question of tenure and academic vita building. How are we to evaluate virtual sociologies if anyone can publish them, skirting the elaborate procedures of submission to refereed journals and book publishers? Should electronic publications "count" as much as refereed pulp publications? Disciplines such as English, which is already engaged with issues of virtuality, have begun to debate these matters. As university library budgets erode and the cost of pulp publishing rises, librarians are insisting that journals be available only online, requiring faculty to download the articles themselves. There are no immediate or automatic answers, no magic algorithms that allow one to "weight" pulp versus electronic intellectual contributions. As journals transition from pulp to pixels, they can of course maintain the "referee" system which requires articles to be evaluated by outside readers before publication. Today, for the most part, only refereed publications "count" toward tenure and promotion. However, as e-journals proliferate and even replace pulp journals, we may decide that quality lies not in whether a paper has been formally refereed by three or four established scholars in the field but whether the paper stands up to scrutiny by three or four thousand (or million) readers, in whose judgment "quality" ultimately lies. As electronic publishing broadens the potential readership of academic writing, we may move from prepublication reviewing to postpublication reviewing carried out by the many readers exposed to the author's or journal's Web page.

In today's academic world, one indicator of the quality of research is whether the work has been published in refereed outlets, which are often ranked by prestige within one's discipline. Another indicator of quality is the extent to which one's work has entered the canon of cited work by other scholars in the same field. Whole citation indices are laboriously compiled and published, and held in university libraries, so that tenure and promotion committees can weigh the value of work. Here, Internet search engines, such as Google, provide instantaneous access to the dissemination of one's work. Try this experiment: Type in the URL www.Google.com and then enter your professor's name, last name first. You will then be provided with a list of entries, sometimes thousands of citations long, of sites on the Web where her or his work has been referenced. Some will be duplicative. Others will refer to another author altogether, especially if you don't supply a middle initial. But a half hour of culling will provide you with a very reliable indication of the impact of your professor's work on her field – where her work is cited and discussed, which university libraries have purchased her latest books, the courses in which other instructors assign her published work, and perhaps even listings of your professor's relative standing in the field. I would argue that such Google searches may be the most valid indicator of a scholar's current standing in the field, even more valid than where she publishes. Although one could argue that very good work goes unnoticed on the Web, there is no denying that not only amateurs but most academics have gone online and are treating the Internet as a vital and viable medium of academic recognition, and thus as a mechanism for measuring scholarly standing. I doubt that few department chairs or deans in the United States are hired without at least some members of the hiring departments having explored their personal Web pages and their departmental home pages, and done Google searches for, in effect, their reputation.

The virtualization of academic life will make it easier to publish, which amounts to posting one's work on the Web, but it will expose one's work to far greater scrutiny. It will also make "reputation" easy to access, as long as Google is available! Although this will initially erode the sacred code of refereed pulp-journal publication, there is no reason why electronic journals cannot subject submitted work to exactly the same vetting that articles now endure. And although exposure of one's work on the Web is much more readily available than an acceptance letter from Harvard University Press, the reality is that only a minority of American faculty members write for publication; most are teachers and have only their course syllabi to post.

In a virtual academia, standards won't be eliminated, as anti-Derrideans often fear. There will simply be multiple indicators of reputation and quality, variables which are strongly correlated. These multiple indicators include the placement of one's work in refereed outlets (including electronic ones), the number of citations one earns, the frequency and nature of one's mention on the Web, the courses in which one's work is adopted, and, perhaps most important, the extent to which one's work has received international recognition. This last feature is a real test of "globality," assessing not only one's reputation in Ames, Iowa but also in Athens, Greece. Although initially the evaluation of quality in an electronic academia will be more ambiguous than it is today, standards will quickly be sorted out, and distinctions between work of greater and lesser quality made. And we have already seen how "reputation" is more easily evaluated using Google than standard citations indexes inasmuch as Google reveals both the extent of adoption of one's work in college courses and the extent of one's international acclaim.

Coda

I have introduced you to the exciting discipline of a virtual sociology, and to other disciplines which enrich sociology. I have done this by discussing changes in our world that are still taking place, notably in the ways we work, communicate, raise families, and entertain ourselves. The virtual world springs from the pulp world, but it is different: As Marshall McLuhan said many years ago, with remarkable foresight, we now occupy a global village, held together by the electronic sinews of rapid information technologies. Our newfound ability to surf the globe instantly is very alluring to people who cannot afford to travel everywhere they want to go. But the price to be paid for the global village is manipulation by corporations and cultures which view the Internet as a new tool for advertising as well as surveillance.

To summarize, a virtual sociology will stress three themes:

1 *Virtuality's impact on self, society, and culture.* Although we haven't yet surpassed modernity, Ford's and FDR's capitalism has been transformed by information, entertainment, surveillance, and transportation technologies. These technologies at once shrink the planet and invade people's minds. They accelerate our lives and transform social institutions, erasing boundaries, for example between public and private, that we have taken for granted since the seventeenth century.

2 *The importance of discourse.* A virtual/Marxist/postmodern sociology will place heavy emphasis on discourse. The Internet helps demonstrate Garfinkel's claim that we constitute social structures through discourse. A media culture also disciplines people in ways suggested by Foucault and the Frankfurt School. Thus, a virtual sociology will link discourse to domination, but at the same time use existentialist, ethnomethodological, and phenomenological insights to demonstrate people's abilities to change the culture, and themselves, through literary agency.

3 *A deprofessionalized sociology blurring the natural and theoretical attitudes.* Derrida helps us understand sociology as a text, a literary project. He empowers readers to become writers, and hence full citizens. They can become sociologists, using intellectual tools such as the Internet. The sociologies they read and write set them free by helping them understand what shaped (and distorted) them. This blurs the boundary between the amateur and the expert, shifting power away from the center to the margins.

Sociologists have generally been slow to address these postmodern developments and their intellectual implications for sociology both because they are fearful of postmodernism, as I discussed in Chapter 3, and because they are a cautious bunch who don't want to add to the hype about the Internet. I used to share this caution, dismissing the Internet as the Next Big Thing that, in the nature of all fads, would fade quickly. Since then, I have been convinced that the Internet's impact on self, society, and culture is vast and growing. What changed my mind is reading books on the Internet, such as Poster's *What's the Matter with the Internet?* and observing my college students and my own children. Recently, a day before spring break at my university, I was in a computer lab in my building, working on final revisions of this book because my office computer's hard drive crashed. It was a gorgeous, lazy Friday and I expected to be all alone in the 65-seat computer room. But I was lucky to find a seat as students clamored to use the high-speed computers. I stole a glance at the users on both sides of me, and one was doing e-mail and the other was Web surfing. Probably a few were doing schoolwork, too! I wondered what these students would have been doing ten years ago, before computing and surfing became so commonplace. I walked over to the university library and it, too, was packed with users, on several floors.

As for the phobia about postmodernism, my advice to critics is "get over it!" Once you cut through Derrida's serpentine sentences, you can excavate insights from such writers about how to view the self in relation to culture, in effect translating postmodern theory into sociology. Sociology will be the better for postmodern insights about discourse, which, as I said above, doesn't replace the concept of social structure but helps us understand social structure in new ways, extending Harold Garfinkel into the land of Foucault. I remain convinced that sociology is the most fruitful discipline to address self, society, and culture, and yet sociology needs to move significantly beyond its reliance on the Holy Grail of scientific method and mathematics in order to ask serious questions about the Internet's impact on selves and on sociology. These questions can best be answered with insights from cultural studies, discourse analysis, political economy, feminist theory, communication theory, enriching sociology and breaking down barriers between disciplines, much as boundaries between social institutions, such as work/family, are melting in this postmodern moment.

I have argued throughout this book that the Internet can be empowering. People can become expert at managing their own lives and dealing with their own problems. They can find connection and gratification, which most of us sorely lack today. They can become practical reasoners, doing Garfinkel's kind of sociology in the natural attitude. The virtual self can become a virtual sociologist, learning from other sociologies and doing her own sociology particularly where the focus is on understanding and undoing the culture industries' influences on us. Although this will not change the world overnight, one of the things we learned from the sixties is that lasting change occurs both on the micro and macro levels, body by body and structure by structure. At the risk of making my sociological colleagues mad, I have argued for a different kind of sociology than is usually published in the journals. Schlosser's book *Fast Food Nation* is far more relevant than most of the articles published in the *American Sociological Review*. Sociology should empower selves to be agents, to know and master their worlds. After all, unless sociology is a required course and you "have" to take it, you probably took the course because you want to understand yourself better and take charge of your life, understanding what has made you the self you are becoming.

To do this, you have to read difficult material and study a lot. Many people have contributed to my intellect, the self I am. Some of these people are found in my bibliography and glossary. Insights into the complex relationship between selves and structures are hard-won. The most interesting facts in sociology's encyclopedia are the surprises: Most murders occur between intimates; capital punishment isn't deterrent; when couples equalize household labor there is more conflict not less (because the male is grumpy); the average income for the lowest fifth of American households is $10,000, far below the poverty line. You can't just know these things intuitively. You must conduct systematic social research and read the writings of others. Studying Derrida and Marx will make you smarter, more insightful about the world around you. I can no longer go to Wal-Mart the same way as before now that I have read Barbara Ehrenreich's book on minimum-wage work *Nickel and Dimed*. What we read changes us, always for the better. Good sociology is not just sitting down and sharing your thoughts with the world, although such exercises, like writing in a diary, help you become a better writer and think more clearly. To be a good sociologist – and you can write this down! – involves relating what you have read to your own life, and the insights you have gained from it. The readings and research you do help frame what you are feeling, giving it shape and substance. If we are lucky, all of us will have read a few books that changed our lives, helping us see ourselves in relation to the world in a new way. Marcuse's *Eros and Civilization* was such a book for me, although there have been others, by Sartre, by Marx, by Derrida, by Foucault, by Arendt, by Schlosser. You too can write books that change lives. I call these books sociologies.

Glossary

agency The existentialist Sartre's term for people's free will, their ability to choose their projects, their lives, their fate.

alienation Marx's term for the tendency of the products and process of one's labor under capitalism to be taken out of the hands of workers, leading them to dislike their jobs and not derive enough economic benefit from them.

bureaucracy The sociological theorist Max Weber identified bureaucracies as workplace organizations, found in both the public and private sectors, in which authority flows from the top down and in which people's work is highly specialized. He worried that bureaucracies, although the most rational form of labor organization, tend to stifle initiative and create "yes people" who blindly follow orders.

capitalism An economic system, such as our own, in which productive wealth such as factories, buildings, technologies is owned privately and in which most people's work is organized bureaucratically, with top-down authority and a division of labor.

commodification Marx's term for the way in which goods and services under capitalism become objects to be purchased in the marketplace. He paid special attention to the way in which human labor becomes a commodity.

critical theory The Frankfurt School's version of Marxist social and cultural theory, which addresses changes in capitalism since Marx wrote in the mid-nineteenth century. Of particular interest to critical theorists is government intervention in the economic system and popular culture's intervention in the psychic lives of people, both of which forestall workers' revolt, expected by Marx.

cultural studies An interdisciplinary movement that began in Britain and Europe that uses theoretical insights from Marxism, feminism, and postmodernism to examine the political ways in which culture and media operate. It broadens culture from "high" culture, such as Shakespeare, to all sorts of popular culture, such as film, television, advertising, videos.

culture industry The Frankfurt School's term for the commercial mass media and popular culture that, by providing distracting entertainments and diversions, assuage people's suffering and lead them to be apolitical and uncritical of the dominant social and economic institutions. This was demonstrated by them in studies of film, television, radio, and journalism.

cyberself The self, and her identity, formed online, which is one of the distinctive features of postmodern culture.

dialectical Hegel and then Marx's term for the tendency of ideas and things to contain contradictions or inconsistencies that, over time, tend to change those ideas and things, negating them and bringing about something new. Dialectical theory views the world as possessing the potential to become something different through the unfolding of these contradictions that lie at the heart of things.

discourse A French postmodern term for all the ways in which we express ourselves and engage in "figuration," including writing words, drawing graphics, producing filmic images, and designing Web pages. Discourse is how we talk, but it includes post-textual media as well.

division of labor Originally, Durkheim's term for the way in which industrial-era work is split into specialized components, for example using the assembly line, unlike the feudal craft era when a single artisan made the whole product.

domination Western Marxists' term for a condition of powerlessness so thorough that people lose their earlier ability (during modernity) to distinguish between true and false ideas. It is a deepened false consciousness, promoted by the culture industries. Marcuse's synonym for this is one-dimensional thinking.

ego Freud's term for the self, the mature individual who has managed to outgrow infancy and adolescence and who is not totally a product of society and socialization but thinks for herself.

empiricism A theory of knowledge that grounds knowledge in sense experience, including direct observation, surveys, experiments. The objects of empirical study were termed phenomena by Kant.

Enlightenment, the A historical blossoming of ideas, intellectual life and science (age of reason), which began in the seventeenth century and, arguably, is still going on.

enlightenment The process of using reason in order to free oneself from myths, religion and dogma, replacing belief with truth that is typically based on empirical evidence.

ethnomethodology Garfinkel's sociological methodology for learning about how people "do" social structure through what he called practical reasoning, the everyday sense-making practices in which we are all involved.

everydayness Having the characteristics of everyday life, a mode of existence approached in what Husserl called the natural attitude—the attitude with which we just accept things the way they are without thinking philosophically or theoretically about the meaning of a table, pen, or the sky.

false consciousness Marx's term for a type of consciousness, typically that of disempowered groups such as the working class, which is misled by dominant groups and classes about the true nature of society. False consciousness typically accepts one's alienation as natural in exchange for the promise of going to heaven or on vacation. Critical theorists are to dispel false consciousness through their intellectual work and consciousness raising.

false needs Marcuse's term for people's wants, such as fatty foods and fast cars, the satisfaction of which is not genuinely fulfilling but even damaging to them. These needs are imposed by advertising, but covertly, so that people think they are free to make these choices.

fast capitalism My term for a capitalism in which production, advertising, shopping, communications, and even childhood are greatly accelerated, making it difficult to reflect on what is happening. This term is similar in meaning to postmodernity, although I contend that our society is still capitalist.

feminism A movement and theory stressing women's rights and their fundamental equality with men.

Fordism A mode of industrial production, initiated by Henry Ford early in the twentieth century, that relies on large-scale production and the assembly line to mass produce commodities, such as cars. This lowers the unit cost and makes them more affordable, thus increasing profit. Units that aren't sold are held as inventory. This mode of production takes place in cities and tends to be relatively inflexible, with few alterations in product type allowed. It also requires a blue-collar labor force which is subject to unionization. This term was developed by the Italian Marxist Antonio Gramsci.

Frankfurt School The name given to the critical theories developed by Adorno, Horkheimer, Marcuse, and later Habermas, beginning in the 1920s as these German Jewish intellectuals asked why Marx's prediction of a socialist revolution had failed to come to pass. Although Marxist in its overtones, the Frankfurt School's theory stresses cultural influences on the self as a relevant political factor in late capitalism.

gender The way in which men and women are supposed to act differently, either as masculine or feminine, based on their biological differentiation. Many feminists question whether we should draw such a sharp line between the genders.

gesture A literary-theory concept that views literary practices, such as writing and art, as human expressive acts. Even science, I would argue, uses gestures such as mathematics, statistics, and graphs.

globalization A distinctive feature of postmodernity or postmodern capitalism in which nations, regions, and cultures are increasingly tied together through commerce, trade, communication, information, thus erasing national boundaries. This creates a global culture of CNN, FedEx, and McDonald's. For most sociologists and theorists, the United States is at the center of this globality.

grounded knowledge A term from phenomenology that views all knowledge as located in a certain social (historical, race, class, gender) context necessarily influencing one's data or results.

historicity Scholars in the Hegelian and Marxian traditions view all social phenomena as unfolding, thus requiring theorists to view those phenomena in the present as a totality of their pasts, presents, and possible futures. To historicize something means to view it from this three-dimensional, process-like perspective and not simply to view it as a timeless, a-historical entity entirely bounded by the present.

hypertext Refers to links within Web pages to other pages, thus allowing one to read a text and immediately connect to other pages to which the original writing refers, such as footnotes and other sources.

identity A psychological term for the self, and how she views herself. Sociologists believe that our identities are largely social products, formed in relation to others and how we think they view us (for example Cooley's concept of the looking-glass self).

intertextuality A literary theory term for the way in which texts that refer to other texts in a sense incorporate them, blurring the boundary between them as distinctive, stand-alone entities. In this sense, all writings are part of a great conversation.

level of analysis A sociological-methodological term for the degree of generality or specificity with which we frame our knowledge. For example, we can analyze world economic inequality or economic inequality in our local county. A standard distinction is between individual-level and aggregate-level analysis, the first referring to the self, the latter referring to the whole population.

lifeworld A term developed by Husserl, synonymous with everyday life, a sphere of experience and existence in which we don't have philosophical doubts about the meaning and stability of things.

methodology Systematic ways of knowing, including quantitative data analysis, qualitative analyses, literature, poetry, art, theory. Our methods are rhetorical, that is they are ways of making arguments for the validity of what we know. As such, they don't solve intellectual problems independent of the process of knowing and writing themselves.

modernity A historical era beginning with the Enlightenment and then continuing through the Industrial Revolution (circa 1750–1920) and taking us up to the present. It is characterized by industry, prosperity, the growth of cities, organized health care and education, literacy, democracy, the nation state.

modernization A sociological term for the tendency of pre-modern, agricultural countries and cultures to become modern, notably through industrialization and the development of economic markets and political democracy.

narcissism A psychological tendency to obsess about oneself and to be self-absorbed. Lasch said that we now inhabit a culture of narcissism, in which people are preoccupied with themselves and not with the larger society.

natural attitude Husserl's term for our mode of consciousness or awareness in everyday life. We take the world largely for granted and don't worry about the ultimate meaning of things, as philosophers or theorists would. We do this in order to negotiate the complex world around us.

object *See* **subject**.

one-dimensionality Marcuse's term for a social condition, prevalent in late capitalism, in which people lose the intellectual ability to criticize the dominant society and to imagine alternatives to it. It occurs because positivism becomes an ideology that prevents people from seeing beyond facts about existing social arrangements. It also occurs because popular culture sedates and diverts people, failing to sharpen their critical insights.

patriarchy Rule by men, in the family and also in society at large.

perspective The vantage from which you see things that necessarily influences "what" you see. Even science is done from perspective, forcing us to reject the ideal of objectivity or value freedom. Acknowledging the influence of all knowledge by perspective doesn't lead to nihilism, relativism, or idealism. There is still a real world.

phenomenology Husserl's philosophy, which grounds all knowledge in everyday life and our raw experience of the world. He argued that philosophers should purge themselves of their prior assumptions about the meaning of the world and instead approach the world naively, so that they could then develop profound understandings.

positivism A particular type of empiricism that views the mind as a blank slate on which phenomena imprint themselves. It requires knowledge to be quantitative and to be expressed in laws (cause and effect statements). Positivists don't worry that the very act of knowing distorts what is known simply by virtue of the scientist's perspective or vantage point, a key insight of postmodernism.

post-Fordism A more flexible mode of production than Fordism, and beginning during the 1970s. Factories are smaller and not always sited in big cities; indeed, many are in third-world countries, where labor is cheaper. Domestic workers tend to have white-collar managerial jobs (think of the computer industry) and don't belong to unions. Production runs are shorter and there is less inventory, utilizing just-in-time-production. Some theorists link the era of post-Fordism with postmodernity.

postmodernism A theory of society and culture that maintains that we have moved beyond modernity in that we no longer rely on urban factories and warehouses with vast inventories, class struggle has been muted, belief in progress has weakened, and science has lost the ability to reveal the world's mysteries. This is a largely French theory developed by Derrida, Foucault, Lyotard, and Baudrillard.

postmodernity A stage of history supposedly beyond modernity, which was characterized by the industrial system, big cities, class conflict, and print and pulp media. Postmodernity is characterized by clean industries, decentralized production, the overcoming of class conflict, and electronic information technologies. French postmodernists embrace the term, but Marxists largely reject it.

practical reason Garfinkel's term, borrowed from the philosopher Kant, to describe the everyday ability of people to make themselves understood and to carry out their projects, despite the imperfections of language and the tendency of people to misunderstand each other.

praxis Marx's Greek term for work that is self-creative (and also productive). He believed we should create a society of praxis, in which people identify with their work, which they freely choose.

productive consumption Shopping, in post-World War II affluent societies, that does not meet basic needs but rather surplus or false needs in order to keep the economic machinery of capitalist production humming. The Frankfurt School stresses that the culture industry must work hard to convince people to engage in this sort of consumption, even beyond people's means (through purchasing on credit).

professionals These are white-collar workers who, like doctors, lawyers and professors, provide certain expert services, hold higher degrees and diplomas, and belong to professional associations that regulate access into the profession.

science aura The reader's impression that one is reading genuine science, produced by literary strategies such as quantification and the use of graphs and tables. Sociologists frequently attempt to produce the science aura in order to upgrade the status and standing of their discipline.

self-alienation Hegel's term for the tendency of human work to create products and artifacts that leave our control by being implanted in the world and nature. He viewed self-alienation as a necessary feature of all work.

sex The biological differentiation between people traditionally called men and women, based on their reproductive differences.

social problems Disturbances of modernity, such as crime and pollution, that could be viewed as unfortunate byproducts of modernization and that can be fixed by the government or state without requiring a wholesale political or economic revolution.

social structures A sociological term for enduring social arrangements that exercise much influence on individual selves. Such structures (or institutions) include the economy, polity, religion, culture and media, education. You cannot necessarily see a structure; it is a theoretical construct, something we believe to be true in order to explain all sorts of social behavior.

state A Marxist term for government and other non-private sector institutions such as education that, since Roosevelt, play a major role in managing the economy and mediating between the capitalist and working classes, notably by providing a measure of social welfare.

stratification A sociological term for structured social and economic inequality, such as class divisions and divisions among races and genders.

subject A philosophical term for the self or person; contrasted with the **object**, which is what the subject knows or deals with. The object can be either nature or other people.

surplus repression One of Marcuse's key concepts, describing how, in an affluent society, the social system must work harder to convince people to go to work, spend, and conform politically, imposing even more repression on them than Freud imagined in an earlier stage of capitalism.

theoretical attitude Husserl's term for our mode of consciousness when we suspend the natural attitude and question the meaning of things, including human existence. We must step back from everyday life in order to ask large questions that, ordinarily, we suspend in order to get on with the business of living.

undecidability Derrida's term for the tendency of all writing to defer final meanings and definitions and thus to elude complete understanding by the reader. We must defer meaning and definitions simply because it is impossible to define all our terms at once, and then the definitions of our definitions, etc. Every text, thus, is somewhat opaque, requiring vigorous interpretation by the reader.

variables Methodologists' term for measurable or observable features of social life that are to be examined for their causal relationship to other such features. For example, income, level of education, occupational prestige are all variables. Independent variables are variables that cause variation in dependent variables (e.g., Durkheim felt that normlessness causes suicide).

virtual self The person who spends a good deal of time online and working with computers and who acquires her identity from this activity, which is at one remove from an everyday reality in which people interact with each other face-to-face. The virtual self experiences the world through the "screen."

virtuality The experience of being online or working with computers, that stands at one remove from reality. Virtuality is real, but in a different way than the world experienced directly and not through the computer screen.

western Marxism In the early 1920s, various Hungarian and German Marxists, such as Georg Lukàcs, reassessed Marxism in light of changes in European and world capitalism since the mid-nineteenth century. They particularly stressed the relevance of class consciousness for understanding the behavior of the working class.

References

Adorno, Theodor W. 1973. *Negative Dialectics*. New York: Seabury Press.

—— 1978. *Minima Moralia*. London: Verso.

—— 1984. *Aesthetic Theory*. London: Routledge and Kegan Paul.

Agger, Ben. 1989a. *Fast Capitalism: A Critical Theory of Significance*. Urbana: University of Illinois Press.

—— 1989b. *Socio(onto)logy: A Disciplinary Reading*. Urbana: University of Illinois Press.

—— 1990. *The Decline of Discourse: Reading, Writing and Resistance in Postmodern Capitalism*. London: Falmer Press.

—— 1991. *Cultural* Studies *as Critical Theory*. London: Falmer Press.

—— 1993. *Gender, Culture and Power: Toward a Feminist Postmodern Critical Theory*. Westport, CN: Praeger.

—— 2000. *Public Sociology: From Social Facts to Literary Acts*. Boulder, CO: Rowman and Littlefield.

—— 2002. *Postponing the Postmodern: Sociological Practices, Selves and Theories*. Boulder, CO: Rowman and Littlefield.

Althusser, Louis. 1970. *For Marx*. London: Allen Lane.

Arendt, Hannah. 1994. *Eichmann in Jerusalem: A Report on the Banality of Evil*. New York: Penguin.

Aronowitz, Stanley. 1988. *Science as Power: Discourse and Ideology in Modern Society*. Minneapolis: University of Minnesota Press.

Barthes, Roland. 1975. *The Pleasure of the Text*. New York: Hill and Wang.

Baudrillard, Jean. 1983. *Simulations*. New York: Semiotext(e).

Bell, Daniel. 1973. *The Coming of Post-Industrial Society*. New York: Basic.

—— 1976. *The Cultural Contradictions of Capitalism*. New York: Basic.

Bendix, Reinhard. 1956. *Work and Authority in Industry*. New York: Wiley.

Benjamin, Walter. 1969. *Illuminations*. New York: Schocken.

Berger, Peter and Thomas Luckmann. 1967. *The Social Construction of Reality.* Garden City: Doubleday.

Bloom, Allan. 1987. *The Closing of the American Mind.* New York: Simon and Schuster.

Blumstein, Philip and Pepper Schwartz 1983. *American Couples: Money, Work and Sex.* New York: Pocket Books.

Braverman, Harry. 1974. *Labor and Monopoly Capital: The Degradation of Work in the 20th Century.* New York: Monthly Review Press.

Breines, Wini. 1982. *Community and Organization in the New Left, 1962–68.* New York: Praeger.

—— 1992. *Young, White and Miserable: Growing up Female in the Fifties.* Boston: Beacon.

Brownmiller, Susan. 1975. *Against Our Will: Men, Women, and Rape.* New York: Simon and Schuster.

Chodorow, Nancy. 1978. *The Reproduction of Mothering.* Berkeley: University of California Press.

Comte, Auguste. 1975. *Auguste Comte and Positivism.* New York: Harper and Row.

Culler, Jonathan. 1982. *On Deconstruction: Theory and Criticism after Structuralism.* Ithaca, NY: Cornell University Press.

Delanty, Gerard. 2000. *Modernity and Postmodernity.* London: Sage.

Derrida, Jacques. 1976. *Of Grammatology.* Baltimore: Johns Hopkins University Press.

—— 1994. *Specters of Marx.* New York: Routledge.

Descartes, Rene. 1956. *Discourse on Method.* Indianapolis: Bobbs-Merrill.

D'Souza, Dinesh. 1991. *Illiberal Education: The Politics of Race and Sex on Campus.* New York: Free Press.

Durkheim, Emile. 1950. *Rules of Sociological Method.* Glencoe, IL: Free Press.

—— 1956. *The Division of Labor in Society.* Glencoe, IL: Free Press.

—— 1951. *Suicide, A Study in Sociology.* Glencoe, IL: Free Press.

Dyer-Witheford, Nick. 1999. *Cyber-Marx: Cycles and Circuits of Struggle in High Technology Capitalism.* Urbana, IL: University of Illinois Press.

Ehrenreich, Barbara. 2001. *Nickel and Dimed: On (Not) Getting By in America.* New York: Metropolitan Books.

Ewen, Stuart. 1976. *Captains of Consciousness: Advertising and the Social Roots of the Consumer Culture.* New York: McGraw-Hill.

Faludi, Susan. 1991. *Backlash: The Undeclared War Against American Women.* New York: Crown.

Fish, Stanley. 1989. *Doing What Comes Naturally.* Durham, NC: Duke University Press.

Foucault, Michel. 1972. *The Archaeology of Knowledge.* New York: Pantheon.

—— 1977. *Discipline and Punish.* New York: Pantheon.

Friedan, Betty. 1963. *The Feminine Mystique.* New York: Norton.

Galbraith, John Kenneth. 1958. *The Affluent Society.* Boston: Houghton Mifflin.

Garfinkel, Harold. 1967. *Studies in Ethnomethodology*. Englewood Cliffs, NJ: Prentice-Hall.

Gergen, Kenneth. 2000. *The Saturated Self: Dilemmas of Identity in Contemporary Life*. New York: Basic.

Gilligan, Carol. 1982. *In a Different Voice*. Cambridge: Harvard University Press.

Gitlin, Todd. 1987. *The Sixties: Years of Hope, Days of Rage*. New York: Bantam.

Gurstein, Penny. 2002. *Wired to the World, Chained to the Home: Telework in Daily Life*. Vancouver: University of British Columbia Press.

Habermas, Jurgen. 1984. *The Theory of Communicative Action*, vol. I. Boston: Beacon Press.

—— 1987. *The Theory of Communicative Action*, vol. II. Boston: Beacon Press.

—— 1989. *The Structural Transformation of the Public Sphere*. Cambridge, MA: MIT Press.

Hardt, Michael and Antonio Negri. 2000. *Empire*. Cambridge: Harvard University Press.

Harrington, Michael. 1962. *The Other America*. New York: Macmillan.

Harvey, David. 1989. *The Condition of Postmodernity*. London: Blackwell.

Hayden, Tom. 1988 *Reunion: A Memoir*. New York: Random House.

Heidegger, Martin. 1962. *Being and Time*. New York: Harper.

Hesse-Biber, Sharlene. 1996. *Am I Thin Enough Yet? The Cult of Thinness and the Commercialization of Identity*. New York: Harper and Row.

Hobbes, Thomas. 1996. *Leviathan*. Cambridge University Press.

Hochschild, Arlie. 1989. *The Second Shift*. New York: Viking.

Horkheimer, Max. 1974. *Eclipse of Reason*. New York: Seabury Press.

Horkheimer, Max and Theodor W. Adorno. 1972. *Dialectic of Enlightenment*. New York: Herder and Herder.

Husserl, Edmund. 1970a. *Crisis of European Sciences and Transcendental Phenomenology*. Evanston: Northwestern University Press.

—— 1970b. *Logical Investigations*. New York: Humanities Press.

Huyssen, Andreas. 1986. *After the Great Divide: Modernism, Mass Culture, Postmodernism*. Bloomington, IN: Indiana University Press.

Irigaray, Luce. 1985. *This Sex Which is Not One*. Ithaca: Cornell University Press.

Jacoby, Russell. 1975. *Social Amnesia: A Critique of Conformist Psychology from Adler to Laing*. Boston: Beacon Press.

—— 1981. *Dialectic of Defeat: Contours of Western Marxism*. New York: Cambridge University Press.

—— 1987. *The Last Intellectuals: American Culture in the Age of Academe*. New York: Basic Books.

Jameson, Fredric. 1991. *Postmodernism, or, the Cultural Logic of Late Capitalism*. Durham, NC: Duke University Press.

Kant, Immanuel. 1956. *Critique of Practical Reason*. New York: Liberal Arts Press.

—— 1966. *Critique of Pure Reason*. Garden City: Doubleday.

Kellner, Doug. 1995. *Media Culture: Cultural Studies, Identity and Politics Between the Modern and the Postmodern*. New York: Routledge.

—— 2003. *Media Spectacle*. New York: Routledge.

Korsch, Karl. 1970. *Marxism and Philosophy*. New York: Monthly Review Press.

Kristeva, Julia. 1980. *Desire in Language: A Semiotic Approach to Literature and Art*. New York: Columbia University Press.

Kroker, Arthur and Michael Weinstein. 1994. *Data Trash: The Theory of the Virtual Class*. New York: St. Martin's.

Kuhn, Thomas. 1970. *The Structure of Scientific Revolutions*. 2nd edn. Chicago: University of Chicago Press.

Lacan, Jacques. 1977. *Ecrits: A Selection*. New York: Norton.

Lasch, Christopher, 1977. *Haven in a Heartless World: The Family Besieged*. New York: Basic.

—— 1979. *The Culture of Narcissism*. New York: Norton.

Lefebvre, Henri. 1984. *Everyday Life in the Modern World*. New Brunswick, NJ: Transaction.

—— 1991. *Critique of Everyday Life*. London: Verso.

Lemert, Charles. 1997. *Postmodernism is not What You Think*. Malden, MA: Blackwell.

—— 2002. *Social Things*. 2nd edn. Boulder, CO: Rowman and Littlefield.

Lenski, Gerhard. 1966. *Power and Privilege: A Theory of Social Stratification*. New York: McGraw-Hill.

Lukàcs, Georg. 1971. *History and Class Consciousness*. London: Merlin Press.

Luke, Timothy W. 1989. *Screens of Power: Ideology, Domination, and Resistance in the Informational Society*. Urbana: University of Illinois Press.

—— forthcoming. *Virtual Ecologies: Social Order and Political Power in Cyberspace*. London: Sage.

Lyotard, Jean-Francois. 1984. *The Postmodern Condition: A Report on Knowledge*. Minneapolis: University of Minnesota Press.

Macpherson, C. B. 1962. *The Political Theory of Possessive Individualism*. Oxford: Clarendon Press.

Mailer, Norman. 2003. *The Spooky Art: Some Thoughts on Writing*. New York: Random House.

Mandel, Ernst. 1978. *Late Capitalism*. London: Verso.

Marcuse, Herbert. 1955. *Eros and Civilization*. New York: Vintage.

—— 1958. *Soviet Marxism*. New York: Vintage.

—— 1964. *One-Dimensional Man*. Boston: Beacon Press.

—— 1969. *An Essay on Liberation*. Boston: Beacon Press.

—— 1973. *Counterrevolution and Revolt*. Boston: Beacon Press.

—— 1978. *The Aesthetic Dimension*. Boston: Beacon Press.

Marx, Karl. 1964. *Early Writings*. Edited by Tom Bottomore. New York: McGraw-Hill.

—— 1967. *Capital: A Critique of Political Economy*. New York: International Publishers.

Marx, Karl and Friedrich Engels. 1947. *The German Ideology*. New York: International Publishers.

—— 1967. *The Communist Manifesto*. New York: Pantheon.

Merleau-Ponty, Maurice. 1964a. *Sense and Non-Sense*. Evanston: Northwestern University Press.

—— 1964b. *Signs*. Evanston: Northwestern University Press.

Merton, Robert. 1957. *Social Theory and Social Structure*. New York: Free Press.

Mill, John Stuart. 1978. *On Liberty*. Indianapolis: Hackett.

Mills, C. Wright. 1959. *The Sociological Imagination*. New York: Oxford University Press.

Negroponte, Nicholas. 1996. *Being Digital*. New York: Knopf.

Nietzsche, Friedrich. 2000. *The Birth of Tragedy*. Oxford: Oxford University Press.

O'Neill, John. 1974. *Making Sense Together: An Introduction to Wild Sociology*. New York: Harper and Row.

Orwell, George. 1981. *1984: A Novel*. New York: New American Library.

Paci, Enzo. 1972. *The Function of the Sciences and the Meaning of Man*. Evanston: Northwestern University Press.

Packard, Vance. 1959. *The Status Seekers*. New York: David McKay.

Parsons, Talcott. 1937. *The Structure of Social Action*. Glencoe, IL: Free Press.

—— 1951. *The Social System*. Glencoe, IL: Free Press.

Piccone, Paul. 1971. "Phenomenological Marxism." *Telos*, 9: 3–31.

Poster, Mark. 1990. *The Mode of Information*. Princeton: Princeton University Press.

—— 2001. *What's the Matter with the Internet?* Minneapolis: University of Minnesota Press.

Poulantzas, Nicos. 1973. *Political Power and Social Classes*. New York: Routledge and Kegan Paul.

Rosenau, Pauline Marie. 1992. *Post-Modernism and the Social Sciences*. Princeton: Princeton University Press.

Rousseau, Jean-Jacques. 1968. *The Social Contract*. Baltimore: Penguin.

Ryan, Michael and Douglas Kellner. 1988. *Camera Politica*. Bloomington, IN: Indiana University Press.

Sartre, Jean-Paul. 1948. *Anti-Semite and Jew: An Exploration of the Etiology of Hate*. New York: Schocken Books.

—— 1956. *Being and Nothingness*. New York: Philosophical Library.

—— 1976. *Critique of Dialectical Reason*. London: New Left Books.

Scheler, Max. 1961. *Ressentiment*. New York: Free Press of Glencoe.

Schlosser, Eric. 2001. *Fast Food Nation: The Dark Side of the All-American Meal*. Boston: Houghton Mifflin..

—— 2003. *Reefer Madness: Sex, Drugs and Cheap Labor in the American Black Market*. Boston: Houghton Mifflin.

Schutz, Alfred. 1967. *The Phenomenology of the Social World*. Evanston: Northwestern University Press.

Sennett, Richard. 1977. *The Fall of Public Man*. New York: Knopf.

Shelton, Beth Anne. 1992. *Women, Men and Time: Gender Differences in Paid Work, Housework and Leisure*. New York: Greenwood.

Sinclair, Upton. 1951. *The Jungle*. New York: Harper.

Slater, Phil. 1975. *Origin and Significance of the Frankfurt School*. London: Routledge and Kegan Paul.

Smith, Adam. 1976. *An Inquiry into the Nature and Causes of The Wealth of Nations*. Oxford: Clarendon.

Spivak, Gayatri Chakravorty. 1999. *A Critique of Postcolonial Reason: Toward a History of the Vanishing Present*. Cambridge, MA: Harvard University Press.

Stacey, Judith. 1998. *Brave New Families: Stories of Domestic Upheaval in Late-Twentieth-Century America*. Berkeley: University of California Press.

Students for a Democratic Society. 1999. "Participatory Democracy.". In Charles Lemert (ed.), *Social Theory: The Multicultural and Classic Readings*. Boulder, CO: Westview, pp. 352–6.

Turkle, Sherry. 1997. *Life on the Screen: Identity in the Age of the Internet*. New York: Touchstone.

Veblen, Thorstein. 1979. *The Theory of the Leisure Class*. New York: Penguin.

Walters, Suzanna. 1992 "Material Girls: Feminism and Cultural Studies." *Current Perspectives in Social Theory*, 12: 59–96.

—— 1995. *Material Girls: Making Sense of Feminist Cultural Theory*. Berkeley: University of California Press.

Weber, Max. 1946. "Science as a Vocation." In Hans Gerth and C. Wright Mills (eds.), *From Max Weber*. New York: Oxford University Press, pp. 129–56.

—— 1978. *Economy and Society: An Outline of Interpretive Sociology*. Berkeley: University of California Press.

Whyte, William, Jr. 1956. *The Organization Man*. New York: Simon and Schuster.

Wiggershaus, Rolf. 1994. *The Frankfurt School: Its History, Theories and Political Significance*. Cambridge, MA: MIT Press.

Willis, Paul. 1977. *Learning to Labour*. Farnborough, UK: Saxon House.

Zaretsky, Eli. 1976. *Capitalism, the Family and Personal Life*. New York: Harper and Row.

Zizek, Slavoj. 1989. *The Sublime Object of Ideology*. London: Verso.

Index